OUR GREAT
REDEEMER

OUR GREAT REDEEMER

365 Days with J. C. Ryle

Compiled by Bryan Schrank

Reformation Heritage Books

Grand Rapids, Michigan

Our Great Redeemer
© 2024 by Bryan Schrank

Reformation Heritage Books
3070 29th St. SE
Grand Rapids, MI 49512
616-977-0889
orders@heritagebooks.org
www.heritagebooks.org

Scripture taken from the King James Version. In the public domain.

Printed in the United States of America
24 25 26 27 28 29/10 9 8 7 6 5 4 3 2 1

Library of Congress Cataloging-in-Publication Data

Names: Ryle, J. C. (John Charles), 1816-1900, author. | Schrank, Brian, compiler.
Title: Our great redeemer : 365 days with J.C. Ryle / compiled by Bryan Schrank.
Description: Grand Rapids, Michigan : Reformation Heritage Books, [2024] |
    Includes index.
Identifiers: LCCN 2024018592 (print) | LCCN 2024018593 (ebook) |
    ISBN 9798886861242 (hardback) | ISBN 9798886861259 (epub)
Subjects: LCSH: Devotional calendars. | Devotional literature.
Classification: LCC BV4811 .R87 2024 (print) | LCC BV4811 (ebook) |
    DDC 242/.2—dc23/eng/20240531
LC record available at https://lccn.loc.gov/2024018592
LC ebook record available at https://lccn.loc.gov/2024018593

The Life and Ministry of J. C. Ryle

When I came to pastor my current church in Grand Rapids, Michigan, in 1986, only a few of the people in our church were reading spiritual classics.[1] At a midweek evening class I was teaching, I held up a seven-volume set of *Expository Thoughts on the Gospels* by J. C. Ryle (1816–1900), encouraging fathers to read portions of these volumes as a starting point for families to engage in daily, intentional, God-glorifying family worship.[2] To my delight, over 150 families signed up. Soon, many in our church were talking about these books. Sixteen years later, a woman told me that she was still reading Ryle's commentary on the Gospels and that every time she reaches the end of the Gospel of John, she starts again in the Gospel of Matthew. In his writing, Ryle has precisely the kind of spiritual appeal and broad readability that encourages readers to come back for more.

J. C. Ryle was an "evangelical champion," wrote the nineteenth-century Baptist preacher C. H. Spurgeon, and "one of the bravest and best of men."[3] Ryle was born in Macclesfield, a town in northwest England, on May 10, 1816.[4] The son of a wealthy banker, he became a good

---

1. This preface is adapted from Joel R. Beeke, *Reformed Preaching: Proclaiming God's Word from the Heart of the Preacher to the Heart of His People* (Wheaton, Ill.: Crossway, 2018), 326–28, 31; and Joel R. Beeke and Douglas Bond, *Evangelical Heroes*, vol. 2 (Grand Rapids: Reformation Heritage Books, 2023), 1–13. Used with permission.
2. J. C. Ryle, *Expository Thoughts on the Gospels*, 7 vols. (1856–1869; repr., Edinburgh: Banner of Truth, 2009).
3. Cited in Gene Fedele, *Heroes of the Faith* (Gainesville, Fla.: Bridge-Logos, 2003), 204.
4. On Ryle, see M. Guthrie Clark, *John Charles Ryle, 1816–1900: First Bishop of Liverpool* (London: Church Book Room Press, n.d.); Ian D. Farley, *J. C. Ryle, First Bishop of Liverpool: A Study in Mission amongst the Masses* (Carlisle, UK: Paternoster, 2000); Marcus L. Loane, *John Charles Ryle, 1816–1900* (London: Hodder & Stoughton, 1983); J. I. Packer, *Faithfulness and Holiness: The Witness of J. C. Ryle* (Wheaton, Ill.: Crossway, 2002); Bennett W. Rogers, *A Tender Lion: The Life, Ministry, and Message of J. C. Ryle* (Grand Rapids: Reformation Heritage Books, 2019); Eric Russel, *J. C. Ryle: That Man of Granite with the Heart of a Child* (Fearn, Ross-shire, Scotland: Christian Focus, 2008); J. C. Ryle, *J. C. Ryle, a Self-Portrait: A Partial Autobiography*, ed. Peter Toon (Swengel, Pa.: Reiner, 1975); Peter Toon and Michael Smout, *John Charles Ryle: Evangelical Bishop* (Cambridge: J. Clarke, 1976).

scholar and athlete (he was a skilled cricketer) at the University of Oxford and appeared destined for greatness in the political or financial world of Victorian England. In his early years, Ryle absorbed his parents' elitist values without serious consideration of the things of God and the gospel of Jesus Christ. But God had a different calling for his life. In 1841 his father's wealth disappeared when the bank failed. Overnight, the family lost their money, their home, and their property valued at a half million pounds (over fifty million dollars today). For the next twenty years, Ryle assisted his father in paying off his family's massive debt.

He might have utterly despaired had not God already introduced him to more enduring riches. In the summer of 1837, while shooting, he swore out loud and was rebuked by a friend, who urged him to "think, repent, and pray." He began to do so, particularly when he fell ill later that year. One Lord's Day afternoon, he attended public worship and passed from death to life while hearing the Scripture lesson slowly and distinctly read from Ephesians 2: "By grace—are ye saved—through faith—and that not of ourselves—it is the gift of God."[5] Later in life, Ryle said that the truths of the sinfulness of sin, Christ's perfect substitution for sinners, the necessity of the new birth by the Holy Spirit, the indispensability of a life of holiness, the necessity of coming out of the world, and the supremacy of the Bible "seemed to flash on me like a sunbeam in the winter of 1837.... Nothing to my mind can account for it, but the free sovereign grace of God."[6]

Enriched in Christ and impoverished among men, Ryle found a new vocation. In 1842 he was ordained to the ministry of the Church of England and served country parishes in Suffolk. From 1844 to 1861, he was the rector of Helmingham (pop. 300), and from 1861 to 1880, the vicar of Stadbroke (pop. 1,300). His first wife, Matilda, died in 1848 after only three years of marriage; his second wife, Jessie, was in nearly constant poor health and died in 1860 after ten years of marriage. He married a third time in 1861 to Henrietta, who died in 1889, eleven years before Ryle passed away in 1900. Ryle also suffered from frequent ill health and prolonged financial troubles. Nevertheless, in 1880, at the age of sixty-four, he was appointed as the first bishop of Liverpool

---

5. Toon and Smout, *John Charles Ryle*, 26–27.
6. Quoted in Packer, *Faithfulness and Holiness*, 28.

through the intervention of none other than Prime Minister Benjamin Disraeli. Ryle served in Liverpool for the next twenty years.

Ryle was a devoted shepherd, a gifted writer, and a very effective administrator. As a bishop, he focused on raising the pay scale and pensions of pastors instead of building a cathedral. He promoted reading the Puritans and similar evangelical preachers from the eighteenth century. He became a leader of evangelical Anglicanism. Today, Ryle is best known for the more than two hundred tracts and twenty books he authored (many tracts at that time were booklets of fifteen to thirty pages). Perhaps most popular today, in addition to his *Expository Thoughts*, is his book *Holiness*, which consists of papers he wrote to advocate the biblical doctrines of sin and sanctification.[7]

When Ryle began his vocation as a preacher, his sermons, by his own admission, were too ornate and florid in style. By ministering to farmers, however, he learned to speak more simply and directly. He divided his thoughts into short sentences and his sermon material into small sections. He made applications in every sermon. He also preached with spiritual urgency, repeated key words, and illustrated abstract concepts with stories of shipwrecks, wars, and compassionate queens in order to personally engage his hearers.[8] He once advised, "Do not be above talking to the poor, and visiting your people from house to house. Sit down with your people by the fireside, and exchange thoughts with them on all subjects. Find out how they think and how they express themselves, if you want them to understand your sermons."[9] The accessibility and practicality of his preaching and writing are evident throughout this devotional. Here you will have that valuable opportunity to sit, as it were, under the teaching of Ryle as he joins you by the hearth.

In Ryle we see simple, straightforward, understandable preaching and teaching that offered Christ to all and demonstrated the difference between saved people and the lost world. His preaching was biblical and

---

7. This classic book is reprinted in many formats, including J. C. Ryle, *Holiness* (Darlington, England: Evangelical Press, 2011). The shorter first edition is contained in Packer, *Faithfulness and Holiness*, 89–246.

8. Farley, *J. C. Ryle, First Bishop of Liverpool*, 6–7, 34–37.

9. J. C. Ryle, *Simplicity in Preaching: A Few Short Hints on a Great Subject* (London: William Hunt, 1882), 43–45.

bold. He dared to tell people who did not live like the sheep of Christ that they were not saved. There was tenderness in his words and compassion for both the saved and the lost. He honored God and His Word, and God honored Ryle's preaching.

One of the greatest tributes given to J. C. Ryle was from his fellow Anglican minister Richard Hobson, writing shortly after Ryle's funeral:

> From his conversion [in 1837] to his burial [in 1900], J. C. Ryle was entirely one-dimensional. He was a one-book man; he was steeped in Scripture; he bled the Bible. As only Ryle could say, *"It is still the first book which fits the child's mind when he begins to learn religion, and the last to which the old man clings as he leaves the world."*

This is *why* his works have lasted—and will last: they bear the stamp of eternity. Today, more than a hundred years after his passing, Ryle's works stand at the crossroads between the historic faith and modern evangelicalism. Like signposts, they direct us to the "old paths." And, like signposts, they are meant to be read.

> [J. C. Ryle] was great through the abounding grace of God. He was great in stature; great in mental power; great in spirituality; great as a preacher and expositor of God's most holy Word; great in hospitality; great as a writer of Gospel tracts; great as a Bishop of the Reformed Evangelical Protestant Church in England, of which he was a noble defender; great as first Bishop of Liverpool. I am bold to say, that perhaps few men in the nineteenth century did as much for God, for truth, and for righteousness, among the English-speaking race, and in the world, as our late Bishop.[10]

Dear reader, you hold in your hands a treasure trove of edifying material from Ryle's sermons from various times in his ministry. Like the families at my church, may you also discover the riches of J. C. Ryle's teaching and preaching over this next year. I trust that many people who would not otherwise read Ryle's work will find many spiritual treasures in the pages to follow that will aid on the pathway to glory. Above all, may you know the Christ whom Ryle so lovingly served, so joyfully glorified, and so boldly proclaimed.

—Joel R. Beeke

---

10. Quoted in Packer, *Faithfulness and Holiness*, 13–14.

Are You Ready for the New Year?

And as it is appointed unto men once to die,
but after this the judgment.
—HEBREWS 9:27

Reader, I ask you a plain question at the beginning of a new year. Are you ready? It is a solemn thing to part company with the old year. It is a still more solemn thing to begin a new one. It is like entering a dark passage. We know not what we may meet before the end. All before us is uncertain. We know not what a day may bring forth, much less what may happen in a year. Reader, are you ready? Are you ready for death? It must come someday. It may come this year. You cannot live always. This very year may be your last. You have no freehold in this world. You have not so much as a lease. You are nothing better than a tenant at God's will. Your last sickness may come upon you and give you notice to exit. The doctor may visit you and exhaust his skill over your case. You may feel yourself drawing near to the coffin, and the grave, and the worm, and an unseen world, and eternity, and God. Reader, if death should come upon you, are you ready?

Are you ready for bereavements? No doubt there are those in the world whom you love. There are those whose names are engraved on your heart, and round whom your affections are entwined. There are those who are the light of your eyes, and the very sunshine of your existence. But they are all mortal. Any one of them may die this year. Before the daisies blossom again, any one of them may be lying in the tomb. Reader, are you ready?

Reader, if you are not ready, I beseech you to make ready without delay. I tell you, in the name of the Lord Jesus Christ, that all things are ready on God's part for your salvation. The Father is ready to receive you. The Lord Jesus is ready to wash your sins away. The Spirit is ready to renew and sanctify you. Angels are ready to rejoice over you. Saints are ready to hold out the right hand to you. Oh, why not make ready this very year?

✤ From the sermon "Are You Ready?"

Do You Pray?

Men ought always to pray.
—LUKE 18:1

I have a question to offer you. It is contained in three words: Do you pray? Only you can answer the question. Whether you attend public worship or not, your minister knows. Whether you have family prayers in your house or not, your relatives know. But whether you pray in private or not is a matter between yourself and God. I beseech you in all affections to attend to the subject I bring before you. Do not say that my question is too close. If your heart is right in the sight of God, there is nothing in it to make you afraid. Do not turn off my question by replying that you say your prayers. It is one thing to say your prayers and another to pray. Do not tell me that my question is unnecessary.

Prayer is the most important subject in practical religion. All other subjects are second to it. Reading the Bible, listening to sermons, attending public worship, going to the Lord's Table—all these are very important matters. But none of them are so important as private prayer. Just as it is with the mind and body, so it is with the soul. There are certain things indispensable to the soul's health and well-being. Each must attend to these things for himself. Each must repent for himself. Each must apply to Christ for himself. And for himself each must speak to God and pray. You must do it for yourself, for by nobody else it can be done. To be prayerless is to be without God, without Christ, without grace, without hope, and without heaven. It is to be on the road to hell. Now can you wonder that I ask the question, Do you pray?

✣ From the sermon "Call to Prayer"

Practice Holiness

Follow peace with all men, and holiness,
without which no man shall see the Lord.
—HEBREWS 12:14

It is as certain as anything in the Bible that "no man shall see the Lord" without holiness (Heb. 12:14). It is equally certain that it is the invariable fruit of saving faith, the real test of regeneration, the only sound evidence of indwelling grace, the certain consequence of vital union with Christ. Holiness is not absolute perfection and freedom from all faults. Nothing of the kind! The wild words of some who talk of enjoying "unbroken communion with God for many months" are greatly to be deprecated because they raise unscriptural expectations in the minds of young believers, and so do harm.

Absolute perfection is for heaven and not for earth, where we have a weak body, a wicked world, and a busy devil continually near our souls. Nor is real Christian holiness ever attained, or maintained, without a constant fight and struggle. The great apostle who said "I keep under my body, and bring it into subjection: lest that by any means, when I have preached to others, I myself should be a castaway" (1 Cor. 9:27) would have been amazed to hear of sanctification without personal exertion, and to be told that believers only need to sit still, and everything will be done for them! Such holiness, I know well, is not common. It is a style of practical Christianity which is painfully rare in these days. But I can find no other standard of holiness in the Word of God, no other which comes up to the pictures drawn by our Lord and His apostles. In an age like this no reader can wonder if I press this subject also on men's attention. Once more let us ask, in the matter of holiness, how is it with our souls? How are we doing?

❖ From the sermon "Self-Inquiry"

Working Out Your Own Salvation

Wherefore, my beloved, as ye have always obeyed, not as in my presence only, but now much more in my absence, work out your own salvation with fear and trembling.
                                                            —PHILIPPIANS 2:12

I address it to all who have manfully taken up the cross and are honestly following Christ. I exhort them to persevere, and not to be moved by difficulties and opposition. You may often find few with you, and many against you. You may often hear hard things said of you. You may often be told that you go too far and that you are extreme. Heed it not. Turn a deaf ear to remarks of this kind. Press on. If there is anything in the world of which a man need not be ashamed, it is the service of Jesus Christ. Of sin, of worldliness, of levity, of trifling, of time wasting, of pleasure seeking, of bad temper, of pride; of making an idol of money, dress, dancing, hunting, shooting, card playing, novel reading, and the like—of all this a man may well be ashamed. Living after this fashion, he makes the angels sorrow and the devils rejoice.

But of living for his soul, caring for his soul, thinking of his soul, providing for his soul, making his soul's salvation the principal and chief thing in his daily life, of all this a man has no cause to be ashamed at all. Believer in Christ, remember this! Remember it in your Bible reading and your private praying. Remember it in your worship of God. In all these things never be ashamed of being wholehearted, real, thorough, and true! The years of our life are fast passing away. Who knows but this year may be the last in his life? Who can tell but that he may be called this very year to meet his God? As ever you would be found ready, be a real and true Christian. Do not be base metal!

✣ From the sermon "Reality"

The Agonies of Hell

Whose fan is in his hand, and he will throughly purge his floor, and gather his wheat into the garner; but he will burn up the chaff with unquenchable fire.
— MATTHEW 3:12

This text describes in words something that should make our ears tingle: Christ shall "burn up the chaff with unquenchable fire" (Matt. 3:12). When the Lord Jesus Christ comes to purge His threshing floor, He shall punish all who are not His disciples with a fearful punishment. All who are found impenitent and unbelieving, all who have held the truth in unrighteousness, all who have clung to sin, stuck to the world, and set their affection on things below, all who are without Christ. All such shall come to an awful end! Christ shall "burn up the chaff"!

Their punishment shall be most severe. There is no pain like that of burning. Put your finger in the candle flame for a moment, if you doubt this, and try. Fire is the most destructive and devouring of all elements. Look into the mouth of a blast furnace and think what it would be to be there. Fire is of all elements most opposed to life. Creatures can live in air, and earth, and water, but nothing can live in fire! Yet fire is the portion to which the Christ-less and unbelieving will come. Christ will "burn up the chaff with unquenchable fire"! Their punishment shall be eternal. Millions of ages shall pass away and the fire into which the chaff is cast shall still burn on. That fire shall never burn low and become dim. The fuel of that fire shall never waste away and be consumed. It is "unquenchable fire." Oh, reader, these are sad and painful things to speak of! I have no pleasure in dwelling on them!

✣ From the sermon "He Will Burn Up the Chaff with Unquenchable Fire"

Hope in the Gospel

And such were some of you: but ye are washed, but ye are sanctified, but ye are justified in the name of the Lord Jesus, and by the Spirit of our God.
—1 CORINTHIANS 6:11

There is hope in the gospel for any man as long as he lives. There is infinite willingness in Christ to pardon sin. There is infinite power in the Holy Spirit to change hearts. There are many diseases of the body which are incurable. The cleverest doctors cannot heal them. But thank God, there are no incurable diseases of the soul! All manner and quantity of sins can be washed away by Christ! The hardest and most wicked of hearts can be changed.

Reader, I say again, while there is life, there is hope. The oldest, the vilest, the worst of sinners may be saved. Only let him come to Christ, confess his sin, and cry to Him for pardon, only let him cast his soul on Christ, and he shall be cured. The Holy Spirit shall be sent down on his heart according to Christ's promise, and he shall be changed by His almighty power into a new creature.

I never despair of anyone becoming a decided Christian, whatever he may have been in days gone by. I know how great the change is from death to life. I know the mountains of division which seem to stand between some men and heaven. I know the hardness, the prejudices, the desperate sinfulness of the natural heart. But I remember that God the Father made the glorious world out of nothing. I remember that the voice of the Lord Jesus could reach Lazarus when four days dead and recall him even from the grave. I remember the amazing victories the Spirit of God has won in every nation under heaven. I remember all this and feel that I never need despair!

✤ From the sermon "The Power of the Holy Spirit"

Jesus Is Coming Again!

He which testifieth these things saith, Surely I come quickly. Amen.
Even so, come, Lord Jesus.   —REVELATION 22:20

What will you see when that great event takes place? You will see the eternal Son of God return in the clouds of heaven with power and great glory. He will come to raise the dead saints and to change the living ones, to punish the wicked and to reward the godly, to summon everyone before His bar, and to give to everyone according to His works. He will come to bind Satan and deprive him of his usurped dominion, to deliver the earth from the curse, and to purify it as the eternal dwelling place of a holy nation; to cast out sin, and all its accursed consequences—disease, death, sorrow, wars, poverty, injustice, and oppression. You see the world defiled now by the presence of evil. You will see it at length restored to its former state, and the days of paradise before the fall brought back again.

What will you get by looking forward to Jesus coming again? You will get that which is the best remedy against disquiet and depression, hope shed abroad in your heart about things to come. When the minds of others are cast down with perplexity, you will feel able to lift up your head and rejoice; when all around seems dark and gloomy, you will see light, and be able to wait patiently for better days. Few things are so remarkable in the present time as the universal anxiety and suspense about the future. On all sides, and among all classes, you hear of lack of confidence and gloomy forebodings of coming evil. Church and state alike seem shaken to their foundations; no one seems to know what to expect next. On one thing alone men seem agreed: they look forward with more fear than hope to the future. In a day like this there is no comfort like that of looking forward to Christ coming again. The Christian who reads his Bible and believes what it contains can behold the shaking of all things round him unmoved!

✢ From the sermon "Are You Looking"

Calvary

And he bearing his cross went forth into a place called the place of a skull, which is called in the Hebrew Golgotha.
                                                            —JOHN 19:17

You probably know that Calvary was a place close to Jerusalem, where the Lord Jesus Christ, the Son of God, was crucified. We know nothing else about Calvary besides this. I am afraid that much ignorance prevails among people on the subject of Jesus Christ's sufferings. I suspect that many see no peculiar glory and beauty in the history of the crucifixion. On the contrary, they think it painful, humbling, and degrading. They do not see much profit in the story of Christ's death and sufferings. They rather turn from it as an unpleasant thing.

People seem to forget that all Christ's sufferings at Calvary were necessary for man's salvation. He had to bear our sins, if ever they were to be borne at all: with His stripes alone could we be healed. This was the one payment of our debts that God would accept; this was the great sacrifice on which our eternal life depended. If Christ had not gone to the cross and suffered in our stead, the just for the unjust, there would not have been a spark of hope for us. There would have been a mighty gulf between ourselves and God that no man ever could have passed. The cross was necessary, in order that there might be an atonement for sin.

People seem to me to forget that all Christ's sufferings at Calvary were foreordained. They did not come on Him by chance or accident: they were all planned, counseled, and determined from all eternity. The cross was foreseen in all the provisions of the everlasting Trinity for the salvation of sinners. Not one throb of pain did Jesus feel, not one precious drop of blood did Jesus shed, that had not been appointed long ago. Infinite wisdom planned that redemption should be by the cross; infinite wisdom brought Jesus to the cross in due time. He was crucified by the determinate counsel and foreknowledge of God.

✣ From the sermon "Calvary"

Cold Time for Believers

The night is far spent, the day is at hand: let us therefore cast off the works of darkness, and let us put on the armour of light.
—ROMANS 13:12

It is a cold time for believers. They meet with much to chill and dampen their zeal and little to cheer and warm their hearts. They have to put up with many crosses and disappointments. They see iniquity abounding, and their own love is apt to become cold. And why? It is night! It is a lonely time for believers. They find little company on the way that leads to heaven. Here and there they fall in with one who loves the Lord Jesus and lives by faith. A few of God's children may be found in one town, and a few in another. But on the whole, the children of the world seem like the Syrian army, which filled the country and the children of God are like a few scattered sheep in a wilderness! And why? It is night.

It is a dangerous time to believers. They often stumble and scarcely discern their path. They often stand in doubt and know not which way to turn. They sometimes are unable to see their tokens and lose sight of their landmarks. At best they travel on in continual fear of enemies. And why? It is night. Reader, I ask you to ponder these things. If time present be night, you will not wonder if we ministers warn Christians to watch and pray. You will count it no strange thing if we tell you to live like soldiers in an enemy's country, and to be always on your guard. Reader, sit down and ask yourself whether you find this world in which you live to be night or day. Is the present time one of conflict, or a time of ease? Do you feel that your best things are here in this life, or that your best things are yet to come? I offer these questions to you as a test of your spiritual state. I place them before you as a gauge and measure of your soul's condition. I tell you plainly, if you never found this world a wilderness and place of darkness, it is a bad sign of your state in the sight of God!

✢ From the sermon "Coming Events and Present Duties"

Privileges of Knowing Christ

And if children, then heirs; heirs of God, and joint-heirs with Christ; if so be that we suffer with him, that we may be also glorified together.

—ROMANS 8:17

Nothing can be conceived more glorious than the prospects of the sons of God. The words of Scripture at the head of this paper contain a rich mine of good and comfortable things. "And if children," says Paul, "then heirs; heirs of God, and joint-heirs with Christ; if so be that we suffer with him, that we may be also glorified together" (Rom. 8:17). True Christians then are "heirs." Something is prepared for them all which is yet to be revealed. They are "heirs of God." To be heirs of the rich on earth is something. How much more then is it to be son and heir of the King of Kings! They are "joint-heirs with Christ." They shall share in His majesty and take part of His glory. They shall be glorified together with Him. And this, we must remember, is for all the children. Abraham took care to provide for all his children, and God takes care to provide for His. None of them are disinherited. None will be cast out. None will be cut off. Each shall stand in his lot and have a portion in the day when the Lord brings many sons to glory.

Who can tell the full nature of the inheritance of the saints in light? Who can describe the glory which is yet to be revealed and given to the children of God? Words fail us. Language falls short. Mind cannot conceive fully, and tongue cannot express perfectly, the things which are comprised in the glory yet to come upon the sons and daughters of the Lord Almighty! Oh, it is indeed a true saying of the apostle John: "Beloved, now are we the sons of God, and it doth not yet appear what we shall be: but we know that, when he shall appear, we shall be like him; for we shall see him as he is" (1 John 3:2)!

�֍ From the sermon "Heirs of God"

Christ in the Sick Room

The LORD will strengthen him upon the bed of languishing: thou wilt make all his bed in his sickness.

—PSALM 41:3

I do say that sickness ought to do us good. And I do say that God sends it in order to do us good. Affliction is a friendly letter from heaven. It is a knock at the door of conscience. It is the voice of the Savior knocking at the heart's door. Happy is he who opens the letter and reads it, who hears the knock and opens the door, who welcomes Christ to the sick room.

Come now and let me show you a few of the lessons which He by sickness would teach us:

1. Sickness is meant to make us think, to remind us that we have a soul as well as a body, an immortal soul, a soul that will live forever in happiness or in misery, and that if this soul is not saved, we had better never have been born.

2. Sickness is meant to teach us that there is a world beyond the grave and that the world we now live in is only a training place for another dwelling where there will be no decay, no sorrow, no tears, no misery, and no sin.

3. Sickness is meant to send us to our Bibles, that blessed book, which in the days of health is too often left on the shelf and is never opened from January to December. But sickness often brings it down from the shelf and throws new light on its pages.

4. Sickness is meant to draw us to Christ. Naturally we do not see the full value of the blessed Savior. We secretly imagine that our prayers, good deeds, and sacrament receiving will save our souls. But when flesh begins to fail, then the absolute necessity of a Redeemer, a Mediator, and an Advocate with the Father stands out before men's eyes like fire, and makes them understand those words, "Simply to Your cross I cling!" as they never did before. Sickness has done this for many—they have found Christ in the sick room!

❖ From the sermon "Christ in the Sick Room"

Signs of Conversion

Bring forth therefore fruits meet for repentance.
—MATTHEW 3:8

Do you think that you are converted? Then give all diligence to make your calling and conversion sure. Leave nothing uncertain that concerns your immortal soul. Labor to have the witness of the Spirit with your spirit, that you are a child of God. Assurance is to be had in this world, and assurance is worth seeking. It is good to have hope; it is far better to feel sure.

Do you think that you are converted? Then do not expect impossibilities in this world.

Do not suppose the day will ever come when you will find no weak point in your heart, no wanderings in private prayer, no distraction in Bible reading, no cold desires in the public worship of God, no flesh to mortify, no devil to tempt, no worldly snares to make you fall. Expect nothing of the kind. Conversion is not perfection! Conversion is not heaven! The old man within you is yet alive, the world around you is yet full of danger; the devil is not dead. Remember at your best, that a converted sinner is still a poor weak sinner, needing Christ every day. Remember this, and you will not be disappointed.

Do you think you are converted? Then show the value you place on conversion by your diligence in trying to do good to others. Do you really believe it is a dreadful thing to be an unconverted man? Do you really think that conversion is an unspeakable blessing? Then prove it, prove it, prove it, by constant zealous efforts to promote the conversion of others. Look around the neighborhood in which you live, have compassion on the multitudes who are yet unconverted. Be not content with getting them to come to your church or chapel; aim at nothing less than their entire conversion to God. Speak to them, read to them, pray for them, stir up others to help them. But never, never, if you are a converted man, never be content to go to heaven alone!

❖ From the sermon "Conversion"

The Visible Church Is a Mixed Body

*Let both grow together until the harvest: and in the time of harvest
I will say to the reapers, Gather ye together first the tares, and bind
them in bundles to burn them: but gather the wheat into my barn.*
—MATTHEW 13:30

First of all, the visible church of Christ will always be a mixed body until
Christ comes again. I there see wise and foolish virgins mingled together
in one company, virgins with oil, and virgins with no oil, all side by
side. And I see this state of things going on until the very moment the
Bridegroom appears. I see all this, and I cannot avoid the conclusion that
the visible church will always be a mixed body until Jesus comes again.
Its members will never be all unbelievers, Christ will always have His
witnesses. Its members will never be all believers, there will always be a
vast proportion of formality, unbelief, hypocrisy, and false profession. I
frankly say that I can find no standing ground for the common opinion
that the visible church will gradually advance to a state of perfection, that
it will become better and better, holier and holier, up to the very end and
that little by little the whole body shall become full of light.

I fully admit that the gospel appears sometimes to make rapid progress in some countries; but that it ever does more than call out an elect
people, I utterly deny. It never did more in the days of the apostles. Out
of all the cities that Paul visited there is not the slightest proof that in any
one city the whole population became believers. It never has done more
in any country, from the time of the apostle down to the present day.
There never yet was a parish or congregation in any part of the world,
however favored in the ministry it enjoyed, in which all the people were
converted. At all events, I never read or heard of it and my belief is the
thing never has been, and never will. I believe that now is the time of
election, not of universal conversion. Now is the time for the gathering
out of Christ's little flock. The time of general obedience is yet to come.

❖ From the sermon "Coming Events and Present Duties"

Christ Is the One

For ye know the grace of our Lord Jesus Christ, that, though he was rich, yet for your sakes he became poor, that ye through his poverty might be rich.
—2 CORINTHIANS 8:9

He is one who is most loving. He loved us so that He left heaven for our sakes and laid aside for a season the glory that He had with the Father. He loved us so that He was born of a woman for our sakes and lived thirty-three years in this sinful world. He loved us so that He undertook to pay our mighty debt to God and died upon the cross to make atonement for our sins. When such a One as this speaks, He deserves a hearing. When He promises a thing, you need not be afraid to trust Him.

He is one who knows the heart of man most thoroughly. He took on Him a body like our own, and was made like man in all things, sin only excepted. He knows by experience what man has to go through. He has tasted poverty and weariness and hunger and thirst and pain and temptation. He is acquainted with all our condition upon earth. He "himself hath suffered being tempted" (Heb. 2:18). When such a one as this makes an offer, He makes it with perfect wisdom. He knows exactly what you and I need and never breaks His word. He always fulfills His promises. He never fails to do what He undertakes. He never disappoints the soul that trusts Him. Mighty as He is, there is one thing which He cannot do, it is impossible for Him to lie (Heb. 6:18). When one like this makes a promise, you need not doubt that He will stand to it. You may depend with confidence on His word.

❖ From the sermon "Christ's Invitation"

Be Content with What You Have

*Let your conversation be without covetousness; and be content with
such things as ye have: for he hath said, I will never leave thee, nor
forsake thee.*

—HEBREWS 13:5

The words which head this paper are soon spoken, and often cost the
speaker very little. Nothing is cheaper than good advice! Everybody
imagines that he can give his neighbor good counsel and tell him exactly
what he ought to do: "Be content with such things as ye have." These
words are very simple. A little child might easily understand them. They
contain no high doctrine; they involve no deep metaphysical question;
and yet, as simple as they are, the duty which these words enjoin on us,
is one of the highest practical importance to all Christians.

Yet to practice the lesson which heads this paper is very hard. To
talk of contentment in the day of health and prosperity is easy enough;
but to be content in the midst of poverty, sickness, trouble, disappointments, and losses, is a state of mind to which very few can attain! Let us
mark how the great apostle to the Gentiles speaks when he would persuade the Hebrew Christians to be content. He backs up his injunction
with a beautiful motive. He does not say nakedly, "Be content," but adds
words which would ring in the ears of all who read his letter, and nerve
their hearts for a struggle: "Be content with such things as ye have: for
he hath said, I will never leave thee, nor forsake thee." Ah! Reader, if you
would be truly happy—and who does not want that?—seek happiness
where alone it can be found. Seek it not in money, seek it not in pleasure,
nor in friends, nor in learning. Seek it in having a will in perfect harmony
with the will of God. Seek it in studying to be content!

✤ From the sermon "Be Content"

Warning against False Teachings

Be not carried about with divers and strange doctrines. For it is a
good thing that the heart be established with grace; not with meats,
which have not profited them that have been occupied therein.
—HEBREWS 13:9

We have here a broad warning in Hebrews 13:9. "Be not carried about with divers and strange doctrines." The meaning of these words is not a hard thing to understand. "Be not tossed back and forth," the apostle seems to say, "by every blast of false teaching, like ships without compass or rudder. False doctrines will arise as long as the world lasts, in many numbers, with varying minor details, in one point alone always the same, strange, new, foreign, and departing from the gospel of Christ. They do exist now. They will always be found within the visible church. Remember this, and do not be carried away." Such is Paul's warning.

The apostle's warning does not stand alone. Even in the midst of the Sermon on the Mount there fell from the loving lips of our Savior a solemn caution: "Beware of false prophets, which come to you in sheep's clothing, but inwardly they are ravening wolves" (Matt. 7:15). Even in Paul's last address to the Ephesian elders, he finds time to warn his friends against false doctrine: "Also of your own selves shall men arise, speaking perverse things, to draw away disciples after them" (Acts 20:30).

If anyone should ask me, "What is the best safeguard against false doctrine?" I answer in one word, "The Bible, the Bible regularly read, regularly prayed over, regularly studied." We must go back to the old prescription of our Master: "Search the scriptures; for in them ye think ye have eternal life: and they are they which testify of me" (John 5:39). If we want a weapon to wield against the plans of Satan, there is nothing like the sword of the Spirit, the Word of God. But to wield it successfully, we must read it habitually, diligently, intelligently, and prayerfully. This is a point on which, I fear, many fail. In an age of hurry and activity, few read their Bibles as much as they should. More books perhaps are read than ever, but less of the one Book which makes man wise to salvation!

❖ From the sermon "All Kinds of Strange Teaching"

Christian Happiness

Happy is that people, that is in such a case: yea, happy is that people, whose God is the LORD.
—PSALM 144:15

Happiness is what all mankind wants to obtain; the desire for it is deeply planted in the human heart. All men naturally dislike pain, sorrow, and discomfort. All men naturally like ease, comfort, and gladness. All men naturally hunger and thirst after happiness. True happiness is not perfect freedom from sorrow and discomfort. Let that never be forgotten. If it were so, there would be no such thing as happiness in the world. Such happiness is for angels who have never fallen, and not for man. The happiness I am inquiring about is such as a poor, dying, sinful creature may hope to attain. Our whole nature is defiled by sin. Evil abounds in the world. Sickness, death, and change are daily doing their sad work on every side. In such a state of things, the highest happiness man can attain to on earth must necessarily be a mixed thing. If we expect to find any literally perfect happiness on this side of the grave, then we expect what we shall not find!

True happiness does not consist in laughter and smiles. The face is very often a poor index of the inward man. There are thousands who laugh loudly and are merry as a grasshopper in company but are wretched and miserable in private and almost afraid to be alone. And the eternal Word of God teaches us that "even in laughter the heart is sorrowful; and the end of that mirth is heaviness" (Prov. 14:13). Tell me not merely of smiling and laughing faces! I want to hear of something more than that, when I ask whether a man is happy. A truly happy man no doubt will often show his happiness in his countenance; but a man may have a very merry face, and yet not be happy at all. Which one are you?

✤ From the sermon "Happiness"

Who Is in the Family of God?

Which were born, not of blood, nor of the will of the flesh, nor of the will of man, but of God.

—JOHN 1:13

The family before us consists of all real Christians, of all who have the Spirit, of all true believers in Christ, of the saints of every age, and church, and nation, and tongue. It includes the blessed company of all faithful people. It is the same as the election of God, the household of faith, the mystical body of Christ, the bride, the living temple, the sheep that never perish, the church of the firstborn. All these expressions are only the family of God under other names.

Membership in the family of God does not depend on any earthly connection. It comes not by natural birth, but by new birth. Ministers cannot impart it to their hearers. Parents cannot give it to their children. You may be born in the godliest family in the land and enjoy the richest means of grace a church can supply, yet never belong to the family of God. To belong to it, you must be born again. None but the Holy Spirit can make a living member of this family. It is His special office and prerogative to bring into the church such as shall be saved. Those who are born again are "born, not of blood, nor of the will of the flesh, nor of the will of man, but of God" (John 1:13).

Outside this family, remember, there is no salvation. None but those who belong to it, according to the Bible, are in the way that leads to heaven. The salvation of our souls does not depend on union with one church or separation from another. They are miserably deceived, who think that it does, and will find it out to their cost one day, except they awake. No, reader, the life of our souls depends on something far more important! This is life eternal, to be a member of the whole family in heaven and earth!

❖ From the sermon "The Family of God"

Beware of Self-Righteousness!

Hearken unto me, ye stouthearted,
that are far from righteousness.
—ISAIAH 46:12

Oh, let us beware of self-righteousness! Open sin kills its thousands of souls. Self-righteousness kills its tens of thousands! Go and study humility with the great Apostle to the Gentiles. Go and sit with Paul at the foot of the cross. Give up your secret pride. Cast away your vain ideas of your own goodness. Be thankful if you have grace, never boast in it for a moment. Work for God and Christ, with heart and soul and mind and strength, but never dream for a second of placing confidence in any work of your own!

Think, you who take comfort in some fancied ideas of your own goodness, think, you who wrap up yourselves in the notion, "all must be right, if I keep to my church," think for a moment what a sandy foundation you are building upon! Think how miserably defective your hopes and pleas will look in the hour of death, and in the day of judgment! Whatever people may say of their own goodness while they are strong and healthy, they will find but little to say of it when they are sick and dying. Whatever merit they may see in their own works here in this world, they will discover none in them when they stand before the tribunal of Christ. The light of that great day of judgment will make a wonderful difference in the appearance of all their doings. It will strip off the tinsel, shrivel up the complexion, expose the rottenness of many a deed that is now called good. Millions of so-called good works will turn out to have been utterly defective and graceless. They passed current and were valued among men but will prove light and worthless in the balance of God. They will be found to have been like the whitened sepulchres of old—fair and beautiful on the outside, but full of corruption on the inside. Alas for the man who can look forward to the day of judgment and lean his soul in the smallest degree on anything of his own now!

❖ From the sermon "The Cross of Christ"

The True Church

And I say also unto thee, That thou art Peter, and upon this rock I will build my church; and the gates of hell shall not prevail against it.
—MATTHEW 16:18

We live in a world in which all things are passing away. Kingdoms, empires, cities, institutions, families—all are liable to change and corruption. One universal law seems to prevail everywhere: in all created things there is a tendency to decay. There is something sad and depressing in this. What profit has a man in the labor of his hands? Is there nothing that shall stand? Is there nothing that shall last? Is there nothing that shall endure? Is there nothing of which we can say, this shall continue forever?

You have the answer to these questions in the words of our text. Our Lord Jesus Christ speaks of something that will continue and not pass away. There is one created thing which is an exception to the universal rule to which I have referred. There is one thing which shall never perish and pass away. That thing is the building founded upon the rock, the church of our Lord Jesus Christ. He declares, in the words you have heard tonight: "Upon this rock I will build my church; and the gates of hell shall not prevail against it."

There is a good time coming for all the people of God, a good time for all the church of Christ, a good time for all believers. But there is a bad time coming for the impenitent and unbelieving—a bad time for those who serve their own lusts and turn their backs on the Lord—but a good time for true Christians. For that good time, let us wait and watch and pray. The scaffolding will soon be taken down, the last stone will soon be brought out, the topstone will be placed upon the edifice. In a little while, and the full beauty of the building shall be clearly seen. The great master builder will soon come Himself. A building shall be shown to assembled worlds, in which there shall be no imperfection. The Savior and the saved shall rejoice together. The whole universe shall acknowledge that in the building of Christ's church all was well done!

✣ From the sermon "The True Church"

Firm Hold upon God's Truth

Prove all things; hold fast that which is good.
—1 THESSALONIANS 5:21

The words of the apostle on this subject are pithy and forcible. "Hold fast," he says, "that which is good." Paul speaks as one who knew what the hearts of all Christians are. He knew that our grasp of the gospel, at our best, is very cold; that our love soon waxes feeble, that our faith soon wavers; that our zeal soon flags; that familiarity with Christ's truth often brings with it a species of contempt; that, like Israel, we are apt to be discouraged by the length of our journey and, like Peter, ready to sleep one moment and fight the next. But, like Peter, we are not ready to watch and pray. All this Paul remembered, and, like a faithful watchman, he cries by the Holy Spirit, "Hold fast that which is good."

He speaks as if he foresaw by the Spirit that the good tidings of the gospel would soon be corrupted, spoiled, and plucked away from the church at Thessalonica. He speaks as one who foresaw that Satan and all his agents would labor hard to cast down Christ's truth. He writes as though he would forewarn men of this danger, and he cries, "Hold fast that which is good." The advice is always needed, as long as the world stands. There is a tendency to decay in the very best of human institutions. The best visible church of Christ is not free from a liability to degenerate. It is made up of fallible men. There is always in it a tendency to leave its first love. We see the leaven of evil creeping into many a church, even in the apostle's time. There were evils in the Corinthian church, evils in the Ephesian church, evils in the Galatian church. All these things are meant to be beacons in these latter times. All show the great necessity laid upon the church to remember the apostle's words: "Hold fast that which is good."

❖ From the sermon "Private Judgment"

Stand, See, Ask

Thus saith the LORD, Stand ye in the ways, and see, and ask for the old paths, where is the good way, and walk therein, and ye shall find rest for your souls. But they said, We will not walk therein.

—JEREMIAH 6:16

Jeremiah says to you, "Stand, see, ask!" I take these words to be a call to thought and consideration. They are as though the prophet said, "Stop and think. Stand still, pause, and reflect. Look within, behind, and before. Do nothing rashly. What are you doing? Where are you going? What will be the end and consequence of your present line of action? Stop and think."

I ask every reader of this paper to consider his ways. Resolve by the grace of God, if you love life, that you will have regular seasons for examining yourself, and looking over the accounts of your soul. "Stand, and see" where you are going, and how matters stand between you and God. Beware of perpetual hurried prayers, hurried Bible reading, hurried churchgoing, hurried communions. Commune at least once a week with your own heart and be still. Cotton, and coal, and iron, and corn, and ships, and stocks, and land, and gold, and liberalism, and conservatism, are not the only things for which we were sent into the world.

Death and judgment and eternity are not illusions but stern realities. Make time to think about them. Stand still and look them in the face. You will be obliged one day to make time to die, whether you are prepared or not. The last enemy, when he knocks at your door, will brook no delay, and will not wait for a convenient season. He must be admitted, and you will have to go. Happy is he who, when the roar of business and politics is dying away on his ear and the unseen world is looming large, can say, "I know whom I have believed, I have often stood and communed with Him by faith; and now I go to see as I have been seen."

✣ From the sermon "The Good Way"

The Christianity Which the World Requires

These that have turned the world upside down are come hither also.
—ACTS 17:6

The Christianity which the world requires is a Christianity for everyday life. No other religion will ever receive much heartfelt attention from mankind. It may exist; but it will never strike deep root and satisfy souls. A mere Sunday religion is not enough. A thing put on and off with our Sunday clothes is powerless. Thinking men feel and know that there are seven days in a week, and that life is not made up of Sundays. A weekly round of forms and ceremonies within consecrated buildings is not enough. Wise men remember that there is a world of duty and trial, outside the walls of the church, in which they have to play their part. They want something that they can carry with them into that world. A faith which cannot flourish except in an ecclesiastical hothouse, a faith which cannot face the cold air of worldly business and bear fruit except behind the fence of retirement and private asceticism, such a faith is a plant which our heavenly Father has not planted, and it brings no fruit to perfection.

The Christianity which the world requires and the Word of God reveals is of a very different stamp. It is a useful everyday religion. It is a healthy, strong, manly plant, which can live in every position and flourish in every atmosphere except that of sin. It is a religion that a man can carry with him wherever he goes and never need leave behind him. In the army or in the navy, at the public school or at college, in the hospital room or at the bar, on the farm or in the shop, true heaven-born Christianity will live and not die. It will wear and stand and prosper in any climate, in winter and in summer, in heat and in cold. Such a religion meets the needs of mankind. The secret of a vigorous, powerful, everyday Christianity is to be ever looking unto Jesus. The glorious company of the apostles, the noble army of martyrs, the saints who in every age and land have made their mark on mankind, and turned the world upside down, all, all have had one common mint stamp upon them. They have been men who lived looking unto Jesus!

❖ From the sermon "Looking unto Jesus"

Most Important Doctrine

For I determined not to know any thing among you, save Jesus Christ, and him crucified.
—1 CORINTHIANS 2:2

There is no doctrine in Christianity so important as the doctrine of Christ crucified.

There is none which the devil tries so hard to destroy. There is none which it is so needful for our own peace to understand. By "Christ crucified," I mean the doctrine that Christ suffered death on the cross to make atonement for our sins, that by His death He made a full, perfect, and complete satisfaction to God for the ungodly, and that through the merits of that death all who believe in Him are forgiven all their sins, however many and great, entirely, and forever.

The doctrine of Christ crucified is the grand peculiarity of the Christian religion. Other religions have laws and moral precepts, forms and ceremonies, rewards and punishments. But other religions cannot tell us of a dying Savior; they cannot show us the cross. This is the crown and glory of the gospel; this is that special comfort which belongs to it alone. Miserable indeed is that religious teaching which calls itself Christian and yet contains nothing of the cross. A man who teaches in this way might as well profess to explain the solar system and yet tell his hearers nothing about the sun. Christ crucified is God's grand ordinance for doing good to men. Whenever a church keeps back Christ crucified or puts anything whatever in that foremost place which Christ crucified should always have, from that moment a church ceases to be useful.

Reader, if you never heard of Christ crucified before this day, I can wish you nothing better than that you may know Him by faith and rest on Him for salvation. If you do know Him, may you know Him better every year you live, till you see Him face to face.

✢ From the sermon "Christ Crucified"

Never Perish!

And I give unto them eternal life; and they shall never perish, neither shall any man pluck them out of my hand.
                                                            —JOHN 10:28

There are two points in religion on which the teaching of the Bible is very plain and distinct. One of these points is the fearful danger of the ungodly. The other is the perfect safety of the righteous. One is the happiness of those who are converted. The other is the misery of those who are unconverted. One is the blessedness of being on the way to heaven. The other is the wretchedness of being on the way to hell.

I hold it to be of the utmost importance that these two points should be constantly impressed on the minds of professing Christians. I believe that the exceeding privileges of the children of God, and the deadly peril of the children of the world, should be continually set forth in the clearest colors before the church of Christ. Reserve on this subject, is a great injury to the souls of men. Wherever such reserve is practiced, the careless will not be aroused, believers will not be established, and the cause of God will receive damage.

Reader, perhaps you are not aware what a vast store of comforting truths which the Bible contains for the peculiar benefit of real Christians. There is a spiritual treasure house in the Word which many may never enter, and some eyes have not so much as seen. There you will find many a golden truth besides the old first principles of repentance, faith and conversion. There you will see in glorious array, the everlasting election of the saints in Christ, the special love with which God loved them before the foundation of the world, their mystical union with their risen Head in heaven, and His consequent sympathy with them, their interest in the perpetual intercession of Jesus, their High Priest, their liberty of daily communion with Father and the Son, their full assurance of hope, their perseverance to the end!

✤ From the sermon "Never Perish"

The World Is a Danger to the Soul

*Depart ye, depart ye, go ye out from thence, touch no unclean thing;
go ye out of the midst of her; be ye clean, that bear the vessels of
the LORD.* —ISAIAH 52:11

The world is the great rock on which thousands of young people are
continually making shipwreck. They do not object to any article of the
Christian faith. They do not deliberately choose evil and openly rebel
against God. They hope somehow to get to heaven at last, and they think
it proper to have some religion. But they cannot give up their idol; they
must have the world. And so, after running well and bidding fair for
heaven while boys and girls, they turn aside when they become men and
women and go down the broad way which leads to destruction. They
begin with Abraham and Moses and end with Demas and Lot's wife.

The last day alone will prove how many souls the world has slain.
Hundreds will be found to have been trained in religious families and
to have known the gospel from their very childhood, and yet missed
heaven. They left the harbor of home with bright prospects, launched
forth on the ocean of life with a father's blessing and a mother's prayers,
then got off the right course through the seductions of the world, and
ended their voyage in shallows and in misery! It is a sorrowful story
to tell; but, alas, it is only too common. I cannot wonder that Paul
says, "Come out…and be ye separate" (2 Cor. 6:17). You will sometimes
see sincere and well-meaning Christians doing things which God never
intended them to do, in the matter of separation from the world, and
honestly believing that they are in the path of duty. Their mistakes often
do great harm. There are few things about which it is so important to
pray for a right judgment and sanctified common sense, as about separation from the world. Have you broken away?

❖ From the sermon "The World"

I Will Give You Rest

Come unto me, all ye that labour and are heavy laden, and I will give you rest.
                                                            —MATTHEW 11:28

Rest is a pleasant thing, and a thing that all seek after. The merchant, the banker, the tradesman, the soldier, the lawyer, the farmer all look forward to the day when they shall be able to rest. But how few can find rest in this world! How many pass their lives in seeking it, and never seem able to reach it! It seems very near sometimes, and they imagine it will soon be their own. Some new personal calamity happens, and they are as far off rest as ever. The whole world is full of restlessness and disappointment, weariness and emptiness. Take warning, young men and women. Do not think that happiness is to be found in any earthly thing. Do not have to learn this by bitter experience. Realize it while young, and do not waste your time in hewing out "cisterns, broken cisterns, that can hold no water" (Jer. 2:13).

But Jesus offers rest to all who will come to Him. "Come unto me," He says, "and I will give you rest." He will give it. He will not sell it, as the Pharisee supposes, so much rest and peace in return for so many good works. He gives it freely to every coming sinner, without money and without price. He will not lend, as the Arminian supposes, so much peace and rest, all to be taken away by and by if we do not please Him. He gives it forever and ever. His gifts are irrevocable. There is a real rest and peace in Christ for all who come to Him. The man that fled to the city of refuge was safe when once within the walls, though perhaps at first he hardly believed it; and so it is with the believer.

✤ From the sermon "Come unto Me"

Fight Till the End

I have fought a good fight, I have finished my course, I have kept the faith.
—2 TIMOTHY 4:7

I know well it is a hard battle that you have to fight, and I want you to know it too. You must fight the good fight of faith and endure hardships if you would lay hold of eternal life; you must make up your mind to a daily struggle if you would reach heaven. There may be shortcuts to heaven invented by man, but ancient Christianity—the good, old way—is the way of the cross, the way of conflict. Sin, the world, and the devil must be actually mortified, resisted, and overcome.

This is the road that saints of old have trodden and left their record on high. When Moses refused the pleasures of sin in Egypt, and chose affliction with the people of God, this was overcoming: he overcame the love of pleasure. When Micaiah refused to prophesy smooth things to King Ahab, though he knew he would be persecuted if he spoke the truth, this was overcoming: he overcame the love of ease. When Daniel refused to give up praying, though he knew the den of lions was prepared for him, this was overcoming: he overcame the fear of death. When Matthew rose from the receipt of custom at our Lord's bidding, left all and followed Him, this was overcoming: he overcame the love of money. When Peter and John stood up boldly before the council and said, "We cannot but speak the things which we have seen and heard" (Acts 4:20), this was overcoming: they overcame the fear of man. When Saul the Pharisee gave up all his prospects of preferment among the Jews and preached that Jesus whom he had once persecuted, this was overcoming: he overcame the love of man's praise.

Reader, the same kind of thing which these men did you must also do, if you would be saved. They were men of like passions with yourself, and yet they overcame. They had as many trials as any you can possibly have, and yet they overcame. They fought, they wrestled, they struggled; you must do the same.

✤ From the sermon "The Great Battle"

My Sheep Hear My Voice

My sheep hear my voice,
and I know them, and they follow me.
—JOHN 10:27

That is a glorious saying, a perfect and complete text; containing all I need to know for my soul's comfort, full of privileges and mercies for true believers and penitent sinners, and at the same time shutting the door effectually against self-righteous Pharisees and whitened sepulchres and painted hypocrites. It shows us two things: the character of real Christians and the spiritual treasures they possess. Or, in other words, it shows what they are to their Savior, and what their Savior is to them.

"My sheep," we read, "hear my voice...and they follow me." The Lord Jesus Christ likens them to sheep. He declares, "They are Mine, and they hear Me and follow Me." True Christians, then, are compared to sheep, and we shall find a great depth of meaning in the comparison if we look into it. Sheep are the most harmless, quiet, inoffensive creatures that God has made. So should it be with Christians: they should be very humble and lowly minded, as disciples of Him who said, "Learn of me; for I am meek and lowly in heart" (Matt. 11:29). They should be known as people of a very gentle and loving spirit who desire to do good to all around them, who would not injure anyone by word or deed; who do not seek the great things of this world, but are content to go straightforward on the path of duty and take whatever it shall please God to send them. They ought to show forth in their lives and outward conversation that the Holy Spirit has given them a new nature, has taken away their old corrupt disposition and planted in them godly thoughts and purposes and desires.

❖ From the sermon "The Character of the True Christian"

All Wish to Go to Heaven

For our conversation is in heaven; from whence also we look for the
Saviour, the Lord Jesus Christ.
—PHILIPPIANS 3:20

You all wish to go to heaven. I know it. I am fully persuaded of it. I am certain of it. There is not one of you, however false may be his views of what he must believe and what he must do, however unscriptural the ground of his hope, however worldly minded he may be, however careless when he gets outside that church door, there is not one of you, I say, who does not wish to go to heaven when he dies. But I do sadly fear that many of you, without a mighty change, will never get there! You would like the crown, but you do not like the cross! You would like the glory, but not the grace! You would like the happiness, but not the holiness! You would like the peace, but not the truth! You would like the victory, but not the fight! You would like the reward, but not the labor! And so I fear that many of you will never get to heaven!

Well, you may say, "These are sharp words, this is hard teaching! We would like to know what sort of people they are, who will be saved." I shall give you a short and very general answer. Those who have the same faith as those holy men whose names are recorded in the Bible, those who walk in that same narrow path which all the saints of God have trodden, such people, and only such, shall have eternal life and never enter into condemnation.

Indeed, beloved, there is but one way to heaven; and in this way every redeemed soul that is now in paradise has walked. This is the way you must yourselves be content to follow; and if you are really wise, if you really love life, as you profess to do, you will take every opportunity of examining the characters of those who have gone before you, you will mark the principles on which they acted, you will note the end they had in view, you will try to profit by their experience, you will follow them so far as they followed Christ.

❖ From the sermon "Enoch Walking with God"

The Rock from Which Justification
and Peace with God Flow

As it is written, Behold, I lay in Sion a stumblingstone and rock of offence: and whosoever believeth on him shall not be ashamed.
—ROMANS 9:33

That rock is Christ. The true Christian is not justified because of any goodness of his own. His peace is not to be traced to any work that he has done. It is not purchased by his prayers and regularity, his repentance and his amendment, his morality and his charity. All these are utterly unable to justify him. In themselves they are defective in many things and need a large forgiveness. And as to justifying him, such a thing is not to be named. Tried by the perfect standard of God's law the best of Christians is nothing better than a justified sinner, a pardoned criminal. As to merit, worthiness, desert, or claim upon God's mercy, he has none.

Peace built on any such foundations as these is utterly worthless. The man who rests upon them is miserably deceived.

This is the one true way of peace: justification by Christ. Beware lest any turn you out of this way and lead you into any of the false doctrines of the Church of Rome. Alas, it is amazing to see how that false church has built a house of error near by the house of truth! Hold fast the truth of God about justification, and be not deceived. Listen not to anything you may hear about other mediators and helpers to peace. Remember there is no mediator but one, Jesus Christ. Remember there is no purgatory for sinners but one, the blood of Christ. Remember there is no sacrifice for sin but one, the sacrifice once made on the cross. Remember there are no works that can merit anything but the work of Christ. Remember there is no priest who can truly absolve but Christ. Stand fast here and be on your guard. Give not to another the glory due to Christ.

Now, is this peace your own? Bought by Christ with His own blood, offered by Christ freely to all who are willing to receive it, is this peace your own? Oh, rest not, rest not until you can give a satisfactory answer to my question, Have you true peace with God?

❖ From the sermon "Justification"

Christian Love

And now abideth faith, hope, charity, these three;
but the greatest of these is charity.
—1 CORINTHIANS 13:13

Love is rightly called the queen of Christian graces. It is a grace which all people profess to admire. It seems a plain practical thing which everybody can understand. It is none of those troublesome doctrinal points about which Christians are disagreed. I want to remind my readers that the Bible contains much about practice as well as about doctrine, and that one thing to which it attaches great weight is love. I turn to the New Testament and ask readers to observe what it says about love. In all religious inquiries there is nothing like letting Scripture speak for itself. There is no surer way of finding out truth than the old way of turning to plain texts.

Let us hear what Paul says to the Colossians: "And above all these things put on charity, which is the bond of perfectness" (Col. 3:14). Let us hear what Paul says to Timothy: "Now the end of the commandment is charity out of a pure heart, and of a good conscience, and of faith unfeigned" (1 Tim. 1:5). Let us hear what Peter says: "And above all things have fervent charity among yourselves: for charity shall cover the multitude of sins" (1 Peter 4:8). Let us hear what our Lord Jesus Christ Himself says, "A new commandment I give unto you, That ye love one another; as I have loved you, that ye also love one another. By this shall all men know that ye are my disciples, if ye have love one to another" (John 13:34–35). To my own mind, the evidence of these texts appears clear, plain, and incontrovertible. They show the immense importance of love, as one of the things that accompany salvation. They prove that it has a right to demand the serious attention of all who call themselves Christians and that those who despise the subject are only exposing their own ignorance of Scripture!

❖ From the sermon "Christian Love"

Communion with Christ

Abide in me, and I in you. As the branch cannot bear fruit of itself,
except it abide in the vine; no more can ye, except ye abide in me.
—JOHN 15:4

By "communion," I mean that habit of "abiding in" Christ which our
Lord speaks of, in the fifteenth chapter of John's gospel, as essential to
Christian fruitfulness (John 15:4–8). Let it be distinctly understood that
union with Christ is one thing and communion is another. There can
be no communion with the Lord Jesus without union first; but unhappily there may be union with the Lord Jesus, and afterward little or no
communion at all. The difference between the two things is not the
difference between two distinct steps, but the higher and lower ends of
an inclined plane. Union is the common privilege of all who feel their
sins, and truly repent, and come to Christ by faith, and are accepted,
forgiven, and justified in Him. Too many believers, it may be feared,
never get beyond this stage! Partly from ignorance, partly from laziness,
partly from the fear of man, partly from secret love of the world, partly
from some unmortified besetting sin, they are content with a little faith
and a little hope and a little peace and a little measure of holiness. And
they live on all their lives in this condition, doubting, weak, hesitant,
and bearing fruit only thirtyfold to the very end of their days!

Communion with Christ is the privilege of those who are continually striving to grow in grace and faith and knowledge and conformity to
the mind of Christ in all things, who "forget what is behind, and "do not
consider themselves yet to have taken hold of it—but "press on toward
the goal to win the prize for which God has called me heavenward in
Christ Jesus" (Phil. 3:13–14).

❖ From the sermon "Self-Inquiry"

The Power of Children's Sin!

The wicked are estranged from the womb:
they go astray as soon as they be born, speaking lies.
—PSALM 58:3

You must not expect to find your children's minds a sheet of pure white paper, and to have no trouble if you only use right means. I warn you plainly you will find no such thing. It is painful to see how much corruption and evil there is in a young child's heart, and how soon it begins to bear fruit. Violent tempers, self-will, pride, envy, irritability, passion, idleness, selfishness, deceit, cunning, lying, hypocrisy, a terrible aptitude to learn what is bad, a painful slowness to learn what is good, a readiness to pretend anything in order to gain their own ends, all these things, or some of them, you must be prepared to see, even in your own flesh and blood. In little ways they will creep out at a very early age; it is almost startling to observe how naturally they seem to spring up. Children require no schooling to learn how to sin.

But you must not be discouraged and depressed by what you see. You must not think it a strange and unusual thing, that little hearts can be so full of sin. It is the only inheritance which our father Adam left us. It is that fallen nature with which we come into the world, that inheritance which belongs to us all. May the awareness of it make you more diligent in using every possible means which seem most likely, by God's blessing, to counteract the evil. Let it make you more and more careful, so far as it lies with you, to keep your children out of the way of temptation.

Never listen to those who tell you your children are good, and well brought up, and can be trusted. Rather, remember that their hearts are always ready to burst into flame like dry tinder. At their very best, they only need a spark to ignite their evil. Parents are seldom too cautious. Remember the natural depravity of your children and be careful!

✣ From the book *The Duties of Parents*

We Must Fight!

Beloved, when I gave all diligence to write unto you of the common salvation, it was needful for me to write unto you, and exhort you that ye should earnestly contend for the faith which was once delivered unto the saints. —JUDE 3

If we mean to preserve Evangelicalism in the Church of England, if we mean to preserve our own position, if we mean to keep the martyrs' candle lighted, then we must boldly change front, alter our tactics, and take up a new position. We must draw the sword and cast away the scabbard! We must stand to our arms and fight. Our warfare no doubt must be waged spiritually, but really. I repeat it, we must fight!

Some Evangelical churchmen, I know, are men of a gentle and tender spirit, have an instinctive horror of controversy, and always shrink from it in dismay. I can understand their feeling. I do not wonder at it. Controversy no doubt is an odious thing and has a desperate tendency to injure our souls. But surely there are times when controversy is a positive duty, when, as the apostle Jude tells us, we must "earnestly contend for the faith." I remind my brethren that we are not weak, if we make a proper use of the scriptural means which God has put into our hands.

I remind my brethren, above all, that we have no other alternative. If we are base enough to draw back and refuse strife and contention for Christ's truth, then there will soon be nothing for us but submission and disgrace. Some men may cry, "Peace, peace! Oh, sacrifice anything for peace!" But there can be no real peace while our church tolerates and fosters popery! Is ecclesiastical peace so sweet that it is worth purchasing at the expense of truth?

God forbid that we should say so!

❖ From the sermon "We Must Unite"

Many Shall Come

And I say unto you, That many shall come from the east and west, and shall sit down with Abraham, and Isaac, and Jacob, in the kingdom of heaven.
—MATTHEW 8:11

The words of Scripture which head this page were spoken by our Lord Jesus Christ. The Bible contains many predictions of things most unlikely and improbable, which have yet proved true. Was it not said of Ishmael, the father of the Arabian race, that "he will be a wild man; his hand will be against every man, and every man's hand against him; and he shall dwell in the presence of all his brethren" (Gen. 16:12). We see the fulfillment of those words at this very day, when we look at the tribes in the Sudan, or observe the ways of the Bedouins. Was it not said of Egypt that it was finally to become "the basest of the kingdoms," and its inhabitants a people who could neither govern themselves nor be governed (Ezek. 29:15)? We see the fulfillment of those words at this very day along the whole valley of the Nile, and every statesman in Europe knows it to his sorrow. It will be just the same with the prophecy before our eyes. "Many…shall sit down…in the kingdom of heaven."

Take the words as a promise. It was spoken for the encouragement of the apostles, and of all Christian ministers and teachers down to the present day. We are often tempted to think that preaching, and teaching, and visiting, and trying to bring souls to Christ does no good, and that our labor is all thrown away. But here is the promise of One who cannot lie and never failed to keep His word. He cheers us with a gracious sentence. He would have us not faint or give way to despair. Whatever we may think, and however little success we may see, there is a Scripture before us which cannot be broken: "Many…shall sit down…in the kingdom of heaven."

❖ From the sermon "Many Shall Come"

Having the Spirit

These be they who separate themselves,
sensual, having not the Spirit.
—JUDE 19

It is vain to attempt to evade the power of this single expression. It teaches plainly that having the Spirit is not the lot of every individual and not the portion of every member of the visible church of Christ. It shows the necessity of finding out some general rule and principle by which the presence of the Spirit in a person may be ascertained. He does not dwell in everyone. Baptism and service in the church are no proofs of His presence. How, then, shall I know whether a person has the Spirit?

The presence of the Spirit in a human soul can only be known by the effects which He produces. The fruits He causes to be brought forth in someone's heart and life are the only evidence which can be depended on. A person's faith, opinions, and practice are the witnesses we must examine if we want to find out whether he or she has the Spirit. This is the rule of the Lord Jesus: "For every tree is known by his own fruit" (Luke 6:44).

In whomever I see the effects and fruits of the Spirit, in that person I see one who has the Spirit. I believe it to be not only charitable to think so, but presumption to doubt it. I do not expect to behold the Holy Spirit with my bodily eyes, or to touch Him with my hands. But I need no angel to come down to show me where He dwells. I need no vision from heaven to tell me where I may find Him. Only show me a man in whom the fruits of the Spirit are to be seen, and I see one who has the Spirit. I will not doubt the inward presence of the almighty cause when I see the outward fact of an evident effect!

✤ From the sermon "Having the Spirit"

The Heart

My son, give me thine heart,
and let thine eyes observe my ways.
—PROVERBS 23:26

The heart is the main thing in true religion. The head is not the principal thing. You may know the whole truth as it is in Jesus, and consent that it is good. You may be clear, correct, and sound in your religious opinions. But all this time you may be walking in the broad way that leads to destruction. It is your heart that is the main point. Is your heart right in the sight of God? Your outward life may be moral, decent, respectable, in the eyes of people. Your minister and friends and neighbors may see nothing very wrong in your general conduct. But all this time you may be hanging on the brink of everlasting ruin. It is your heart that is the main thing. Is that heart right in the sight of God?

Wishes and desires are not enough to make a Christian. You may have many good feelings about your soul. You may, like Balaam, long to "die the death of the righteous" (Num. 23:10). You may sometimes tremble at the thought of judgment to come or be melted to tears by the tidings of Christ's love. But all this time you may be slowly drifting downward into hell. It is your heart that is the main thing. Is that heart right in the sight of God?

Is your heart right? Then be hopeful about the hearts of other people. Who has made you to differ? Why should not anyone in the world be changed, when such a one as you has been made a new creature? Work on. Pray on. Speak on. Write on. Labor to do all the good you can to souls. Never despair of anyone being saved so long as he is alive. Surely the man who has been changed by grace ought to feel that there are no desperate cases. There are no hearts which it is impossible for Christ to cure!

❖ From the sermon "The Heart"

Death Is before Us

Then shall the dust return to the earth as it was: and the spirit shall return unto God who gave it. —ECCLESIASTES 12:7

Let us remember, furthermore, that death is before us! We cannot live always. There must be an end, one day, of all our scheming and planning, and buying and selling, and working and toiling. A visitor will come to our house who will take no denial. The king of terrors will demand admission and serve us with notice to quit. Where are the rulers and kings who governed millions of subjects a hundred years ago? Where are the rich people who made fortunes and founded houses? Where are the clergymen who performed services and preached sermons? Where are the children who played in the sunshine as if they would never be old? Where are the old people who leaned on their sticks and gossiped about the days when they were young? There is but one answer. They are all dead, dead, dead! Strong and beautiful and active as they once were, they are all dust and ashes now. Mighty and important as they all thought their business, it all came to an end. And we are traveling in the same way. A few more years and we also shall be lying in our graves!

Let us remember, furthermore, that resurrection and judgment await us. All is not over when the last breath is drawn and our bodies become a lump of cold clay. No, all is not over! The realities of existence then begin. The ears that would not obey the churchgoing bell shall be obliged to obey another summons. The proud wills that would not submit to listen to sermons shall be compelled to listen to the judgment of God. The great white throne shall be set, the books shall be opened. Every man, woman, and child shall be arraigned at that great assize. Everyone shall be judged according to his works. The sins of everyone shall be answered for.

Let us think of these things. Surely in remembrance of that day you must allow that my subject deserves attention. Surely you must confess that it is of the utmost importance to have your sins cleansed away. Surely you will consider, "How am I going to be judged?"

❖ From the sermon "Where Are Your Sins?"

Daniel Was Found Faithful

Then said these men, We shall not find any occasion against this Daniel, except we find it against him concerning the law of his God.
—DANIEL 6:5

It would be impossible, I think, to imagine a higher testimony to a man's character than you have heard in these words. You know how ready the world is to find fault with a Christian, how closely his conduct is watched, how eagerly his shortcomings are proclaimed, and happy indeed are those who by grace are so enabled to live, that the godless and profane can find no occasion against them.

Daniel, who was a prince of the royal family of Judah, and descended directly from David, had been carried to Babylon as a prisoner, with many other Jews, when Jerusalem was destroyed. While there, it pleased God to bring him into favor with the heathen kings of Babylon, and he was advanced to great dignity and honor. Nor was his honor ever taken from him; for when Belshazzar was overthrown, and the kingdom of Babylon was taken by the Medes and Persians, the Lord inclined the heart of Darius the Mede to make Daniel the first among his counselors, who ordered all things under the king. But the wicked followers of Darius became jealous of Daniel. They made a conspiracy against him, and for a while they succeeded; for they obtained a decree that Daniel should be cast into the den of lions. But God, whom he served, here came to his assistance: he was miraculously preserved; his enemies were condemned and perished in his stead; and King Darius gave glory to God.

Yes, God's ways are often difficult and mysterious to His people; we cannot see the meaning of many things that happen around us. We think them hard; we almost quarrel with the Lord's arrangements. But those who are really wise will be patient, will wait to see the end, and lay to heart the words of the Lord Jesus: "What I do thou knowest not now; but thou shalt know hereafter" (John 13:7).

❖ From the sermon "Daniel Was Found Faithful"

The Prayer Life of Daniel

Now when Daniel knew that the writing was signed, he went into his house; and his windows being open in his chamber toward Jerusalem, he kneeled upon his knees three times a day, and prayed, and gave thanks before his God, as he did aforetime. Then these men assembled, and found Daniel praying and making supplication before his God. —DANIEL 6:10–11

Notice Daniel's habit of private prayer. This was the hidden cause of all his steadiness, and it was discovered accidentally on this occasion. It seems that his enemies had obtained a decree of the king, that whoever should ask a petition of any God for thirty days should be cast into the den of lions. And having laid this snare for this holy man, we read that they assembled and found Daniel praying and making supplication before God.

We are also told that he was in the habit of kneeling upon his knees and praying three times a day; this was the practice of holy David, as we read in the Psalms, and this was the spirit of the centurion in Acts, who prayed to God always. So Paul exhorts the Ephesians to pray always with all prayer and supplications, and the Thessalonians to pray without ceasing. And such has been the habit of all the most eminent saints of God. They have not been content with a few cold, heartless words every morning and every night, they have lived in the spirit of prayer, and sent up many a short earnest petition throughout the day.

Moreover, we are told that Daniel prayed with his windows open toward Jerusalem, and this is a most important circumstance. We know that he had all the cares of government upon his shoulders; he must have been surrounded with the business and affairs of nations, but none of these things prevented him from drawing near to God. He knew that God would keep him. Mark well, beloved, the habit of private prayer: here is the secret of that steadiness which Daniel showed in Babylon, here was the staff which preserved him upright in the middle of temptations.

✣ From the sermon "Daniel Was Found Faithful"

The Character of Daniel

Then said these men, We shall not find any occasion against this Daniel, except we find it against him concerning the law of his God.
—DANIEL 6:5

Consider his steady walk with God. He was now ninety years of age. He had spent more than the ordinary life of man in the very heart of a wicked city and a corrupt court. He had riches and honors and everything to make this world enjoyable, but he never turned aside from the narrow way, either to the right hand or the left. The eyes of all were fixed upon him; many envied and hated him. They examined his public conduct; they inquired into his private character; they sifted his words and actions, but they sought in vain for any ground of accusation. He was so steady, so upright, so conscientious, that they could find no occasion of fault in him, they could not find any charge against him, except as concerning the law of his God.

Oh, what an unanswerable argument is a believer's life! Oh, what an epistle of Christ is the daily conduct of a child of God! Men cannot see your hearts, nor understand your principles, but they can see your lives! And if they find that pious masters, servants, brothers, friends, sisters, husbands, wives, do far exceed all others in their several positions, then you are bringing glory to God and honor to your Redeemer. Think not that your profession is worth anything, if it is not known of others by its godly fruit; without this it is little better than sounding brass and a tinkling cymbal. We do not find that Daniel blew his trumpet before him and talked everywhere about his own experience, but he walked close to God, and his life spoke for him, and his character became known in Babylon, and even his enemies were obliged to confess: The hand of God is here, the Lord is truly with this man!

❖ From the sermon "Daniel Was Found Faithful"

Daniel's Confidence in God

Then the king commanded, and they brought Daniel, and cast him into the den of lions. Now the king spake and said unto Daniel, Thy God whom thou servest continually, he will deliver thee.
—DANIEL 6:16

The last point to be observed in Daniel's character is his faith, his confidence in God. The decree appeared, forbidding all sorts of worship for thirty days on pain of death. And oh, how many professors of our generation would have held their peace! How many would have said, "It is but a short time, we need not give offense; the Lord does not require us to lose our lives in His service"? But look at Daniel: he knew that the writing was signed, he knew that he was watched, he knew that his life was at stake, and yet he went to his house and kneeled on his knees and prayed as he did before. He did not on the one hand run into danger, nor did he on the other flinch from it. Here was no carnal policy, no timeserving, no crooked contrivance, no love of expediency. He made a straight path for his feet; he did as usual, neither more nor less; and why? Look at verse 23: "he believed in his God." Mark here the fruits of daily communion with God; see how a habit of prayer will produce quietness and assurance in the hour of trial and difficulty.

There never have been lacking lewd men of the baser sort who say, "Where is the use of your praying? What good will it do you?" But wait until the days of affliction come upon you and the Lord will provide you with an answer. A habit of prayer will impart special reliance upon God in time of danger; it will give a special boldness; it will secure a special deliverance, for those who honor God He will honor. Happy indeed are those who, like Daniel, pray without ceasing. They will find within them the same spirit of faith; they never need fear being surprised; they are like him, always the same and always ready.

❖ From the sermon "Daniel Was Found Faithful"

Seasons of Darkness

Then the king commanded, and they brought Daniel, and cast him into the den of lions. Now the king spake and said unto Daniel, Thy God whom thou servest continually, he will deliver thee. And a stone was brought, and laid upon the mouth of the den; and the king sealed it with his own signet, and with the signet of his lords; that the purpose might not be changed concerning Daniel.

—DANIEL 6:16–17

Who would have supposed that God would have allowed iniquity so far to triumph as to leave Daniel in the hands of enemies! Who would have thought that this pious old man would be cast into the den of lions. But God's ways are not as our ways, and strange as it may appear, the wicked were permitted to work their will for a season. Daniel was accused of breaking the laws; he was pronounced guilty; he was condemned to death; the king labored to deliver him, but he could not; the decree could not be altered, Daniel must die! He was let down into this pit, the den of savage beasts, and a stone was laid upon the mouth of the den.

Pause here, beloved, for an instant. This hour of darkness seems to you a mystery. Do you not often see things hard to understand in the world around you? How often the wicked prosper and have all that man could desire; how often iniquity abounds, and the love of God waxes cold, and the righteous are oppressed and silenced and afraid. How often it seems as if the Lord has forgotten this earth and cares not though His servants are persecuted and His name blasphemed. How often we feel disposed to cry, "How long, O Lord, holy and true, will You not judge and avenge Yourself on the ungodly!"

Fear not because you sometimes walk in darkness and have no light. Remember that you cannot understand the mind of the Lord or the meaning of His dealings. But when the clouds compass you about, believe in God as Daniel did; trust in the Lord Jesus at all times. Be sure, be very sure, he who believes shall never be ashamed.

❖ From the sermon "Daniel Was Found Faithful"

Daniel Delivered

Then said Daniel unto the king, O king, live for ever. My God hath sent his angel, and hath shut the lions' mouths, that they have not hurt me: forasmuch as before him innocency was found in me; and also before thee, O king, have I done no hurt. —DANIEL 6:21–22

Come now and hear how the darkness was scattered and the light returned. Heaviness may endure for a night, but joy comes in the morning. Daniel, you have seen, was allowed to go through the furnace of tribulation, but the time came at last when God intervened on His servant's behalf and made His dealings clear and plain. Daniel was cast into the lions' den, but the Lord was with him and therefore he was safe. We read that the king, Darius, came very early in the morning to the mouth of the cave, and cried with an anxious and lamentable voice, "Daniel… is thy God…able to deliver thee?" (Dan. 6:20). And oh, how joyful must his feelings have been when he heard the holy man's reply: "O king, live forever. My God has sent his angel and shut the lions' mouths, that they have not hurt me: forasmuch as before him innocency was found in me" (vv. 21–22)!

And need I tell you that Daniel was brought forth, and honored and exalted; while his enemies, in their turn, were cast into the den and the lions destroyed them all? So true it is that light is sown for the righteous, that God will keep in perfect peace, those whose minds are stayed on Him. So true is Psalm 91, which tells us that the one who lives under the protection of the Most High dwells in the shadow of the Almighty. He Himself will deliver you from the hunter's net, from the destructive plague. He will cover you with His feathers; you will take refuge under His wings. His faithfulness will be a protective shield!

❖ From the sermon "Daniel Was Found Faithful"

Hope That Rests Entirely on Jesus Christ

To whom God would make known what is the riches of the glory of this mystery among the Gentiles; which is Christ in you, the hope of glory.
—COLOSSIANS 1:27

The person who has a good hope founds all his expectations of pardon and salvation on the mediation and redeeming work of Jesus, the Son of God. He knows his own sinfulness; he feels that he is guilty, wicked, and lost by nature, but he sees forgiveness and peace with God offered freely to him through faith in Christ. He accepts the offer, he casts himself with all his sins on Jesus, and rests on Him. Jesus and His atonement on the cross, Jesus and His righteousness, Jesus and His finished work, Jesus and His all-prevailing intercession—Jesus, and Jesus only, is the foundation of the confidence of his soul.

Let us beware of supposing that any hope is good which is not founded on Christ. All other hopes are built on sand. They may look well in the summertime of health and prosperity, but they will fail in the day of sickness and the hour of death. "For other foundation can no man lay than that is laid, which is Jesus Christ" (1 Cor. 3:11). Church membership is no foundation of hope. We may belong to the best of churches and yet never belong to Christ.

We may fill our pew regularly every Sunday and hear the sermons of orthodox, ordained clergymen, and yet never hear the voice of Jesus or follow Him. If we have nothing better than church membership to rest upon we are in a poor plight. We have nothing solid beneath our feet.

Christ Himself is the only true foundation of a good hope. He is the rock; His work is perfect. He is the stone, the sure stone, the tried cornerstone. He is able to bear all the weight that we can lay upon Him. He only that builds and "believeth on him shall not be confounded" (1 Peter 2:6; see also Deut. 32:4; Isa. 28:16).

✤ From the sermon "Our Hope"

The Best Friend

His mouth is most sweet: yea, he is altogether lovely.
This is my beloved, and this is my friend.
—SONG OF SOLOMON 5:16

A friend is one of the greatest blessings on earth. Tell me not of money, love is better than gold; sympathy is better than lands. He is a poor man who has no friends! This world is full of sorrow because it is full of sin. It is a dark place. It is a lonely place. It is a disappointing place. The brightest sunbeam in it is a friend. Friendship halves our troubles and doubles our joys!

A real friend is scarce and rare. There are many who will eat and drink and laugh with us in the sunshine of prosperity. There are few who will stand by us in the days of darkness—few who will love us when we are sick, helpless, and poor—few, above all, who will care for our souls. Does any reader of this paper want a real friend? I write to recommend one to your notice this day. I know of one "friend that sticketh closer than a brother" (Prov. 18:24)! I know of one who is ready to be your friend for time and for eternity, if you will receive Him. Hear me while I try to tell you something about Him.

Man is the neediest creature on God's earth because he is a sinner. There is no need as great as that of sinners: poverty, hunger, thirst, cold, sickness, all are nothing in comparison. Sinners need pardon and are utterly unable to provide it for themselves; they need deliverance from a guilty conscience and the fear of death, but have no power of their own to obtain it. This need the Lord Jesus Christ came into the world to relieve. He came into the world to save sinners! The friend I want you to know is Jesus Christ. Happy is that family in which Christ has the foremost place! Happy is that person whose chief friend is Christ!

✣ From the sermon "The Best Friend"

Preach Christ's Cross

For the preaching of the cross is to them that perish foolishness;
but unto us which are saved it is the power of God.
—1 CORINTHIANS 1:18

The cross is the foundation of a church's prosperity. No church will ever be honored in which Christ crucified is not continually lifted up, nothing whatever can make up for the lack of the cross. Without it all things may be done decently and in order; without it there may be splendid ceremonies, beautiful music, gorgeous churches, learned ministers, crowded Communion tables, huge collections for the poor. But without the cross no good will be done; dark hearts will not be enlightened, proud hearts will not be humbled, mourning hearts will not be comforted, fainting hearts will not be cheered.

Sermons about the church and an apostolic ministry, sermons about baptism and the Lord's Supper, sermons about unity and schism, sermons about fasts and Communion, sermons about fathers and saints—such sermons will never make up for the absence of sermons about the cross of Christ. They may amuse some; they will feed none. A gorgeous banqueting room and splendid gold plate on the table will never make up to a hungry man for the lack of food. Christ crucified is God's ordinance for doing good to people. Whenever a church keeps back Christ crucified or puts anything whatever in that foremost place which Christ crucified should always have, from that moment a church ceases to be useful. Without Christ crucified in her pulpits, a church is little better than a cumberer of the ground, a dead carcass, a well without water, a barren fig tree, a sleeping watchman, a silent trumpet, a speechless witness, an ambassador without terms of peace, a messenger without tidings, a lighthouse without fire, a stumbling block to weak believers, a comfort to infidels, a hotbed for formalism, a joy to the devil, and an offense to God!

✤ From the sermon "The Cross of Christ"

Edify One Another

Wherefore comfort yourselves together,
and edify one another, even as also ye do.
—1 THESSALONIANS 5:11

Let us believers take more pains to edify others! It is incredible and sad to see how Scripture speaks on this matter and then to observe the conduct of many of Christ's people. Paul tells the Corinthians that the members of Christ "should have the same care one for another" (1 Cor. 12:25). He says to the Thessalonians, "Edify one another, even as also ye do" (1 Thess. 5:11). He says to the Hebrews, "Exhort one another daily... lest any of you be hardened through the deceitfulness of sin" (Heb. 3:13) and again, "Consider one another to provoke unto love and to good works...exhorting one another: and so much the more, as ye see the day approaching" (Heb. 10:24–25). Brethren, I fear we fall very short of the New Testament Christians in this respect. We are sadly apt to lose sight of this edifying one another when we are in the company of believing friends. Prayer and the Word and godly conversation are not put in the foremost place, and so we separate, being nothing the better, but rather worse. Far too often there is so much coldness, and restraint, and reserve, and backwardness, that a man might imagine we were ashamed of Christ, and that we thought it proper to hold our tongues, and not make mention of the name of the Lord.

Let us bring out the Bible more when we get together. We none of us know it all yet; our brother may have found some pearl in it which has escaped our eyes, and we perhaps may show him something in return. It is the common map by which we all journey; let us not behave as if we had each a private map to be studied in a corner and kept to ourselves. Oh, that the Word were like a burning fire shut up in our bones, so that we could not forbear speaking of it! He who tries to promote holiness in others shall reap a blessed reward in his own soul. He waters others, and he shall be watered himself.

✣ From the sermon "Consider Your Ways"

Our Need of Forgiveness

I write unto you, little children,
because your sins are forgiven you for his name's sake.
—1 JOHN 2:12

All people need forgiveness because all people are sinners. He who does not know this knows nothing in religion. It is the very ABCs of Christianity that a man should know his right place in the sight of God and understand his deserts. We are all great sinners. "There is none righteous, no, not one" (Rom. 3:10) and "all have sinned, and come short of the glory of God" (3:23). Sinners we were born and sinners we have been all our lives. We take to sin naturally from the very first. No child ever needs schooling and education to teach it to do wrong. No devil or bad companion ever leads us into such wickedness as our own hearts. And "the wages of sin is death" (Rom. 6:23). We must either be forgiven or lost eternally.

We are all guilty sinners in the sight of God. We have broken His holy law. We have transgressed His precepts. We have not done His will. There is not a commandment in all the ten which does not condemn us. If we have not broken it in deed we have in word; if we have not broken it in word, we have in thought and imagination, and that continually. All the world is "guilty before God" (Rom. 3:19). "And as it is appointed unto men once to die, but after this the judgment" (Heb. 9:27). We must either be forgiven or perish everlastingly.

When I walk through the crowded streets of London I see hundreds and thousands of whom I know nothing beyond their outward appearance. I see some bent on pleasure, and some on business, some who look rich, and some who look poor, some rolling in their carriages, some hurrying along on foot. Each has his own object in view. But one thing I know for a certainty as I look upon them: they are all sinners. There breathes not the man or woman in that crowd but must die forgiven, or else rise again to be condemned forever at the last day.

✤ From the sermon "Forgiveness"

Jellyfish Christianity

For the time will come when they will not endure sound doctrine;
but after their own lusts shall they heap to themselves teachers, hav-
ing itching ears. —2 TIMOTHY 4:3

The consequences of this widespread dislike to doctrine are very serious in the present day. Whether we like to allow it or not, it is an epidemic which is doing great harm. It produces what I must venture to call, if I may coin the phrase, a jellyfish Christianity in the churches. A Christianity without bone, or muscle, or sinew, without any distinct teaching about the atonement, or the work of the Spirit, or justification, or the way of peace with God—a vague, foggy, misty Christianity, of which the only watchwords seem to be, "You must be liberal and kind. You must condemn no man's doctrinal views. You must think everybody is right, and nobody is wrong."

A jellyfish, as everyone knows who has been much by the seaside, is a pretty and graceful object when it floats in the sea, contracting and expanding like a little, delicate, transparent umbrella. Yet the same jellyfish, when cast on the shore, is a mere helpless lump, without capacity for movement, self-defense, or self-preservation. Alas! It is a vivid type of much of the religion of this day, of which the leading principle is, "No dogma, no distinct tenets, no positive doctrine." We have hundreds of jellyfish clergymen who seem not to have a single bone in their body of divinity. They have no definite opinions. They belong to no school or party. They are so afraid of "extreme" views that they have no views at all. We have thousands of jellyfish sermons preached every year, sermons without an edge or a point. They are as smooth as billiard balls, awakening no sinner, and edifying no saint.

They are tossed to and fro, like children, by every wind of doctrine! They are often carried away by any new excitement and sensational movement. They are ever ready for new things, because they have no firm grasp on the old Scripture truths!

❖ From the tract *Jellyfish Christianity*

Assurance Leads to Fruitfulness

*Being confident of this very thing, that he which hath begun a good
work in you will perform it until the day of Jesus Christ.*
—PHILIPPIANS 1:6

Generally speaking, none do so much for Christ on earth as those who
enjoy the fullest confidence of a free entrance into heaven. That sounds
wonderful, I daresay, but it is true. A believer who lacks an assured hope
will spend much of his time in inward searchings of heart about his own
state. He will be full of his own doubtings and questionings, his own
conflicts and corruptions. In short, you will often find that he is so taken
up with this internal warfare that he has little leisure for other things,
little time to work for God.

Now a believer who has, like Paul, an assured hope is free from these
harassing distractions. He does not vex his soul with doubts about his
own pardon and acceptance. He looks at the covenant sealed with blood,
at the finished work and never-broken word of his Lord and Savior,
and therefore counts his salvation a settled thing. And thus he is able to
give undivided attention to the Lord's work, and so in the long run to
do more.

None will do so much for the Lord who bought them as the believer
who sees that title clear. The joy of the Lord will be that man's strength.
"Restore unto me," says David, "the joy of thy salvation…then will I
teach transgressors thy ways" (Ps. 51:12–13). Never were there such
working Christians as the apostles. They seemed to live to labor. Christ's
work was their food and drink. They counted not their lives dear; they
spent and were spent; they laid down health, ease, worldly comfort at
the foot of the cross. And one cause of this, I believe, was their assured
hope. They were men who said, "We know that we are of God."

⊹ From the sermon "Assurance"

The Things of This World

Ye adulterers and adulteresses, know ye not that the friendship of the world is enmity with God? whosoever therefore will be a friend of the world is the enemy of God. —JAMES 4:4

What then shall I say of the things of this world, which men appear to think so valuable—money, houses, land, clothes, fine food and drink, learning, honors, titles, pleasures, amusements, and the like? Beloved, I shall say two things. First, they are all really worthless! Such things are capable, no doubt, of being turned to a good use (every creature of God, says the Bible, is good if sanctified by the word of God and prayer), but I mean this—that if you suppose they are in themselves able to make you really happy, you are woefully deceived! If any unconverted person in this parish could have just as much as he wished of every earthly good thing, he would still find in a very short time that he was not one whit happier than before.

Second, I say that all the things of the world are perishable! Surely, dear friends, this cannot require any evidence. You must have seen with your own eyes that none of the things I have mentioned are sure, lasting, permanent, incorruptible, and to be depended on. Money and property may be lost; health may fail; friends may be deceitful; and unless we can make a covenant with death and hell, we ourselves may suddenly be cut off in the midst of our days and hurried to our final judgment!

Job said, "Man that is born of a woman is of few days and full of trouble. He cometh forth like a flower, and is cut down: he fleeth also as a shadow, and continueth not" (Job 14:1–2). "There is hope of a tree, if it be cut down, that it will sprout again.... But man dieth, and wasteth away: yea, man giveth up the ghost, and where is he" (Job 14:7, 10)? Such is the world! "And the world passeth away, and the lust thereof: but he that doeth the will of God abideth for ever" (1 John 2:17)!

❖ From the sermon "Profit and Loss"

Sickness

And we know that all things work together for good to them that love God, to them who are the called according to his purpose.
—ROMANS 8:28

I invite the attention of my readers to the subject of sickness. The subject is one which we ought frequently to look in the face. We cannot avoid it. It needs no prophet's eye to see sickness coming to each of us in turn one day. In the midst of life we are in death. Let us turn aside for a few moments, and consider sickness as Christians. The consideration will not hasten its coming, and by God's blessing may teach us wisdom.

Sickness is everywhere. In Europe, in Asia, in Africa, in America; in hot countries and in cold, in civilized nations and in savage tribes, men, women, and children sicken and die.

Sickness is among all classes. Grace does not lift a believer above it. The universal prevalence of sickness is indirect evidence that the Bible is true. The Bible explains it. The Bible answers the questions about it which will arise in every inquiring mind. No other systems of religion can do this. They all fail here. They are silent. They are confounded. The Bible alone looks the subject in the face. It boldly proclaims the fact that man is a fallen creature, and with equal boldness proclaims a vast remedial system to meet his needs.

Now what can we make of this great fact—the universal prevalence of sickness? How shall we account for it? What explanation can we give of it?

The only explanation that satisfies me is that which the Bible gives. Something has come into the world which has dethroned man from his original position and stripped him of his original privileges. And what is that something? I answer, in one word, it is sin. "Sin entered into the world, and death by sin" (Rom. 5:12.) Sin is the cause of all the sickness and disease and pain and suffering which prevail on the earth. They are all a part of that curse which came into the world when Adam and Eve ate the forbidden fruit and fell. There would have been no sickness if there had been no fall. There would have been no disease if there had been no sin.

❖ From the sermon "Sickness"

The Means of Regeneration

So then faith cometh by hearing,
and hearing by the word of God.
—ROMANS 10:17

The preaching of the Word is the great means which God has appointed for regeneration: "So then faith cometh by hearing, and hearing by the word of God" (Rom. 10:17). This change is one which can only be known and discerned by its effects. Its beginnings are a hidden and secret thing. We cannot see them. Our Lord Jesus Christ tells us this most plainly: "The wind bloweth where it listeth, and thou hearest the sound thereof, but canst not tell whence it cometh, and whither it goeth: so is every one that is born of the Spirit" (John 3:8). This change is one which no man can give to himself, nor yet to another. It would be as reasonable to expect the dead to raise themselves, or to require an artist to give life to a marble statue. The sons of God are born "not of blood, nor of the will of the flesh, nor of the will of man, but of God" (John 1:13). Sometimes the change is ascribed to God the Father: "Blessed be the God and Father of our Lord Jesus Christ, which according to his abundant mercy hath begotten us again unto a lively hope by the resurrection of Jesus Christ from the dead" (1 Peter 1:3).

Would we know if we are regenerate? We must try the question by examining what we know of the effects of regeneration. Those effects are always the same. The ways by which true Christians are led in passing through their great change are certainly various. But the state of heart and soul into which they are brought at last is always the same. Ask them what they think of sin, Christ, holiness, the world, the Bible, and prayer, and you will find them all of one mind!

✤ From the sermon "Regeneration"

Out of Great Tribulation

And I said unto him, Sir, thou knowest. And he said to me, These are they which came out of great tribulation, and have washed their robes, and made them white in the blood of the Lamb. Therefore are they before the throne of God, and serve him day and night in his temple: and he that sitteth on the throne shall dwell among them. They shall hunger no more, neither thirst any more; neither shall the sun light on them, nor any heat. —REVELATION 7:14–16

That is, they have come out of a world full of sin and danger, a world in which they have so much to encounter which is hurtful to their souls that you may truly call it a place of great tribulation. How strange that seems! This earth so fair and lovely as it appears, so full of everything to make life enjoyable; this earth on which millions set all their affections and have not a thought beyond it, is a wilderness beset with trials and difficulties to every true believer. Write this down on the tablet of your memory, that if you make up your mind to follow Christ and have your soul saved, you will sooner or later have to go through great tribulation.

Brethren, why are these things so? Because the world you live in is a fallen world, the devil is the prince of it, and by far the greater part of the men and women in it have shut their eyes and given themselves up to his service. Once you become a follower of Christ, you will see iniquity abounding on every side, you will see your blessed Savior's laws trampled underfoot, you will find the immense majority of those around you to be spiritually dark, sleeping, and dead, some altogether thoughtless, some resting on a form of godliness without the power. And if you love the Lord Jesus in sincerity, to see your Redeemer thus despised will make the world a place of tribulation.

✜ From the sermon "The Blood of the Lamb"

Importance of Public Worship

But in vain they do worship me,
teaching for doctrines the commandments of men.
—MATTHEW 15:9

Public worship, I am bold to say, has always been one mark of God's servants. As a general rule, man is a social being and does not like to live separate from his fellows. In every age God has made use of that mighty principle and has taught His people to worship Him publicly as well as privately, together as well as alone. I believe the last day will show that wherever God has had a people, He has always had a congregation. His servants, however few in number, have always assembled themselves together, and approached their heavenly Father in company. They have been taught to do it for many wise reasons, partly to bear a public testimony to the world; partly to strengthen, cheer, help, encourage, and comfort one another; and above all, to train and prepare them for the general assembly in heaven. "Iron sharpeneth iron; so a man sharpeneth the countenance of his friend" (Prov. 27:17). That man can know little of human nature, who does not know that to see others doing and professing the same things that we do in religion, is an immense help and encouragement to our souls.

You see it throughout the whole New Testament. The Lord Jesus Himself gives a special promise of His presence wherever two or three are assembled in His name. The apostles, in every church they founded, made the duty of assembling together a first principle in their list of duties. Their universal rule was "not forsaking the assembling of ourselves together" (Heb. 10:25). These are ancient things, I know, but it is well to be reminded of them. Just as you may lay it down as a certainty that where there is no private prayer, there is no grace in a man's heart, so you may lay it down as the highest probability that where there is no public worship, there is no church of God, and no profession of Christianity.

❖ From the sermon "Worship"

100,000 Sins!

Order my steps in thy word:
and let not any iniquity have dominion over me.
—PSALM 119:133

I say this boldly, and without the least hesitation. I know not who you are, or how the time past of your life has been spent. But I know, from the Word of God, that every son and daughter of Adam is a great sinner in the sight of God. There is no exception. Sin is the common disease of the whole family of mankind in every quarter of the globe. From the king on his throne, to the beggar by the roadside; from the landlord in his hall, to the laborer in his cottage; from the fine lady in her drawing room, to the humblest maidservant in the kitchen; from the clergyman in the pulpit, to the little child in the Sunday school, we are all by nature guilty, guilty, guilty in the sight of God!

Sit down and take pen and paper and count up the sins that you have probably sinned since you first knew good from evil. Sit down, I say, and make a sum. Grant for a moment that there have been on average fifteen hours in every twenty-four during which you have been awake and an active and accountable being. Grant for a moment that in each one of these fifteen hours you have sinned only two sins. Surely you will not say that this is an unfair supposition. Remember we may sin against God in thought, word, or deed. And now add up the sins of your life and see to what sum they will amount.

At the rate of fifteen waking hours in a day, you have sinned every day thirty sins! At the rate of seven days in a week, you have sinned 210 sins every week! At the rate of four weeks in every month, you have sinned 840 sins every month! At the rate of twelve months in every year, you have sinned 10,080 sins every year! And, in short, not to go further with the calculation, every ten years of your life you have sinned, at the lowest computation, more than 100,000 sins!

✤ From the sermon "Where Are Your Sins?"

The Way to Peace

Let him eschew evil, and do good; let him seek peace, and ensue it.
—1 PETER 3:11

You want peace! Then seek it without delay from Him who alone is able to give it, Christ Jesus the Lord. Go to Him in humble prayer and ask Him to fulfill His own promises and look graciously on your soul. Tell Him you have read His compassionate invitation to the "laboring and heavy laden." Tell Him that this is the plight of your soul, and implore Him to give you rest. Do this and do it without delay. Seek Christ Himself, and do not stop short of personal dealings with Him. Rest not in regular attendance on Christ's ordinances. Be not content with becoming a communicant and receiving the Lord's Supper. Think not to find solid peace in this way. You must see the King's face and be touched by the golden scepter. You must speak to the physician and open your whole case to Him. You must be closeted with the Advocate and keep nothing back from Him.

Seek Christ and wait for nothing. Wait not until you feel you have repented enough. Wait not until your knowledge is increased. Wait not until you have been sufficiently humbled because of your sins. Wait not until you have no raveled tangle of doubts and darkness and unbelief all over your heart. Seek Christ just as you are. You will never be better by keeping away from Him. Alas, it is not humility, but pride and ignorance that make so many anxious souls hang back from closing with Jesus. They forget that the sicker a man is, the more need he has of the physician. The worse a man feels his heart, the more readily and speedily ought he to flee to Christ.

Seek Christ, and do not fancy you must sit still. Let not Satan tempt you to suppose that you must wait in a state of passive inaction, and not strive to lay hold upon Jesus. How you can lay hold upon Him I do not pretend to explain. But I am certain that it is better to struggle toward Christ and strive to lay hold than to sit still with our arms folded in sin and unbelief.

✣ From the sermon "Justification"

The Day Is Soon at Hand

The night is far spent, the day is at hand: let us therefore cast off the works of darkness, and let us put on the armour of light.
—ROMANS 13:12

There is a time coming, when believers shall have joy and gladness and sorrow and sighing shall flee far away. Every tear shall be wiped away, every cross laid down, every anxiety removed, every bitter cup taken away! Persecution, temptation, sickness, mourning, parting, separation, and death shall be at end! Surely that will be sunshine. It will be day. There is a time coming when the whole family of Christ shall be gathered together. They shall rise from their narrow beds and each put on a glorious body. They shall awake from their long sleep refreshed, strengthened, and far more beautiful than when they lay down. They shall leave behind them in their graves, every imperfection, and meet without spot or wrinkle, to part no more. Surely that will be a joyful morning. It will be day.

There is a time coming when believers shall no longer see through a glass darkly, but face-to-face. They shall see as they have been seen and know as they have been known. They shall cease to wrangle and dispute about outward matters and shall think of nothing but eternal realities. They shall behold their crucified Lord and Savior with the eye of sense and no longer follow Him by faith. They shall see one another free from all corruption, misunderstanding one another's motives and conduct no more. Surely that will be day.

There is a day before you, a glorious day. You sometimes feel now as if you walked in darkness and had no light. You often have a hard battle to fight with the world, the flesh, and the devil. You sometimes imagine that you will never win your way home and must faint along the way. Your flesh and heart are ready to fail. You are sorely tempted to give up and to sit down in despair. But take comfort in the thought of things yet to come. There is a good time before you. Your day has yet to dawn!

❖ From the sermon "Coming Events and Present Duties"

The Importance of Dogma

For the which cause I also suffer these things: nevertheless I am not ashamed: for I know whom I have believed, and am persuaded that he is able to keep that which I have committed unto him against that day.
—2 TIMOTHY 1:12

"Dogma" is a word that simply means a definite ascertained truth, which is no longer the subject of inquiry, simply because inquiry has ended, and the result has been accepted. Wherever there is any fixed ascertained truth whatever, there must be dogma. If there is no dogma, then there is no known truth. It is the duty of ministers to speak like men who have quite made up their minds, who have grappled with Pilate's question "What is truth?" and are prepared to give the question an unhesitating answer. In short, if men mean to be faithful ministers of the New Testament, they must hold and teach dogma.

It was dogma in the apostolic ages that emptied the heathen temples and shook Greece and Rome. It was dogma that awoke Christendom from its slumbers at the time of the Reformation and spoiled the pope of one-third of his subjects. It was dogma that, a hundred years ago, revived the Church of England in the days of Whitefield, Wesley, Venn, and Romaine and blew up our dying Christianity into a burning flame. It is dogma at this moment that gives power to every successful mission, whether at home or abroad. It is doctrine, doctrine, clear ringing doctrine, that, like the rams' horns at Jericho, casts down the opposition of the devil and sin. Let us go on clinging to dogma and doctrine, whatever some may please to say; and we shall do well for ourselves, well for others, well for the Church of England, and well for Christ's cause in the world!

✣ From the sermon "The Importance of Dogma"

Guard against Idolatry

Wherefore, my dearly beloved, flee from idolatry.
—1 CORINTHIANS 10:14

Idolatry is a sin that we all need to watch and pray against continually. It creeps into our religious worship insensibly and is upon us before we are aware. Idolatry is that sin which God has especially denounced in His Word. One commandment out of ten is devoted to the prohibition of it. Not one of all the ten contains such a solemn declaration of God's character, and of His judgments against the disobedient: "Thou shalt not bow down thyself to them, nor serve them: for I the LORD thy God am a jealous God, visiting the iniquity of the fathers upon the children unto the third and fourth generation of them that hate me" (Ex. 20:5). Not one, perhaps, of all the ten is so emphatically repeated and amplified, and especially in the fourth chapter of the book of Deuteronomy.

Idolatry is the sin, of all others, to which the Jews seem to have been most inclined before the destruction of Solomon's temple. What is the history of Israel under their judges and kings, but a melancholy record of repeated falling away into idolatry? Again and again, we read of high places and false gods. Again and again, we read of captivities and chastisements on account of idolatry. Again and again, we read of a return to the old sin. It seems as if the love of idols among the Jews was naturally bone of their bone and flesh of their flesh. The besetting sin of the Old Testament church, in one word, was idolatry! In the face of the most elaborate ceremonial ordinances that God ever gave to His people, Israel was incessantly turning aside after idols, and worshiping the work of men's hands.

Let us gather up these things in our minds and ponder them well. Idolatry is a subject that, in every church of Christ that would keep herself pure, should be thoroughly examined, understood, and known. It is not for nothing that Paul lays down the stern command, "Flee from idolatry" (1 Cor. 10:14).

❖ From the sermon "Coming Events and Present Duties"

Zealous Christians

But it is good to be zealously affected always in a good thing, and not only when I am present with you. —GALATIANS 4:18

Zeal is a subject, like many others in religion, most sadly misunderstood. Many would be ashamed to be thought zealous Christians. Many are ready to say of zealous people what Festus said of Paul: "Paul, thou art beside thyself; much learning doth make thee mad" (Acts 26:24). But zeal is a subject that no reader of the Bible has any right to pass over. If we make the Bible our rule of faith and practice, we cannot turn away from it. We must look it in the face. What says the apostle Paul to Titus? "Who gave himself for us, that he might redeem us from all iniquity, and purify unto himself a peculiar people, zealous of good works" (Titus 2:14). What says the Lord Jesus to the Laodicean church? "Be zealous therefore, and repent" (Rev. 3:19)!

Zeal in religion is a burning desire to please God, do His will, and advance His glory in the world in every possible way. It is a desire which no man feels by nature, which the Spirit puts in the heart of every believer when he is converted, but which some believers feel so much more strongly than others, that they alone deserve to be called zealous Christians. This desire is so strong when it really reigns in a man that it impels him to make any sacrifice, to go through any trouble, to deny himself to any amount to suffer, to work, to labor, to toil, to spend himself and be spent, and even to die, if only he can please God and honor Christ. A zealous man in religion is preeminently a man of one thing. It is not enough to say that he is earnest, hearty, uncompromising, thoroughgoing, wholehearted, fervent in spirit. He sees one thing, he cares for one thing, he lives for one thing, he is swallowed up in one thing, and that one thing is to please God!

✤ From the sermon "Christian Zeal"

I Shall Never Be Cast Away

All that the Father giveth me shall come to me; and him that cometh to me I will in no wise cast out. —JOHN 6:37

Would I gather arguments for hoping that I shall never be cast away? Where shall I go to find them? Shall I look at my own graces and gifts? Shall I take comfort in my own faith and love and penitence and zeal and prayer? Shall I turn to my own heart, and say, "This same heart will never be false and cold"? Oh, no! God forbid! I will look at the cross of Christ. This is my grand argument. This is my mainstay. I cannot think that He who went through such sufferings to redeem my soul, will let that soul perish after all, when it has once cast itself on Him. Oh, no! What Jesus paid for, Jesus will surely keep. He paid dearly for it. He will not let it easily be lost. He called me to Himself when I was a dark sinner, He will never forsake me after I have believed. When Satan tempts us to doubt whether Christ's people will be kept from falling, we should tell Satan to look at the cross!

And now, will you marvel that I said all Christians ought to boast in the cross? Will you not rather wonder that any can hear of the cross and remain unmoved? I declare I know no greater proof of man's depravity, than the fact that thousands of so-called Christians see nothing in the cross. Well may our hearts be called stony, well may the eyes of our mind be called blind, well may our whole nature be called diseased, well may we all be called dead, when the cross of Christ is heard of and yet neglected. Surely we may take up the words of the prophet, and say, "Hear, O heavens, and be astonished O earth; an astounding and a horrible thing is done," if Christ was crucified for sinners, and yet many Christians live as if He was never crucified at all!

✣ From the sermon "The Cross of Christ"

Every One of Us Has an Undying Soul

*For what is a man profited, if he shall gain the whole world, and
lose his own soul? or what shall a man give in exchange for his soul?*
—MATTHEW 16:26

The saying of our Lord Jesus Christ, which stands at the head of this
page, ought to ring in our ears like a trumpet blast. It concerns our
highest and best interests. It concerns our souls. What a solemn question these words of Scripture contain! What a mighty sum of profit and
loss they propound to us for calculation! Where is the accountant who
could reckon it up? Where is the clever arithmetician who would not
be baffled by that sum? "For what is a man profited, if he shall gain the
whole world, and lose his own soul?" (Matt. 16:26).

I cannot forget that the world is just now fixing its attention on material things to a most extravagant extent. We live in an age of progress, an
age of steam engines and machinery, of locomotion and invention. We
live in an age when the multitude are increasingly absorbed in earthly
things—in railways and docks and mines and commerce and trade and
banks and shops and cotton and corn and iron and gold. We live in an
age when there is a false glare on the things of time, and a great mist
over the things of eternity. In an age like this it is the bound duty of the
ministers of Christ to fall back upon first principles. Necessity is laid
upon us. Woe is unto us, if we do not press home on men our Lord's
question about the soul! Woe is unto us, if we do not cry aloud, "This
present world is not all. The life that we now live in the flesh is not the
only life. There is a life to come. We have souls!" Let us establish it in
our minds as a great fact, that we all carry within our bosoms something
that will never die!

✣ From the sermon "Our Souls"

No More Crying

And God shall wipe away all tears from their eyes; and there shall be no more death, neither sorrow, nor crying, neither shall there be any more pain: for the former things are passed away.
—REVELATION 21:4

What is this place? It is heaven. It is the place to which all godly people go when they are dead. In heaven, there all is joy and happiness. There no tears are shed. There sorrow and pain and sickness and death can never enter in. There can be no crying in heaven because there is nothing that can cause grief.

There will be no more work in heaven. People will no longer need to labor for their food.

The head will no longer have to ache with thinking. The hands will no longer be painful with toiling. There will be an eternal rest for all the people of God. There will be no sickness in heaven. Pain and disease and weakness and death will not be known. The people who dwell there shall never say, "I am sick." They will be always well. There will be nothing but health and strength forevermore. There will be no sin in heaven. There will be no bad tempers, no unkind words, no spiteful actions. The great tempter, the devil, will not be allowed to come in and spoil the happiness. There shall be nothing but holiness and love forevermore.

Best of all, the Lord Jesus Christ Himself will be in the midst of heaven. His people shall at last see Him face-to-face and never leave His presence! He shall gather His lambs into His bosom and wipe away all tears from all eyes. Where He is will be fullness of joy, and at His right hand shall be pleasures forevermore. Jesus is the way and the door into heaven. He has the key to heaven in His hand. Children, if you want to go to heaven, you must ask Jesus Christ to let you in!

❖ From the sermon "No More Crying"

The Flock of Christ

I am the good shepherd, and know my sheep,
and am known of mine.
—JOHN 10:14

This is the only church of which not one member can perish. Once enrolled in the lists of this church, sinners are safe for eternity. They are never cast away. The election of God the Father, the continual intercession of God the Son, the daily renewing and sanctifying power of God the Holy Spirit, surround and fence them in like a garden enclosed. Not one bone of Christ's mystical body shall ever be broken. Not one lamb of Christ's flock shall ever be plucked out of His hand.

This is the church which does the work of Christ upon earth. Its members are a little flock and few compared with the children of the world—one or two here, and two or three there, a few in this parish, and a few in that. But these are those who shake the universe. These are those who change the fortunes of kingdoms by their prayers. These are those who are the active workers for spreading the knowledge of pure religion and undefiled. These are the lifeblood of a country, the shield, the defense, the stay, and the support of any nation to which they belong.

This is the church to which a man must belong if he would be saved. Until we belong to this true church, we are nothing better than lost souls. We may have the form, the husk, the skin, and the shell of religion, but we have not got the substance and the life. Yes! We may have countless outward privileges, we may enjoy great light and knowledge and opportunities, but if we do not belong to the body of Christ, then our light, and knowledge and privileges and opportunities will not save our souls.

✥ From the sermon "The Church"

Your Faith May Be Feeble

The eternal God is thy refuge,
and underneath are the everlasting arms.
—DEUTERONOMY 33:27

Your faith may be very feeble, your grace may be very weak, your strength may be very small, you may feel that in spiritual things you are but a child. Yet fear not, neither be afraid. It is not on the quantity of a man's grace, but on the truth and genuineness of it, which the promise turns. A penny is as truly a current coin of the country as a dollar, though it is not so valuable. Wherever sin is truly repented of and Christ is truly trusted and holiness is truly followed, there is a work which shall never be overthrown. It shall stand when the earth and all the works thereof shall be burned up.

Reader, there are yet some things to be said about perseverance, to which I must request your special attention. Without them the account of the doctrine would be imperfect and incomplete. The mention of them may clear up some of the difficulties which surround the subject and throw light on some points of Christian experience that God's children find hard to understand.

Remember, then, that when I tell you believers shall persevere to the end, I do not for a moment say that they shall never fall into sin. They may fall sadly, foully, and shamefully, to the scandal of true religion, to the injury of their own deep and bitter sorrow. Noah once fell into drunkenness. Abraham twice said falsely that Sarah was only his sister. Jacob deceived his father, Isaac. David committed horrible adultery. Solomon lost his first love and was led away by his many wives. Peter denied his Lord three times with an oath. The apostles all forsook Christ in the garden. All these are cases in point. They are all melancholy proofs that Christians may fall. But believers shall never fall totally, finally, and completely. They shall always rise again from their falls by repentance and renew their walk with God. Though sorely humbled and cast down, they never entirely lose grace.

✠ From the sermon "Never Perish"

The Lord's Supper

But let a man examine himself, and so let him eat of that bread, and drink of that cup. —1 CORINTHIANS 11:28

It was ordained for the continual remembrance of the sacrifice of the death of Christ, and of the benefits which we thereby receive. The bread, which in the Lord's Supper is broken, given, and eaten, is meant to remind us of Christ's body given on the cross for our sins. The wine, which is poured out and received, is meant to remind us of Christ's blood shed on the cross for our sins. He who eats that bread and drinks that wine is reminded, in the most striking and forceful manner, of the benefits Christ has obtained for his soul, and of the death of Christ as the hinge and turning point on which all those benefits depend.

In subjects like this we must call no man master. It matters little what great theologians and learned preachers have thought fit to put forth about the Lord's Supper. If they teach more than the Word of God contains, they are not to be believed. I take up my Bible and turn to the New Testament. There I find no less than four separate accounts of the first appointment of the Lord's Supper. Matthew, Mark, Luke, and Paul—all four describe it and agree in telling us what our Lord did on this memorable occasion. Only two tell us the reason why our Lord commanded that His disciples were to eat the bread and drink the cup. Paul and Luke both record the remarkable words, "This do in remembrance of me" (Luke 22:19). Paul adds his own inspired comment: "For as often as ye eat this bread, and drink this cup, ye do shew the Lord's death till he come" (1 Cor. 11:25–26). When Scripture speaks so clearly, why can't men be content with it? Why should we mystify and confuse a subject which in the New Testament is so simple?

❖ From the sermon "The Lord's Supper"

Salvation in Christ Alone

Neither is there salvation in any other: for there is none other name
under heaven given among men, whereby we must be saved.
—ACTS 4:12

Let us make sure that we rightly understand what the apostle means. He says of Christ, "Neither is there salvation in any other: for there is none other name under heaven given among men, whereby we must be saved!" Now, what does this mean? On our clearly seeing this very much depends. He means that no one can be saved from sin, its guilt, its power, and its consequences, except by Jesus Christ.

He means that no one can have peace with God the Father, obtain pardon in this world, and escape wrath to come in the next, except through the atonement and mediation of Jesus Christ. In Christ alone, God's rich provision of salvation for sinners is treasured up. By Christ alone, God's abundant mercies come down from heaven to earth. And the apostle adds emphatically, "Neither is there salvation in any other: for there is none other name under heaven given among men, whereby we must be saved!" There is no other person commissioned, sealed, and appointed by God the Father to be the Savior of sinners except Christ. The keys of life and death are committed to His hand, and all who would be saved must go to Him.

There was but one place of safety in the day when the flood came on the earth; that place was Noah's ark. All other places and devices, mountains, towers, trees, rafts, boats—all were alike useless. In the same way, there is but one hiding place for the sinner who would escape the storm of God's anger; he must venture his soul on Christ. Such is the doctrine of the text: "No salvation but by Jesus Christ, in him, there is plenty of salvation, salvation to the uttermost, salvation for the very chief of sinners!"

✣ From the sermon "Only One Way of Salvation"

We Must Be Holy

And ye shall be holy; for I am holy.
—LEVITICUS 11:44

We must be holy on earth before we die if we desire to go to heaven after death! If we hope to dwell with God forever in the life to come, we must endeavor to be like Him in the life that now is. We must not only admire holiness, and wish for holiness, we must be holy.

Holiness cannot justify and save us. Holiness cannot cover our iniquities, make satisfaction for transgressions, pay our debts to God. Our best works are no better than filthy rags, when tried by the light of God's law. The righteousness that Jesus Christ brought in must be our only confidence, and the blood of His atonement our only hope. All this is perfectly true, and yet we must be holy.

We must be holy because God in the Bible plainly commands it: "But as he which hath called you is holy, so be ye holy in all manner of conversation; because it is written, Be ye holy; for I am holy" (1 Peter 1:15–16). We must be holy, because this is one great end for which Christ came into the world. "And that he died for all, that they which live should not henceforth live unto themselves, but unto him which died for them, and rose again" (2 Cor. 5:15).

We must be holy, because this is the only sound evidence that we have a saving faith in Christ. "Even so faith, if it hath not works, is dead, being alone" (James 2:17) and "For as the body without the spirit is dead, so faith without works is dead also" (2:26).

Last, we must be holy because without holiness on earth, we should never be prepared and fit for heaven. It is written of the heavenly glory, "And there shall in no wise enter into it any thing that defileth, neither whatsoever worketh abomination, or maketh a lie: but they which are written in the Lamb's book of life" (Rev. 21:27).

❖ From the sermon "We Must Be Holy"

The Bible Is What the Bible Is

All scripture is given by inspiration of God, and is profitable for doctrine, for reproof, for correction, for instruction in righteousness: that the man of God may be perfect, thoroughly furnished unto all good works. —2 TIMOTHY 3:16–17

All through the Bible, from Genesis down to Revelation, there is only one simple account of the way in which a man or woman must be saved. It is always the same: only by our Lord Jesus Christ, through faith; never by our own works and righteousness. You see it dimly revealed at first: it looms through the mist of a few promises, but there it is. You see it more clearly later: it is taught by the pictures and symbols of the law of Moses. You have it still more clearly as time goes by: the prophets saw in visions many particulars about the Redeemer who was to come.

In fact, this truth appears to me to be the great focus of the Bible, and all the different parts and portions of the book are meant to pour light on it. I can gather from it no ideas of pardon and peace with God except in connection with this truth. If I could read of one soul in it who was saved without faith in the Savior, I might perhaps not speak so confidently. But when I see that faith in Christ, whether in a coming Christ or a crucified Christ, was the prominent feature in the religion of all who went to heaven—when I see Abel owning Christ in his better sacrifice at one end of the Bible and the saints in glory in John's vision rejoicing in Christ at the other end—when I see a man like Cornelius, who was devout and feared God and gave to the poor and prayed, told in effect that in order to be saved, he was to send for Peter and hear of Christ—when I see all these things I say, I feel bound to believe that the doctrine of the text is the doctrine of the whole Bible. No salvation, no way to heaven, except through Jesus Christ!

✤ From the sermon "Only One Way—Christ!"

Confession of Sin

If we confess our sins, he is faithful and just to forgive us our sins,
and to cleanse us from all unrighteousness.
—1 JOHN 1:9

Without confession there is no salvation. The love of God toward sinners is infinite. The readiness of Christ to receive sinners is unbounded. The blood of Christ can cleanse away all sin. But we must plead guilty before God can declare us innocent. We must acknowledge that we willingly surrender before we can be pardoned and let go free. Sins that are known and not confessed, are sins that are not forgiven; they are yet upon us and daily sinking us nearer to hell. "He that covereth his sins shall not prosper: but whoso confesseth and forsaketh them shall have mercy" (Prov. 28:13).

Without confession, there is no inward peace. Conscience will never be at rest, so long as it feels the burden of unacknowledged transgression. It is a load of which man must get rid if he means to be really happy. It is a worm at the root of all comfort. It is a blight on joy and mirth. "When I kept silence," says David, "my bones waxed old through my roaring all the day long. For day and night thy hand was heavy upon me: my moisture is turned into the drought of summer. Selah. I acknowledge my sin unto thee, and mine iniquity have I not hid. I said, I will confess my transgressions unto the LORD; and thou forgavest the iniquity of my sin" (Ps. 32:3–5). There is no gainsaying these things. They stand out plainly on the face of Scripture, as if they were written with a sunbeam! They are so clear that he who runs may read. Confession of sin is absolutely necessary to salvation. It is a habit that is an essential part of repentance unto life!

❖ From the sermon "Confession"

Shining More and More Every Day

But ye are a chosen generation, a royal priesthood, an holy nation,
a peculiar people; that ye should shew forth the praises of him who
hath called you out of darkness into his marvellous light.
—1 PETER 2:9

I wish the elect of God to be indeed a holy nation and the sons of adoption to live as becomes the children of a King. I want those who are light in the Lord to walk as children of light, shining more and more every day. And I say it for the good of the world. You are almost the only book that worldly people read. Surely your lives should be epistles of Christ, so plain that he who runs may read them. The world cares little for doctrine, the world knows nothing of experience, but the world can understand a close walk with God. And not least I say it because of the times you live in. I write it down deliberately; I believe there never were so many lukewarm saints as there are now. There never was a time in which a low and carnal standard of Christian behavior so much prevailed. There never were so many babes in grace in the family of God; so many who seem to sit still and live on old experience; so many who appear to have need of nothing and to be neither hungering nor thirsting after righteousness, as at the present time. I write this with all sorrow. It may be too painful to please some. But I ask you, as in God's sight, is it not true?

Brethren, these are the reasons why I write so strongly. I want your Christianity to be unmistakable. I want you all to grow really, and to do more than others. Let us bury our idols. Let us put away all strange gods. Let us cast out the old leaven. Let us lay aside every weight and besetting sin. Let us cleanse ourselves from all filthiness of flesh and spirit, and perfect holiness in the fear of God. Let us aim at the highest and best things. Let us resolve by God's blessing to be more holy, and then I know and am persuaded we shall be more useful and more happy!

✣ From the sermon "Consider Your Ways"

Suddenness of Christ's Return

But know this, that if the goodman of the house had known in what
watch the thief would come, he would have watched, and would not
have suffered his house to be broken up. Therefore be ye also ready:
for in such an hour as ye think not the Son of man cometh.
—MATTHEW 24:43–44

I do not know when Christ will come. I am no prophet, though I love
the subject of prophecy. I dislike date fixing, and I think it has done
great harm. I only assert positively that Christ will come again one day
in person to set up His kingdom, and that whether the day be near or
whether it be far off, it will take the church and world exceedingly by
surprise. It will come on men suddenly. It will break on the world all at
once. It will not have been talked over, prepared for, and looked forward
to by everybody. It will awaken men's minds like a cry of fire at midnight. It will startle men's hearts like a trumpet blown by their bedsides
in their first sleep. Like Pharaoh and his army, men will know nothing
until the very waters are upon them. Before they can recover their breath
and know where they are, they shall find that the Lord has come.

I suspect there is a vague notion floating in men's minds that the
present order of things will not end quite so suddenly. I suspect men
cling to the idea that there will be a time when all will know the Lord's
Day is near, a time when all will be able to cleanse their consciences,
look up their best garment, shake off their earthly business, and prepare
to meet the Lord. If anyone here has got such a notion, I charge him to
give it up forever. If anything is clear in unfulfilled prophecy, this one
fact seems clear, that the Lord's coming will be sudden and take men
by surprise; and any view of prophecy that destroys the possibility of its
being a sudden event appears to carry about with it a fatal defect.

❖ From the sermon "The Ten Virgins"

Contentment Is One of the Rarest of Graces

But godliness with contentment is great gain. For we brought nothing into this world, and it is certain we can carry nothing out.
—1 TIMOTHY 6:6–7

Contentment is one of the rarest graces. Like all precious things, it is most uncommon.

The fallen angels had heaven itself to dwell in, before they fell, and the immediate presence and favor of God, but they were not content. Adam and Eve had the garden of Eden to live in, with a free grant of everything in it excepting one tree, but they were not content. Ahab had his throne and kingdom, but so long as Naboth's vineyard was not his, he was not content. Haman was the chief favorite of the Persian king, but so long as Mordecai sat at the gate, he was not content.

It is just the same everywhere in the present day. Murmuring, dissatisfaction, discontent with what we have meet us at every turn. To say with Jacob "I have enough" seems flatly contrary to the grain of human nature. To say "I want more" seems the mother tongue of every child of Adam. Our little ones around our family hearths are daily illustrations of the truth of what I am saying. They learn to ask for more much sooner than they learn to be satisfied.

They are far more ready to cry for what they want, than to say thank you when they have got it. There are few readers of this very paper, I will venture to say, who do not want something or other different from what they have, something more or something less. What you have does not seem as good as what you have not. If you only had this or that thing granted, you imagine that you would be quite happy. This is why contentment is one of the rarest of graces.

❖ From the sermon "Be Content"

Let Us Not Neglect Little Duties

How shall we escape, if we neglect so great salvation; which at the first began to be spoken by the Lord, and was confirmed unto us by them that heard him?
—HEBREWS 2:3

Let us resolve to make conscience of little things in our daily religion. Let us not neglect little duties, let us not allow ourselves in little faults. Whatever we may like to think, nothing is really of small importance that affects the soul. All diseases are small at the beginning. Many a deathbed begins with a little cold. Nothing that can grow is large all at once; the greatest sin must have a beginning. Nothing that is great comes to perfection in a day; characters and habits are all the result of little actions.

Believers, do not forget how full the Epistles are of instruction about the particulars of Christian life. The apostles seem to take nothing for granted. They do not think it sufficient to say, "be holy"; they take care to specify and name the things in which holiness is shown. See how they dwell on the duties of husbands and wives, masters and servants, parents and children, rulers and subjects, old people and young. See how they single out and urge upon us industry in business, kindness in temper, forgivingness in disposition, honesty, truthfulness, temperance, meekness, gentleness, humility, charity, patience, courtesy.

See how they exhort us to honor all men, to govern our tongues, to season our speech with grace, to abstain from foolish talking and jesting, not to please ourselves only, to redeem the time, to be content with such things as we have, and whether we eat or drink, to do all in the name of the Lord Jesus. Brethren, some people think that to dwell on such things is bondage, but I believe it good to remind you of them; I am sure it is safe. If the Spirit of God thought it wise to dwell so much on them in the Word, I cannot doubt it must be wise for us to attend to them in our walk.

✤ From the sermon "Consider Your Ways"

Are You Heavy Laden?

Come unto me, all ye that labour and are heavy laden, and I will give you rest.   —MATTHEW 11:28

The Lord Jesus addresses all who labor and are heavy laden. The expression is deeply comforting and instructive. It is wide, sweeping, and comprehensive. It describes the ease of millions in every part of the world. To what class do the laboring and heavy laden belong to? They belong to every class; there is no exception. They are to be found among masters as well as among servants; among rich as well as among poor; among kings as well as among subjects; among learned as well as among ignorant people. In every class you will find trouble, care, sorrow, anxiety, murmuring, discontent, and unrest. What does it mean?

Reader, sin and departure from God are the true reasons why men are everywhere laboring and heavy laden. Sin is the universal disease which infects the whole earth. Sin brought in thorns and thistles at the beginning, and obliged man to earn his bread by the sweat of his brow. Sin is the reason why the whole creation groans and travails in pain, and the foundations of the earth are out of course; sin is the cause of all the burdens which now press down mankind. Most men know it not, and weary themselves in vain to explain the state of things among them. But sin is the great root and foundation of all sorrow, whatever proud man may think. How much men ought to hate sin!

Reader, if you are laboring and heavy laden, you are the very person to whom the Lord Jesus Christ sends an invitation this day. If you have an aching heart and a sore conscience; if you want rest for a weary soul and know not where to find it; if you want peace for a guilty heart and are at a loss which way to turn; you are the man, you are the woman, to whom Jesus speaks today. There is hope for you. I bring you good tidings. "Come unto me," says Jesus, "and I will give you rest."

❖ From the tract *Come*

God Is Everywhere!

The eyes of the LORD are in every place,
beholding the evil and the good.
—PROVERBS 15:3

The teaching of the Bible on this point is clear, plain, and unmistakable. God is everywhere! There is no place in heaven or earth where He is not. There is no place in air or land or sea, no place above ground or underground, no place in town or country, no place in Europe, Asia, Africa, or America where God is not always present. Enter into your closet and lock the door—God is there. Climb to the top of the highest mountain, where not even an insect moves—God is there. Sail to the most remote island in the Pacific Ocean, where the foot of man never trod—God is there. He is always near us, seeing, hearing, observing; knowing every action and deed and word and whisper and look and thought and motive and secret of every one of us, wherever we are.

What says the Scripture? It is written in Job, "For his eyes are upon the ways of man, and he seeth all his goings. There is no darkness, nor shadow of death, where the workers of iniquity may hide themselves" (Job 34:21–22). It is written in Proverbs, "The eyes of the LORD are in every place, beholding the evil and the good" (Prov. 15:3). It is written in Jeremiah, "Great in counsel, and mighty in work: for thine eyes are open upon all the ways of the sons of men: to give every one according to his ways, and according to the fruit of his doings" (Jer. 32:19).

However hard it is to comprehend this doctrine, it is one that is most useful and wholesome for our souls. To keep continually in mind that God is always present with us; to live always as in God's sight; to act and speak and think as always under His eye—all this is eminently calculated to have a good effect upon our souls.

❖ From the sermon "The Real Presence"

The Darkness of This Age

Who gave himself for our sins, that he might deliver us from this present evil world, according to the will of God and our Father.
—GALATIANS 1:4

Are there few saved? Then, if you are one, use every opportunity to try to do good to souls. Settle it down in your mind that the vast majority of people around you are in dreadful danger of being lost forever. Work every engine for bringing the gospel to bear upon them. Help every Christian enterprise for plucking brands from the burning. Give liberally to every society which has for its object to spread the everlasting gospel. Throw all your influence heartily and unreservedly into the cause of doing good to souls. Live like one who thoroughly believes that time is short and eternity near, the devil strong and sin abounding, the darkness very great and the light very small, the ungodly very many and the godly very few, the things of the world mere transitory shadows, and heaven and hell the great substantial realities.

Alas, indeed, for the lives that many believers live! How cold are many, and how frozen, how slow to do decided things in religion, and how afraid of going too far, how backward to attempt anything new, how ready to discourage a good movement, how ingenious in discovering reasons why it is best to sit still, how unwilling ever to allow that "the time" for active exertion is come, how wise in finding fault, how shiftless in devising plans to meet growing evils! Truly a man might sometimes think, when he looks at the ways of many who are counted believers, that all the world was going to heaven, and hell was nothing but a lie.

Let us all beware of this state of mind! Whether we like to believe it or not, hell is filling fast. Christ is daily holding out His hand to a disobedient people. Many are in the broad way that leads to destruction! Few are in the way that leads to life! Many, many are likely to be lost. Few, few are likely to be saved!

✤ From the sermon "Few Saved"

Prayer Is One of the Surest Marks of a Christian

For ye have not received the spirit of bondage again to fear; but ye have received the Spirit of adoption, whereby we cry, Abba, Father.
—ROMANS 8:15

All the children of God on earth are alike in this respect. From the moment there is any life and reality about their religion, they pray. Just as the first sign of the life of an infant when born into the world is the act of breathing, so the first act of men and women when they are born again is praying. This is one of the common marks of all the elect of God, they "cry day and night unto him" (Luke 18:7). The Holy Spirit who makes them new creatures, works in them a feeling of adoption, and makes them cry, "Abba, Father" (Rom. 8:15). The Lord Jesus, when He quickens them, gives them a voice and a tongue and says to them, "Be dumb no more." God has no dumb children. It is as much a part of their new nature to pray as it is of a child to cry. They see their need of mercy and grace. They feel their emptiness and weakness. They cannot do otherwise than they do. They must pray.

I have looked carefully over the lives of God's saints in the Bible. I cannot find one whose history much is told us, from Genesis to Revelation, who was not a person of prayer. I find it mentioned as a characteristic of the godly, that "they call on the Father," that "they call upon the name of the Lord Jesus Christ." I find it recorded as a characteristic of the wicked, that they "call not upon the LORD" (Ps. 14:4; see also 1 Cor. 1:2; 1 Peter 1:17). Christians must pray!

❖ From the sermon "Call to Prayer"

Sons of God!

But as many as received him, to them gave he power to become the sons of God, even to them that believe on his name. —JOHN 1:12

I know no higher and more comfortable word that could have been chosen. To be servants of God, to be subjects, soldiers, disciples, friends—all these are excellent titles; but to be the sons of God is a step higher still. What does the Scripture say? "And the servant abideth not in the house for ever: but the Son abideth ever" (John 8:35). To be a son of the rich and noble in this world, to be son of the princes and kings of the earth, this is commonly reckoned a great advantage and privilege. But to be a son of the King of Kings and Lord of Lords, to be a son of the High and Holy One who inhabits eternity, this is something far higher. And yet this is the portion of every true Christian.

The son of an earthly parent looks naturally to his father for affection, maintenance, provision, and education. There is a home always open to him. There is a love which, generally speaking, no bad conduct can completely extinguish. All these are things belonging even to the sonship of this world. Think then how great the privilege of that poor sinner is who can say of God, "He is my Father."

Men become sons of God in the day that the Spirit leads them to believe on Jesus Christ for salvation, and not before. What says the epistle to the Galatians? "For ye are all the children of God by faith in Christ Jesus" (Gal. 3:26). What says the first epistle to the Corinthians? "But of him are ye in Christ Jesus" (1 Cor. 1:30). What says the gospel of John? "But as many as received him, to them gave he power to become the sons of God, even to them that believe on his name" (John 1:12).

✤ From the sermon "Heirs of God"

Christ's Work on Your Behalf

*For Christ also hath once suffered for sins, the just for the unjust,
that he might bring us to God, being put to death in the flesh, but
quickened by the Spirit.*   —1 PETER 3:18

Christ has stood in the place of the true Christian. He has become his
surety and his substitute. He undertook to bear all that was to be borne,
and to do all that was to be done, and what He undertook He performed. Hence the true Christian is a justified man (Isa. 53:6). Christ
has suffered for sins, the "just for the unjust." He has endured our punishment in His own body on the cross. He has allowed the wrath of
God, which we deserved, to fall on His own head. Hence the true Christian is a justified man (1 Peter 3:18).

Christ has paid the debt the Christian owed, by His own blood.
He has reckoned for it and discharged it to the uttermost farthing by
His own death. God is a just God and will not require his debts to be
paid twice over. Hence the true Christian is a justified man (Acts 20:28;
1 Peter 1:18–19). Christ has obeyed the law of God perfectly. The devil,
the prince of this world, could find no fault in Him. By so fulfilling it
He brought in an everlasting righteousness, in which all His people are
clothed in the sight of God. Hence the true Christian is a justified man
(Dan. 9:24; Rom. 10:4).

Christ, in one word, has lived for the true Christian. Christ has died
for him. Christ has gone to the grave for him. Christ has risen again for
him. Christ has ascended up on high for him and gone into heaven to
intercede for his soul. Christ has done all, paid all, suffered all that was
needful for his redemption. Hence arises the true Christian's justification; hence his peace. In himself there is nothing but sin, but in Christ
he has all things that his soul can require (Col. 2:3; 3:11).

✤ From the sermon "Justification"

The Christian Race

Wherefore seeing we also are compassed about with so great a cloud of witnesses, let us lay aside every weight, and the sin which doth so easily beset us, and let us run with patience the race that is set before us, looking unto Jesus the author and finisher of our faith; who for the joy that was set before him endured the cross, despising the shame, and is set down at the right hand of the throne of God.
—HEBREWS 12:1–2

We have all a race to run. By this you are not to understand that our own arm and our own strength can ever open for us the gates of everlasting life, and win us a place in heaven. Far from it: that is all of grace, it is another question. It simply means that all who take up the cross and follow Christ must make up their minds to meet with many a difficulty, they must calculate on labor and toil and trouble, they have a mighty work to do, and there is need for all their attention and energy. Without there will be fightings, within there will be fears; there will be snares to be avoided, and temptations to be resisted; there will be your own treacherous hearts, often cold and dead and dry and dull; there will be friends who will give you unscriptural advice, and relations who will even war against your soul. In short, there will be stumbling blocks on every side. There will be occasion for all your diligence and watchfulness and godly jealousy and prayer. You will soon find that to be a real Christian is no light matter.

But those who are taught and called of God may soon be distinguished from the sleeping children of this world. These have no leisure for vain amusements; their eyes are fixed, and their thoughts are engaged upon the narrow path they have to tread and the crown they hope to receive. They have counted the cost and come out from the world, and their only wish is that they may finish their course with joy.

✤ From the sermon "The Christian Race"

Our Home!

Lord, thou hast been our dwelling place in all generations.
—PSALM 90:1

The first thought that I will offer you is this: I will show you what the world is. It is a beautiful world in many respects, I freely admit. Its seas and rivers, its sunrises and sunsets, its mountains and valleys, its harvests and its forests, its fruits and its flowers, its days and its nights—all are beautiful in their way. Cold and unfeeling must that heart be which never finds a day in the year when it can admire anything in nature! But as beautiful as the world is, there are many things in it to remind us that it is not home. It is an inn, a tent, a tabernacle, a lodging, a training school, but it is not home.

It is a changing world. All around us is continually moving, altering, and passing away. Families, properties, landlords, tenants, farmers, laborers, tradesmen, all are continually on the move. To find the same name in the same dwelling for three generations running is so uncommon, that it is the exception and not the rule. A world so full of change cannot be called home. It is a trying and disappointing world. Trials in married life and trials in single life, trials in children and trials in brothers and sisters, trials in money matters and trials in health, how many they are! Their name is legion. And not the tenth part of them perhaps ever comes to light. Few indeed are the families which have not a skeleton in the closet. A world so full of trial and disappointment cannot be called home.

These are ancient things. It is useless to be surprised at them. They are the bitter fruit of sin, and the sorrowful consequence of the fall. Change, trial, death, and division all entered the world when Adam and Eve transgressed. We must not murmur. We must not fret. We must not complain. We must accept the situation in which we find ourselves. We must each do our best to lighten the sorrows and increase the comforts of our position. We must steadily resolve to make the best of everybody and everything around us. But we must never, never, never, forget that the world is not home!

✣ From the sermon "Our Home"

In My Father's House

In my Father's house are many mansions: if it were not so, I would
have told you. I go to prepare a place for you. And if I go and prepare
a place for you, I will come again, and receive you unto myself; that
where I am, there ye may be also. And whither I go ye know, and
the way ye know.
—JOHN 14:2–4

We have in this passage a very comfortable account of heaven, or the
future abode of saints. It is but little that we understand about heaven
while we are here in the body, and that little is generally taught to us in
the Bible by negative descriptions much more than positive descriptions.
But here, at any rate, there are some plain things. heaven is a "Father's
house," the house of that God of whom Jesus says, "I ascend unto my
Father, and your Father" (John 20:17). It is, in a word, home: the home
of Christ and Christians. This is a sweet and touching expression. Home,
as we all know, is the place where we are generally loved for our own
sakes and not for our gifts or possessions; the place where we are loved
to the end, never forgotten, and always welcome. This is one idea of
heaven. Believers are in a strange land and at school in this life. In the
life to come, they will be at home.

Heaven is a place of "many mansions." There will be room for all
believers and room for all sorts, for little saints as well as great ones, for
the weakest believer as well as for the strongest. The feeblest child of God
need not fear that there will be no place for him. None will be shut out
but impenitent sinners and obstinate unbelievers! Let these things sink
down into our minds. To the worldly and careless they may seem nothing at all. To all who feel in themselves the working of the Spirit of God,
they are full of unspeakable comfort. If we hope to be in heaven, it is
pleasant to know what heaven is like.

❖ From the sermon "A Brief Account of Heaven"

Do You Have a New Heart?

A new heart also will I give you, and a new spirit will I put within you: and I will take away the stony heart out of your flesh, and I will give you an heart of flesh. —EZEKIEL 36:26

The right heart is "a new heart" (Ezek. 36:26). It is not the heart with which a man is born, but another heart put in him by the Holy Spirit. It is a heart which has new tastes, new joys, new sorrows, new desires, new hopes, new fears, new likes, new dislikes. It has new views about the soul and sin and God and Christ and salvation and the Bible and prayer and heaven and hell and the world and holiness. It is like a farm with a new and good tenant. "Old things are passed away; behold, all things are become new" (2 Cor. 5:17).

The right heart is a "broken and a contrite heart" (Ps. 51:17). It is broken off from pride, self-conceit, and self-righteousness. Its former high thoughts of self are cracked, shattered, and shivered to atoms. It thinks itself guilty, unworthy, and corrupt. Its former stubbornness, heaviness, and insensibility have thawed, disappeared, and passed away. It no longer thinks lightly of offending God. It is tender, sensitive, and jealously fearful of running into sin (2 Kings 22:19). It is humble, lowly, and self-abased and sees in itself no good thing.

A right heart is a heart that believes on Christ alone for salvation and in which Christ dwells by faith (Rom. 10:10; Eph. 3:17). It rests all its hopes of pardon and eternal life on Christ's atonement, Christ's mediation, and Christ's intercession. It is sprinkled in Christ's blood from an evil conscience (Heb. 10:22). It turns to Christ as the compass needle turns to the north. It looks to Christ for daily peace, mercy, and grace, as the sunflower looks to the sun. It feeds on Christ for its daily sustenance, as Israel fed on the manna in the wilderness. It sees in Christ a special fitness to supply all its needs and requirements. It leans on Him, hangs on Him, builds on Him, cleaves to Him, as its physician, guardian, husband, and friend!

✤ From the sermon "The Heart"

Guard against False Doctrine

These were more noble than those in Thessalonica, in that they received the word with all readiness of mind, and searched the scriptures daily, whether those things were so. —ACTS 17:11

Let us be on our guard against false doctrine. Unsound faith will never be the mother of really sound practice, and in these latter days, departures from the faith abound. See then that your loins be girt about with truth, and be very jealous of receiving anything which cannot be proved by the Bible. Do not think for a moment that false doctrine will meet you face-to-face, saying, "I am false doctrine, and I want to come into your heart." Satan does not go to work in that way. He dresses up false doctrine like Jezebel, he paints her face and attires her hair, and tries to make her like truth. Do not think that those who preach error will never preach anything that is true. Error would do little harm if that was the case. No! Error will come before you mingled with much that is sound and scriptural.

The sermon will be all right except for a few sentences. The book will be all good except for a few pages. And this is the chief danger of religious error in these times. It is like the subtle poisons of days gone by. It works so deceitfully that it throws men off their guard.

Brethren, take care. Remember, that even Satan himself is transformed into an angel of light. Keep clear of any system of religion which confounds the world with true believers, and makes no broad distinction between those who are true children of God in a congregation and those who are not. Do not be carried away by an appearance of great self-denial and humility. It is far easier to fast and wear sackcloth, and be of a sad countenance, than to receive thoroughly the doctrine of justification by faith without the deeds of the law. Take heed, lest your minds be corrupted from the simplicity that is in Christ!

❖ From the sermon "Consider Your Ways"

The World Is Passing Away

And the world passeth away, and the lust thereof: but he that doeth the will of God abideth for ever.
                                                                —1 JOHN 2:17

That man must be blind indeed who cannot realize this. Everything around us is decaying, dying, and coming to an end. There is a sense, no doubt, in which matter is eternal. Once created, it will never entirely perish. But in a popular practical sense, there is nothing undying about us except our souls. We are all going, going, going—whether high or low, gentle or simple, rich or poor, old or young. We are all going and shall soon be gone.

Humbling and painful as these truths may sound, it is good for us to realize them and lay them to heart. The houses we live in, the homes we love, the riches we accumulate, the professions we follow, the plans we form, the relations we enter into, they are only for a time. "And they that use this world, as not abusing it: for the fashion of this world passeth away" (1 Cor. 7:31). The thought is one which ought to rouse everyone who is living only for this world. If his conscience is not utterly seared, it should stir in him great searchings of heart.

The same thought ought to cheer and comfort every true Christian. Your trials, crosses, and conflicts are all temporary. They will soon have an end; and even now they are working for you "a far more exceeding and eternal weight of glory" (2 Cor. 4:17). Take them patiently; bear them quietly; look upward, forward, onward, and far beyond them. Fight your daily fight under an abiding conviction that it is only for a little time, and that rest is not far off. Carry your daily cross with an abiding recollection that it is one of the "things seen" which are temporary. The cross shall soon be exchanged for a crown, and you shall sit down with Abraham, Isaac, and Jacob in the kingdom of God!

✤ From the sermon "Thoughts on Immortality"

Christ Crucified

For I determined not to know any thing among you, save Jesus Christ, and him crucified. —1 CORINTHIANS 2:2

Let your faith's eye daily look on Christ crucified, and rest in the sight. What will you see as you look at Jesus on the cross? You will see the eternal Son of God suffering, bleeding, agonizing, dying in order to pay your soul's debt and make satisfaction for your sins. You will see the most wonderful transaction taking place that ever took place since the foundation of the world. You will see a divine substitute suffering in your stead, the just for the unjust; bearing your sins, carrying your transgressions, allowing Himself to be reckoned a curse and sin for you in order that you, sinner as you are, might be set free from all guilt and counted innocent before God.

Reader, look steadily at Jesus on the cross if you want to feel inward peace. Look to anything of your own, and you will never feel comfortable. Your own life and doings, your own repentance and amendment, your own morality and regularity, your own church going and sacrament receiving, your own Bible reading and your prayers, what, what are they all but a huge mass of imperfection? Rest not upon them for a moment in the matter of your justification. As evidences of your wishes, feelings, bias, tastes, habits, inclinations, they may be useful helps occasionally. As grounds of acceptance with God they are worthless rubbish. They cannot give you comfort; they cannot bear the weight of your sins; they cannot stand the searching eye of God. Rest on nothing but Christ crucified and the atonement He made for you on Calvary. This, this alone, is the way of peace.

Look steadily to Jesus on the cross and listen not to those who would persuade you to look elsewhere. Reader, you will never have cause to be ashamed of the doctrine of the cross. Let the first look of your soul to Jesus be a look backward. Look at Him dying for your sins on the cross, and as you look, say to yourself, "This was done for me!"

✣ From the sermon "Are You Looking?"

Hell Is Real

So shall it be at the end of the world: the angels shall come forth,
and sever the wicked from among the just, and shall cast them into
the furnace of fire: there shall be wailing and gnashing of teeth.
—MATTHEW 13:49–50

I know very well that some believe there is a hell but never like it to be spoken of. It is a subject that should always be kept back. They see no profit in bringing it forward and are rather shocked when it is mentioned. This also is an immense help to the devil. "Hush, hush!" says Satan, "say nothing about hell." The fowler wishes to hear no noise when he lays his snare. The wolf would like the shepherd to sleep while he prowls round the fold. Just so, the devil rejoices when Christians are silent about hell.

Do you believe the Bible? Then depend upon it, hell is real and true. It is as true as heaven, as true as justification by faith, as true as the fact that Christ died upon the cross. There is not a fact or doctrine which you may not lawfully doubt if you doubt hell. Disbelieve hell, and you unscrew, unsettle, and unpin everything in Scripture! You may as well throw your Bible away at once. From "no hell" to "no God" there is but a series of steps. Do you believe the Bible? Then depend upon it, hell will have inhabitants. The wicked shall certainly be sent into hell, and all the people that forget God. These shall go away into everlasting punishment. The same blessed Savior who now sits on a throne of grace will one day sit on a throne of judgment, and men will see there is such a thing as the wrath of the Lamb! The same lips that now say "Come, come unto Me," will one day say "Depart from Me, you who are cursed!" Alas, how awful the thought of being condemned by Christ Himself, judged by the Savior, sentenced to eternal misery by the Lamb!

✣ From the sermon "He Will Burn Up the Chaff with Unquenchable Fire"

Do You Have a Priest?

Seeing then that we have a great high priest, that is passed into the heavens, Jesus the Son of God, let us hold fast our profession.
—HEBREWS 4:14

The question before your eyes deserves your best attention. Whether you know it or not, it is a question of deep and wide importance. He who wishes to have any comfort in religion must have a priest. A religion without a priest is a poor, unhappy, useless, powerless thing. Now what is your religion? Have you a priest?

You and I are such sinful, corrupt creatures that we are unfit by ourselves to have anything to do with God. God is so holy a being that He cannot bear that which is evil, and so high a being that His majesty makes us afraid. We are such sinful, defective, and guilty beings that we naturally shrink from God and dare not speak to Him or look Him in the face. We need an almighty friend between us. We need a mediator and advocate, able, willing, loving, commissioned, tried, proved, and ready to help us. Have you a priest?

The Christian religion provides the very thing that man's soul and conscience require. It is the glory of God's Word that it reveals to man the very friend and mediator that he needs, the God-man Christ Jesus! It tells us of the very Priest who meets our needs, even Jesus, the Son of God. It sets Him fully before us, in the epistle to the Hebrews, as the very person that our longing hearts could desire. If Christ is the Priest of your soul, live always like one who looks for His second coming. Live like one who longs to see face-to-face the Savior in whom he believes. Happy is the Christian who lives the life of faith in Christ, dying, interceding, and coming again! There is a crown laid up for all "that love his appearing" (2 Tim. 4:8). Let us give diligence as long as we live, that this crown may be ours!

✤ From the sermon "Do You Have a Priest?"

Let Any Man Come!

In the last day, that great day of the feast, Jesus stood and cried, say-
ing, If any man thirst, let him come unto me, and drink. He that
believeth on me, as the scripture hath said, out of his belly shall flow
rivers of living water.
　　　　　　　　　　　　　　　　　　　　　　　—JOHN 7:37–38

The text at the head of this paper contains one of those mighty sayings
of Christ that deserves to be printed in letters of gold. All Scripture is
given by inspiration of God, but that heart must indeed be cold and dull
which does not feel that some verses are particularly rich and full. Of
such verses this text is one.

In order to see the whole force and beauty of the text, we must
remember the place, time, and occasion when it comes in. The place,
then, was Jerusalem—the metropolis of Judaism and stronghold of priests
and scribes, of Pharisees and Sadducees. The occasion was the Feast of
Tabernacles, one of those great annual feasts when every Jew, if he could,
went up to the temple, according to the law. The time was the last day of
the feast when all the ceremonies were drawing to a close, when the water
drawn from the fountain of Siloam had been solemnly poured on the
altar, and nothing remained for worshipers but to return home.

At this critical moment our Lord Jesus Christ stood forward on a
prominent place and spoke to the assembled crowds. I doubt not He
read their hearts. He saw them going away with aching consciences and
unsatisfied minds, having got nothing from their blind teachers, the
Pharisees and Sadducees, and carrying away nothing but a barren recollection of pompous forms. He saw and pitied them, and cried aloud, like
a herald, "If any man thirsts, let him come unto me, and drink"! I doubt
that this was all our Lord said on this memorable occasion. I suspect it is
only the keynote of His address. But this, I believe, was the first sentence
that fell from His lips: "If any man thirsts, let him come unto me." If
anyone wants living, satisfying water, "let him come unto me"!

❖ From the sermon "Let Any Man Come"

Casting Off the Works of Darkness

The night is far spent, the day is at hand: let us therefore cast off the works of darkness, and let us put on the armour of light.
— ROMANS 13:12

Reader, you and I are in a world which is rapidly rolling on toward the day of judgment.

There is an hour before us all when the earth and its works shall be burned up, and the inhabitants thereof shall all stand before the bar of Christ. There is a day to come whose issues are of greatest importance. Surely it befits us to think of that day. Are we ready for it? Is it possible that we may live to see it? Is it near, or is it far off? What time is it?

Come with me this day and consider the thoughts of an inspired apostle on this solemn subject. He says, "The night is far spent, the day is at hand: let us therefore cast off the works of darkness, and let us put on the armour of light." These words ought to come home to our consciences like the blast of a trumpet. They ought to rouse our sleeping minds to a sense of the eternal realities which are before us. They call upon us to lay aside all trifling, lingering, and carelessness about our Christianity. They summon us to a close walk with God. There are four things brought before my mind by the words just quoted:

1. You have here the present condition of the world. It is night.
2. You have the condition of the world which is yet to come. It will be day.
3. You have the particular time in which our lot is cast. The night is far spent, and the day is at hand.
4. You have the duty of all believers who know the time. They ought to cast off the works of darkness and put on the armor of light.

❖ From the sermon "Coming Events and Present Duties"

What Is Your Hope?

But I will hope continually, and will yet praise thee more and more.
—PSALM 71:14

Reader, what is your hope about your soul? Have you any, or have you none? Can you tell me in what way you expect to be accounted righteousness before God? Depend upon it, these are very serious questions. You and I are dying men. After death comes the judgment. What is your hope of acquittal in that solemn day? What are we going to plead on our behalf before God?

Shall we say that we have done our duty to God? Shall we say that we have done our duty to our neighbor? Shall we bring forward our prayers, our good works, our morality, our church going, our amendments? Shall we ask to be accepted by God for any of these things? Which of these things will stand God's eye? Which of them will actually justify you and me?

Which of them will carry us clear through judgment, and land us safe in glory? Absolutely none! Take any commandment of the ten and let us examine ourselves by it. We have broken it repeatedly. We cannot answer God. Take any of us and look narrowly into our ways—and we are nothing but sinners. There is but one verdict. We are all guilty, we all ought to die, we all deserve hell. How then can we come before God?

We must come in the name of Jesus, standing on no other ground, pleading no other plea than this: "Christ died on the cross for the ungodly, and I trust in Him." Oh, believe me, Christ must be all the hope of everyone who would be justified and saved. You must be content to go to heaven as a beggar, saved by free grace alone, simply as a believer in Jesus, or you will never be saved at all. "For by grace are ye saved through faith; and that not of yourselves: it is the gift of God: not of works, lest any man should boast" (Eph. 2:8–9).

❖ From the sermon "What Is Your Hope?"

The Path of Happiness

Oh how great is thy goodness, which thou hast laid up for them that fear thee; which thou hast wrought for them that trust in thee before the sons of men!
—PSALM 31:19

There is a sure path which leads to happiness if people will only take it. There never lived the person who traveled in that path and missed the object that he sought to attain. It is a path open to all. It needs neither wealth, nor rank, nor learning in order to walk in it. It is for the servant as well as for the master. It is for the poor as well as for the rich. None are excluded but those who exclude themselves. The way to be happy is to be a real, thoroughgoing, truehearted Christian! Scripture declares it, experience proves it. The converted individual, the believer in Christ, the child of God—this person alone is one who is happy. It sounds too simple to be true, it seems at first sight so plain a formula that it is not believed. But the greatest truths are often the simplest. The secret which many of the wisest on earth have utterly failed to discover, is revealed to the humblest believer in Christ. I repeat it deliberately and defy the world to disprove it, the true Christian is the only happy human being.

The one I have in view is the Christian in heart and life, taught by the Spirit really to feel his or her sins, who really rests all hopes on the Lord Jesus Christ and His atonement. This is one who has been born again and really lives a spiritual, holy life, whose religion is not a mere Sunday coat, but a mighty constraining principle governing every day of his or her life—this is the person I mean when I speak of a true Christian!

✤ From the sermon "Happiness"

Be an Overcoming Christian

And they overcame him by the blood of the Lamb, and by the word
of their testimony; and they loved not their lives unto the death.
—REVELATION 12:11

Resolve, by the grace of God, to be an overcoming Christian. I do fear much for many professing Christians: I see no sign of fighting in them, much less of victory; they never strike one stroke on the side of Christ. They are at peace with His enemies: they have no quarrel with sin. Reader, I warn you, that this is not Christianity; this is not the way to heaven.

Men and women who hear the gospel regularly, I often fear much for you. I fear lest you become so familiar with the sounds of its doctrines, that insensibly you become dead to its power. I fear lest your religion should sink down into a little vague talk about your own weakness and corruption, and a few sentimental expressions about Christ, while real practical fighting on Christ's side is altogether neglected. Oh, beware of this state of mind! "Be ye doers of the word, and not hearers only" (James 1:22). No victory, no crown! Fight and overcome!

Believers in the Lord Jesus of every church and rank in life, I feel much for you. I know your course is hard. I know it is a sore battle you have to fight. I know you are often tempted to say, "It is of no use" and lay down your arms altogether. Cheer up, dear brethren and sisters. Take comfort, I entreat you; look at the bright side of your position. Be encouraged to fight on; the time is short, the Lord is at hand, the night is far spent. Millions as weak as you have fought the same fight; not one of all those millions has been finally led captive by Satan. Mighty are your enemies, but the Captain of your salvation is mightier still. His arm, His grace, and His Spirit shall hold you up! Cheer up! Be not cast down!

✤ From the sermon "The Great Battle"

Unbelief, a Marvel

And he marvelled because of their unbelief. And he went round about the villages, teaching. —MARK 6:6

The text which heads this page is a very remarkable one. Of all the expressions in the four Gospels which show that the Lord Jesus Christ was very man, none perhaps is more startling than this. That He who was born of the virgin Mary and had a body like our own should hunger and thirst and weep and rejoice and be weary and suffer pain—all this we can, in some degree, understand. He who knew what was in man, that He should marvel at anything here below, may well fill us with astonishment! But what says the Scripture? There it is written in plain words, which no ingenuity can explain away, "He marvelled because of their unbelief."

What is there in unbelief that made even the Lord Jesus, the Son of God marvel? No doubt there was something peculiar and extraordinary in the unbelief of the Jews. That the children of Israel—brought up from their infancy in the knowledge of the law and the prophets, trained from their earliest years to look for the Messiah, to expect a mighty "prophet like unto Moses," to believe in the possibility of miracles, familiar with the story of miracle-working men—that they should reject Jesus of Nazareth and not be moved by the mighty works that He did among them, all this was truly astonishing and surprising! Astonishing that they should have such privileges and yet make such a bad use of them! Astonishing that the door of life should be open and heaven so near and they should refuse to enter in!

Some of my readers, I dare say, are often troubled with skeptical doubts about the truth of Christianity. You are not professed unbelievers; God forbid that I should say this. But you see many things in the Bible that you cannot quite understand. You see not a few men of powerful and commanding intellect rejecting Christianity almost entirely. You hear many slighting things said and depreciatory remarks made cleverly and smartly about the facts and doctrines of the Bible that you are unable to answer. All this puzzles you. You stand in doubt. Unless you take heed, they may land you in infidelity.

❖ From the sermon "Unbelief, a Marvel"

Being Filled with the Spirit

And be not drunk with wine, wherein is excess;
but be filled with the Spirit.
—EPHESIANS 5:18

If you have the Spirit, seek to "be filled with the Spirit." Drink deep of the living waters. Do not be content with a little religion. Pray that the Spirit may fill every corner and chamber of your heart and that not an inch of room may be left in it for the world and the devil. If you have the Spirit, "grieve not the holy Spirit of God" (Eph. 4:30). It is easy for believers to weaken their sense of His presence and deprive themselves of His comfort. Little sins not mortified, little bad habits of temper or of tongue not corrected, little compliances with the world, are all likely to offend the Holy Spirit. Oh, that believers would remember this! There is far more of heaven on earth to be enjoyed than many of them attain to, and why do they not attain to it? They do not watch sufficiently over their daily ways and so the Spirit's work is damped and hindered. The Spirit must be a thoroughly sanctifying Spirit if He is to be a comforter to your soul.

If you have the Spirit, labor to bring forth all the fruits of the Spirit. "But the fruit of the Spirit is love, joy, peace, longsuffering, gentleness, goodness, faith, meekness, temperance: against such there is no law. And they that are Christ's have crucified the flesh with the affections and lusts" (Gal. 5:22–24). Read over the list the apostle has drawn out and see that not one of these fruits is neglected. Oh, that believers would seek for more love and more joy! Then would they do more good to all people; then would they feel happier themselves; then would they make religion more beautiful in the eyes of the world!

Join with me in praying that the Spirit may be poured out from on high with more abundant influence than He has ever been yet. Pray that He may be poured out on all believers, at home and abroad, that they may be more united and more holy!

❖ From the sermon "Having the Spirit"

Boast in the Cross

But God forbid that I should glory, save in the cross of our Lord Jesus Christ, by whom the world is crucified unto me, and I unto the world.
—GALATIANS 6:14

What do we think and feel about the cross of Christ? We live in a Christian land. We probably attend the worship of a Christian church. We have, most of us, been baptized in the name of Christ. We profess and call ourselves Christians. All this is well, it is more than can be said of millions in the world. But what do we think and feel about the cross of Christ?

I want to examine what one of the greatest Christians who ever lived, thought of the cross of Christ. He has written down his opinion, he has given his judgment in words that cannot be mistaken. The man I mean is the apostle Paul. The place where you will find his opinion is in the letter that the Holy Spirit inspired him to write to the Galatians. The words in which his judgment is set down are these: "But God forbid that I should glory, save in the cross of our Lord Jesus Christ."

Now what did Paul mean by saying this? He meant to declare strongly that he trusted in nothing but Jesus Christ crucified for the pardon of his sins and the salvation of his soul. Let others, if they would, look elsewhere for salvation; let others, if they were so disposed, trust in other things for pardon and peace, for his part the apostle was determined to rest on nothing, lean on nothing, build his hope on nothing, place confidence in nothing, boast in nothing, except in the cross of Jesus Christ. Paul boasted in nothing but the cross. Strive to be like him. Set Jesus crucified fully before the eyes of your soul. Listen not to any teaching that would interpose anything between you and Him. Do not give Christ's honor to another. "He that glorieth, let him glory in the Lord" (1 Cor. 1:31).

✢ From the sermon "The Cross of Christ"

Ryle's Thoughts on Missions in Light of the End Times

Therefore I endure all things for the elect's sakes, that they may also obtain the salvation which is in Christ Jesus with eternal glory.
—2 TIMOTHY 2:10

I fully admit that missions are doing a great work among the heathen, and that schools and district-visiting are rescuing thousands from the devil at home. I do not undervalue these things. I would to God that all professing Christians would value them more. But men appear to me to forget that gospel religion is often withering in one place, while it is flourishing in another. They look at the progress of Christianity in the west of Europe. They forget how fearfully it has lost ground in the east. And as for any signs that all the ends of the earth shall turn to the Lord, under the present order of things, there are none. God's work is going forward as it always has done. The gospel is being preached for a witness to every quarter of the globe. The elect are being brought to Christ one by one and there is everything to encourage us to persevere. But more than this, no missionary can report in any station in the world.

I long for the conversion of all mankind as much as anyone. But I believe it is utterly beyond the reach of any instrumentality that man possesses. I quite expect that the earth will one day be filled with the knowledge of the glory of the Lord. But I believe that day will be in an entirely new dispensation—it will not be until after the Lord's return. I would not hesitate to preach the gospel and offer Christ's salvation to every man and woman alive. But that there always will be a vast amount of unbelief and wickedness until the second advent, I am fully persuaded. The gospel net may perhaps be spread far more widely than it has been till now, but the angels shall find abundance of bad fish in it as well as good fish in the last day. The gospel laborers may possibly be multiplied a thousandfold, and I pray God it may be so. But however faithfully they may sow, a large proportion of tares will be found growing together with the wheat at the time of harvest.

❖ From the sermon "Coming Events and Present Duties"

The Fruit of Christian Love

But the fruit of the Spirit is love.
—GALATIANS 5:22

Christian love will show itself in a believer's doings. It will make one ready to do kind acts to everyone within his reach, "both to their bodies and souls." It will not let one be content with soft words and kind wishes. It will make one diligent in doing all that lies in his or her power to lessen the sorrow and increase the happiness of others. Like his Master, he will care more for ministering than for being ministered to and will look for nothing in return. Like his Master's great apostle, he will very willingly spend and be spent for others, even though they repay him with hatred and not with love. True love does not want wages. Its work is its reward.

Christian love will show itself in a believer's readiness to bear evil as well as to do good.

It will make one patient under provocation, forgiving when injured, meek when unjustly attacked, quiet when slandered. It will make one bear much and forbear much, put up with much and look over much, submit often and deny himself or herself often, all for the sake of peace. It will make one put a strong bit on the temper, and a strong bridle on the tongue. True love is not always asking, "What are my rights? Am I treated as I deserve?" but, "How can I best promote peace? How can I do that which is most edifying to others?" Christian love will show itself in the general spirit and demeanor of a believer. It will make him kind, unselfish, good-natured, good-tempered, and considerate for others. It will make him gentle, affable, and courteous, in all the daily relations of private life. It will make him thoughtful for others' comfort, tender for others' feelings, and more anxious to give pleasure than to receive!

❖ From the sermon "Christian Love"

Those Old Sins Shall Never Rise Again

For Christ is not entered into the holy places made with hands, which are the figures of the true; but into heaven itself, now to appear in the presence of God for us.　　　　　—HEBREWS 9:24

Those old sins shall never rise again, nor stand up to condemn the child of God. For what says the Scripture, "For Christ is not entered into the holy places made with hands, which are the figures of the true; but into heaven itself, now to appear in the presence of God for us" (Heb. 9:24). Christ, to use a legal phrase, is ever "putting in an appearance" in the court of heaven on behalf of those who believe in Him. There is not a year, nor a month, nor a day, nor an hour, nor a minute but there is One living in the presence of God to make an appearance there on behalf of all the saints. Christ is ever appearing before God the Father on behalf of the men and women who believe in Him. His blood and His sacrifice are ever in God's sight. His work, His death, His intercession, are always sounding in God the Father's ears.

The wounds of the Lord Jesus Christ are ever before God the Father. The nail prints in His hands and feet, the marks of the spear in His side, the thorn marks upon His forehead, the marks of all that He suffered as a slain Lamb are, in a certain sense, ever before God the Father in heaven. While Christ is in heaven the believer's old sins will never rise in judgment against him. Christ lives, and those old sins will not condemn him. We have an ever-living, ever-interceding Priest. Christ is not dead but alive.

How shall a man get through the day with comfort, fill his office in the world, do his duty in the position to which God has called him? Let him lay hold upon the intercession of Jesus Christ. Let him grasp the great thought, that Christ not merely died for him, but rose again, and still lives for him.

❖ From the sermon "Christ's Power to Save"

Victory!

For whatsoever is born of God overcometh the world: and this is the victory that overcometh the world, even our faith. Who is he that overcometh the world, but he that believeth that Jesus is the Son of God? —1 JOHN 5:4–5

Consider the special mark that John supplies of the man who is a true Christian. He says, "Whatsoever is born of God overcometh the world." The three great spiritual enemies of man are the world, the flesh, and the devil. It is hard to say which does most harm to the soul. The last day alone will settle that point. But I venture boldly to say that at no former period has the world been so dangerous and so successful in injuring Christ's church as it is just now. Every age is said to have its own peculiar epidemic disease. I suspect that worldliness is the peculiar plague of Christendom in our own era.

Even in days of persecution under heathen emperors, these spiritual enemies slew their thousands; and in days like our own of ease and luxury and free thought, they slay their tens of thousands. The subtle influence of the world nowadays seems to infect the very air we breathe. It creeps into families like an angel of light and leads myriads captive, who never know that they are slaves. The enormous increase of English wealth and consequent power of self-indulgence and the immense growth of a passionate relish for recreations and amusements of all kinds; the startling rise and progress of a so-called liberality of opinion, which refuses to say anybody is wrong (whatever he does) and loudly asserts that, as in the days of the Judges, everyone should think and do what is right in his own eyes and never be checked—all these strange phenomena of our age give the world an amazing additional power and make it doubly needful for Christ's ministers to cry aloud, "Beware of the world!"

In the face of this aggravated danger, we must never forget that the word of the living God changes not. "Love not the world!" (1 John 2:15). "Be not conformed to this world!" (Rom. 12:2). "Whosoever therefore will be a friend of the world is the enemy of God" (James 4:4). These mighty sayings of God's statute book remain still unrepealed.

❖ From the sermon "Victory"

He Will Give You Rest

Take my yoke upon you, and learn of me; for I am meek and lowly in heart: and ye shall find rest unto your souls. —MATTHEW 11:29

He will give you rest from guilt of sin. The sins of the one who comes to Christ are completely taken away; they are forgiven, pardoned, removed, blotted out. They can no longer appear in condemnation against him! They are sunk in the depths of the sea. Ah! Brethren, that is rest. He will give you rest from fear of law. The law has no further claim on the person who has come to Christ. Its debts are all paid; its requirements are all satisfied. Christ is the end of the law for righteousness. Christ has redeemed us from the curse of law. And that is rest.

He will give you rest from fear of hell. Hell cannot touch the man who has come to Christ. The punishment has been borne, the pain and suffering have been undergone by Jesus, and the sinner is free. And that, too, is rest. He will give you rest from fear of the devil. The devil is mighty, but he cannot touch those who have come to Christ. Their Redeemer is strong. He will set a hedge around them that Satan cannot overthrow. Satan may sift and buffet and vex, but he cannot destroy such. And that, too, is rest.

He will give you rest from fear of death. The sting of death is taken away when a man comes to Christ. Jesus has overcome death, and it is a conquered enemy. The grave loses half its terrors when we think it is the place where the Lord lay. The believer's soul is safe whatever happens to his body. His flesh rests in hope. This also is rest. He will give you rest in the storm of affliction. He will comfort you with comfort the world knows nothing of. He will cheer your heart and sustain your fainting spirit. He will enable you to bear loss patiently and to hold your peace in the day of trouble. Be advised and seek rest in Christ. There is enough in Him and to spare. You have a rest even now, and you shall have more abundantly!

❖ From the sermon "Come unto Me"

Benefits of Sickness

It is good for me that I have been afflicted;
that I might learn thy statutes.
—PSALM 119:71

I speak of the benefits of sickness on purpose and advisedly. I know the suffering and pain that sickness entails. I admit the misery and wretchedness that it often brings in its train. But I cannot regard it as an unmixed evil. I see in it a wise permission of God. I see in it a useful provision to check the ravages of sin and the devil among men's souls. Here are a few points:

1. Sickness helps to remind men of death. Most live as if they were never going to die. They follow business or pleasure or politics or science as if earth was their eternal home. A heavy illness sometimes goes far in dispelling these delusions. It awakens men from their daydreams and reminds them that they have to die as well as live. Now this I say emphatically is a mighty good.

2. Sickness helps to make men think seriously of God and their souls and the world to come. The most in their days of health can find no time for such thoughts. They dislike them. They put them away. They count them troublesome and disagreeable. Now a severe disease has sometimes a wonderful power of mustering and rallying these thoughts and bringing them up before the eyes of a man's soul.

We have no right to murmur at sickness and repine at its presence in the world. We ought rather to thank God for it. It is God's witness. It is the soul's adviser. It is an awakener to the conscience. It is a purifier to the heart. Surely I have a right to tell you that sickness is a blessing and not a curse, a help and not an injury, a gain and not a loss, a friend and not a foe to mankind. So long as we have a world wherein there is sin, it is a mercy that it is a world wherein there is sickness.

❖ From the sermon "Sickness"

Simplicity That Is in Christ

But I fear, lest by any means, as the serpent beguiled Eve through his subtilty, so your minds should be corrupted from the simplicity that is in Christ.
                                                    —2 CORINTHIANS 11:3

Now the expression before us is somewhat remarkable and stands alone in the New Testament. One thing at any rate is abundantly clear: the word "simplicity" means that which is single and unmixed, in contradistinction to that which is mixed and double. Following out that idea, some have held that the expression means "singleness of affection toward Christ"; we are to fear lest we should divide our affections between Christ and any other. This is no doubt very good theology, but I question whether it is the true sense of the text. I prefer the opinion that the expression means the simple, unmixed, unadulterated, unaltered doctrine of Christ, the simple truth as it is in Jesus on all points, without addition, subtraction, or substitution.

Departure from the simple genuine prescription of the gospel, either by leaving out any part or adding any part, was the thing Paul would have the Corinthians especially to fear.

The expression is full of meaning and seems especially written for our learning in these last days. We are to be ever jealously on our guard, lest we depart from and corrupt the simple gospel which Christ once delivered to the saints. The expression before us is exceedingly instructive. The principle it contains is of unspeakable importance. If we love our souls and would keep them in a healthy state, we must endeavor to adhere closely to the simple doctrine of Christ in every jot, tittle, and particular. Once we add to it or take away anything from it, and we risk spoiling the divine medicine and may even turn it into poison. Let your ruling principle be, "No other doctrine but that of Christ, nothing less, and nothing more!" Lay firm hold on that principle, and never let it go. Write it on the tablet of your heart and never forget it!

❖ From the sermon "Apostolic Fears"

The Security of the True Church of Christ

And I say also unto thee, That thou art Peter, and upon this rock I will build my church; and the gates of hell shall not prevail against it.
—MATTHEW 16:18

There is a glorious promise given by the mighty Builder: "The gates of hell will not overcome it." He who cannot lie has pledged His royal word that all the powers of hell shall never overthrow His church. It shall continue and stand in spite of every assault. It shall never be overcome. All other created things perish and pass away, but not the church of Christ. The hand of outward violence or the moth of inward decay prevail over everything else, but not over the church that Christ builds. Empires have risen and fallen in rapid succession. Egypt, Assyria, Babylon, Persia, Tyre, Carthage, Rome, Greece, Venice—where are all these now? They were all the creations of human hands and have passed away. But the church of Christ lives on. The mightiest cities have become heaps of ruins.

Has the true church been oppressed in one country? It has fled to another. Has it been trampled on and oppressed in one soil? It has taken root and flourished in some other climate. Fire, sword, prisons, fines, punishments have never been able to destroy its vitality. Its persecutors have died and gone to their own place, but the Word of God has lived and grown and multiplied.

Weak as this true church may appear to the eye of man, it is an anvil that has broken many a hammer in times past and perhaps will break many more before the end. He who lays hands on it is touching the apple of God's eye! The true church is Christ's army. The Captain of our salvation loses none of His soldiers. His plans are never defeated. His supplies never fail. His roll call is the same at the end as it was at the beginning! Christ will ever provide for His own church! Christ will take care that the gates of hell shall not prevail against it! All is going on well, though our eyes may not see it. The kingdoms of this world shall yet become the kingdoms of our God and of His Christ.

❖ From the sermon "The True Church"

What Ought We to Do?

For I am not ashamed of the gospel of Christ: for it is the power of God unto salvation to every one that believeth; to the Jew first, and also to the Greek.
—ROMANS 1:16

What ought we to do? This, after all, is the point to which I want to bring your mind. Seeing and feeling are good. But doing is the life of religion. Passive impressions that do not lead to action have a tendency to harden the conscience and do us positive harm. What ought we to do? We ought to do much more than we have ever done yet. We might all probably do more. The honor of the gospel, the state of the missionary field abroad, the condition of our overgrown cities at home, all call upon us to do more.

Need we stand still and be ashamed of the weapons of our warfare? I assert boldly that we have no cause to be ashamed of the gospel at all. It is not worn out. It is not effete. It is not behind the times. We need nothing new, nothing added to the gospel, nothing taken away. We need nothing but "the old paths," the old truths fully, boldly, affectionately proclaimed. Only preach the gospel fully, the same gospel which Paul preached, and it is still "the power of God unto salvation to every one that believeth," and nothing else called religion has any real power at all (Rom. 1:16).

Need we stand still and be ashamed of the results of preaching the gospel? Shall we hang down our heads and complain that "the faith once delivered to the saints" has lost its power, and does no good? We have no cause to be ashamed at all. What can we do now but humble ourselves for the past, and endeavor, by God's help, to do more for time to come? Let us open our eyes more and see. Let us open our hearts more, and feel. Let us stir up ourselves to do more work by self-denying gifts, by zealous cooperation, by bold advocacy, by fervent prayer. Let us do something worthy of our cause. The cause for which Jesus left heaven and came down to earth deserves the best that we can do.

❖ From the sermon "Athens"

The Nature of Sanctification

Sanctify them through thy truth: thy word is truth.
—JOHN 17:17

Sanctification is that inward spiritual work which the Lord Jesus Christ works in a person by the Holy Spirit when He calls someone to be a true believer. He not only washes him or her from all sins in His own blood but also separates the new believer from his or her natural love of sin and the world, puts a new principle in the heart, and makes a person practically godly in life. The instrument by which the Spirit effects this work is generally the Word of God, though He sometimes uses afflictions and providential visitations "without the word" (1 Peter 3:1). The subject of this work of Christ by His Spirit is called in Scripture a sanctified man.

He is, thus, not only their "righteousness" but their "sanctification" (1 Cor. 1:30).

Let us hear what the Bible says: "And for their sakes I sanctify myself, that they also might be sanctified through the truth" (John 17:19). "Christ also loved the church, and gave himself for it; That he might sanctify and cleanse it" (Eph. 5:25–26). Christ "gave himself for us, that he might redeem us from all iniquity, and purify unto himself a peculiar people, zealous of good works" (Titus 2:14). Christ "bare our sins in his own body on the tree, that we, being dead to sins, should live unto righteousness: by whose stripes ye were healed" (1 Peter 2:24). Christ "hath…reconciled [you] in the body of his flesh through death, to present you holy and unblameable and unreproveable in his sight" (Col. 1:21–22). Let the meaning of these five texts be carefully considered. If words mean anything, they teach that Christ undertakes the sanctification, no less than the justification, of His believing people. Both are alike provided for in that "everlasting covenant, ordered in all things, and sure" (2 Sam. 23:5), of which the Mediator is Christ. In fact, Christ in one place is called "he that sanctifieth" and His people "they who are sanctified" (Heb. 2:11).

❖ From the sermon "Are We Sanctified"

Why Social Reforms Fail

And the scripture, foreseeing that God would justify the heathen through faith, preached before the gospel unto Abraham, saying, In thee shall all nations be blessed. —GALATIANS 3:8

After eighteen hundred years, human nature is still the same. Selfishness, oppression, cruelty, robbery, and even murder are still to be found in every quarter of the globe. The slave trade of Africa, which goes on even now on the east coast and in the Sudan; the massacres of the Indian Mutiny and recently in Egypt; the treatment of women, children, the sick, and the poor in almost every heathen country; the social disorders that disgrace some parts of Christendom; the robberies, murders, and deeds of violence. The plain truth is that the suffering and the downtrodden, the victims of oppression and robbery and violence are everywhere. Political and social reforms labor in vain because they ignore the fall of Adam and original sin. These are great stubborn facts that ruin all their calculations. Without acknowledging the reality and consequences of sin, the great problems of human nature can never be solved. How much we ought to long and strive to promote the progress of the gospel of Christ! This, after all, is the only true reformer of mankind. Just in proportion as men are brought under the influence of the despised old gospel will be the increase of peace on earth and goodwill among men!

The more Christ is known and loved and the more the Bible is read, the more will the inhabitants of the earth love one another. If pure and undefiled religion prevailed everywhere, then such plagues and pests and nuisances as quarreling, robbing, murder, drunkenness, immorality, swindling, gambling, idleness, lying, and cheating would be comparatively unknown. Half the prisons and workhouses would soon be shut. Lawyers and policemen would have little to do. Taxes would be cut in half. He is the truest friend to human happiness who does the most to spread the knowledge of Christ and evangelize the world. Men may laugh and mock at missions if they will. But the despised evangelical missionary, at home and abroad, the preacher of Christ and justification by faith, the preacher of the Holy Spirit and sanctification is the best friend of mankind!

✣ From the sermon "The Parable of the Good Samaritan"

The Lord's Garden

A garden inclosed is my sister, my spouse;
a spring shut up, a fountain sealed.
—SONG OF SOLOMON 4:12

The Lord Jesus Christ has a garden. It is the company of all who are true believers in Him. They are His garden. Jesus calls His people a garden because they are altogether different from the men of the world. The world is a wilderness; it brings forth little but thorns and thistles; it is fruitful in nothing but sin. The children of this world are an untilled wilderness in God's sight. With all their arts and sciences, intellect and skill, eloquence and statesmanship, poetry and refinement—with all this they are a wilderness, barren of repentance, faith, holiness, and obedience to God. The Lord looks down from heaven, and where He sees no grace, there the Lord can see nothing but a wilderness state of things. The Lord Jesus Christ's believing people are the only green spot on the earth, the only oasis amid barren deserts; they are His garden.

He calls His people a garden because they are sweet and beautiful to His mind. He looks on the world, and it grieves Him to the heart, He looks on the little flock of His believing people and is well pleased. He sees in them the fruit of His travail and is satisfied. He rejoices in spirit when He sees the kingdom revealed to babes, though the wise and prudent receive it not. As in the day of Noah's sacrifice, He smells a sweet aroma and is refreshed. It is very wonderful, very mysterious! Believers are vile in their own eyes and feel themselves miserable sinners; yet Jesus says, "Thou art fair, for sweet is thy voice, thy countenance is comely, Thou art beautiful, O my love, as Tirzah, comely as Jerusalem, terrible as an army with banners" (see Song 1:15; 4:7; 2:14; 6:4, 10). Oh, the depths! It sounds incomprehensible and almost incredible, but it is true! He calls His people a garden because He delights to walk among them!

✣ From the sermon "The Lord's Garden"

Greatest Shortcoming in the Church

But the day of the Lord will come as a thief in the night.
—2 PETER 3:10

I have long felt that it is one of the greatest shortcomings of the church of Christ that we ministers do not preach enough about this advent of Christ, and that private believers do not think enough about it. A few of us here and there receive the doctrine and profess to love it, but the number of such people is comparatively very small. And, after all, we none of us live on it, feed on it, act on it, work from it, take comfort in it, as much as God intended us to do. In short, the Bridegroom tarries and we all slumber and sleep! For myself, I can only give my own individual testimony. But the little I know experimentally of the doctrine of Christ's second coming makes me regard it as most practical and precious, and makes me long to see it more generally received.

I find Christ's second coming to be a powerful spring and stimulus to holy living, a motive for patience, for moderation, for spiritual-mindedness, a test for the employment of time, and a gauge for all my actions: "Would I like my Lord to find me in this place? Would I like Him to find me so doing?" I find Christ's second coming to be the strongest argument for missionary work. The time is short. The Lord is at hand. The gathering out from all nations will soon be accomplished. The heralds and forerunners of the King will soon have proclaimed the gospel in every nation. The night is far spent. The King will soon be here!

And now, is there any one among the readers of this address who cannot receive the doctrine of Christ's second advent and kingdom? I invite that man to consider the subject calmly and dispassionately. Dismiss from your mind traditional interpretations. Separate the doctrine from the mistakes and blunders of many who hold it. Do not reject the foundation because of the wood, hay, and stubble that some have built upon it. Do not condemn it and cast it aside because of injudicious friends. It is a sad truth, but a truth never to be forgotten, that none have injured the doctrine of the second coming so much as its overzealous friends.

❖ From the sermon "Coming Events and Present Duties"

Five Marks of Forgiven Souls

Blessed is he whose transgression is forgiven,
whose sin is covered.
—PSALM 32:1

Let me set down in order the leading marks of a forgiven soul.

1. Forgiven souls hate sin. If you and sin are friends, you and God are not yet reconciled. You are not fit for heaven; for one main part of heaven's excellence is the absence of all sin.

2. Forgiven souls love Christ. This is that one thing they can say, if they dare say nothing else, they do love Christ. His person, His offices, His work, His name, His cross, His blood, His words, His example, His ordinances—all, all are precious to forgiven souls. The ministry which exalts Him most is that which they enjoy most. The books which are most full of Him are most pleasant to their minds. The people on earth they feel most drawn to are those in whom they see something of Christ.

3. Forgiven souls are humble. They cannot forget that they owe all they have and hope for to free grace, and this keeps them lowly. They are brands plucked from the fire, debtors who could not pay for themselves, captives who must have remained in prison forever but for undeserved mercy, wandering sheep who were ready to perish when the Shepherd found them! We have nothing we can call our own but sin and weakness. Surely there is no garment that befits us so well as humility.

4. Forgiven souls are holy. Their chief desire is to please Him who has saved them, to do His will, to glorify Him in body and in Spirit, which are His. Pardon of sin and love of sin are like oil and water; they will never go together. All who are washed in the blood of Christ are also sanctified by the Spirit of Christ.

5. Forgiven souls are forgiving. They do as they have been done by. They look over the offenses of their brethren. They remember how God for Christ's sake forgave them and endeavor to do the same toward their fellow creatures. Surely we know nothing of Christ's love to us but the name of it if we do not love our brethren.

✣ From the sermon "Forgiveness"

Advancing World Missions

Yea, so have I strived to preach the gospel, not where Christ was named, lest I should build upon another man's foundation.
—ROMANS 15:20

There is needed among us more of a working spirit. I mean just simply what I say. We need more vigorous working to advance the cause of missions, more active, businesslike exertion to set forward its prosperity. The way to advance any cause is to keep it continually in mind, to be always thinking of it, always speaking of it, always trying to bring it under the notice of others, always endeavoring to keep it before their eyes.

We need to have this done for the missionary cause. The heathen are perishing daily. Nothing but the gospel can save them. Every person who is in earnest about his own soul should look on missions as his own affair and should consider, "What can I do to help them?" The nations are shaking, and thrones and principalities are being cast down. The kingdom draws near which can never be shaken. The King Himself cannot be far off. The Judge stands at the door. The night is coming when no man can work. God seems to be crying in His wonderful providences, "Who is on the Lord's side?" Oh! Let us each say, "I am!"

The state of the heathen demands it. North and south, east and west, souls are perishing for lack of knowledge. Sin is reigning and Satan carrying men captive at his will. If we are not infidels, if we are not sham Christians, if we are really in earnest in our religion, let us have pity on them and send to help them. Above all, the well-being of our own souls demands it. We little know how much depends on working for God in the matter of our spiritual comfort. Exercise is the secret of a healthy body and active working for God one secret of a healthy soul. This is the path in which God will meet us and give us more peace and strength. He who waters others shall be watered himself!

❖ From the sermon "Work to Be Done"

Train Your Children in Obedience

Children, obey your parents in the Lord: for this is right.
—EPHESIANS 6:1

This is a goal which is worth any amount of effort to attain. No habit, I believe, has such an influence over our lives as this. Parents, determine to make your children obey you, though it may cost you a lot of trouble and cost them many tears. Let there be no questioning and reasoning and disputing and delaying. When you give them a command, let them clearly see that you expect them to do it.

Obedience is the only reality. It is faith visible, faith acting, and faith manifest. It is the test of real discipleship among the Lord's people. Jesus said, "Ye are my friends, if ye do whatsoever I command you" (John 15:14). It ought to be the mark of well-trained children that they do whatever their parents command them. Where, in fact, is the honor that the fifth commandment directs if fathers and mothers are not obeyed cheerfully, willingly, and at once?

Parents, do you want to see your children happy? Be careful, then, that you train them to obey when they are spoken to, to do as they are told. Believe me, we are not made to be entirely independent; we are not fit for it. Even those whom Christ has set free have a yoke to wear, "for ye serve the Lord Christ" (Col. 3:24). Children cannot learn too soon that this is a world in which not everyone was intended to rule and that we are never in our right place until we know how to obey those over us. Teach them to obey while they are young, or else they will be protesting against God all their lives and wear themselves out with the vain idea of being independent of His control. Parents, if you love your children, let obedience be a motto and a watchword continually before their eyes.

❖ From the book *The Duties of Parents*

The Danger of Double-Mindedness

A double minded man is unstable in all his ways.
—JAMES 1:8

You may starve your soul to death by trifling and indecision. You may idle through life with a name upon the baptismal register but not inscribed in the Lamb's Book of Life, with a form of godliness but without the power. You may trifle on year after year, taking no interest in that which is good, content to sneer at the inconsistencies of professors, and flattering yourself because you are no bigot, or party man, or professor, it will be all right with your soul at last. "Let no man deceive you with vain words" (Eph. 5:6). Indecision is just as ruinous to the soul as a false religion or no religion at all. The stream of life can never stand still. Whether you are sleeping or waking, you are floating down that stream. You are coming nearer and nearer to the rapids. You will soon pass over the falls, and, if you die without a decided faith, be cast away for all eternity!

Let me say plainly that we ministers are full of fears about many who profess and call themselves Christians. We fear lest they should lose at last their precious souls. We fear lest that archimposter, Satan, should cheat them out of salvation and lead them captive at his will. We fear lest they should wake up in eternity and find themselves lost forevermore! We fear because we see so many living in sinful habits, so many resting in forms and ceremonies which God never commanded, so many trifling with all religion whatever—so many, in short, ruining their own souls! We see these things and are afraid.

It is just because I feel that souls are in danger that I write this paper and invite men to read it. If I thought there was no such place as hell I would not write as I do. If I thought that as a matter of course all people would go to heaven at last, I would be quiet and leave them alone. But I dare not do so. I see danger ahead, and I would sincerely warn every man to flee from the wrath to come.

❖ From the sermon "Our Souls"

A Word to Christian Soldiers

Thou therefore endure hardness, as a good soldier of Jesus Christ. No man that warreth entangleth himself with the affairs of this life; that he may please him who hath chosen him to be a soldier.
—2 TIMOTHY 2:3–4

Let us all remember that the Christian soldier's best time is yet to come. Here in this world we are often injured and hindered in our warfare. There are many hard things to be done and borne. There are wounds and bruises; there are watchings and fatigues; there are reverses and disappointments. But the end of all things is at hand. For those who overcome there will be a conqueror's crown, when the Captain of our salvation and His victorious soldiers shall at length meet face-to-face. What tongue can tell the happiness of that time when we shall lay aside our armor and say to the sword, "Rest, and be still!" What mind can conceive the blessedness of that hour when we shall see the King in His beauty and hear these words: "Well done, good and faithful servant and soldier, enter you into the joy of your Lord"? For that glorious day let us wait patiently, for it cannot be far off. In the hope of it let us work and watch and pray and fight on and resist the world. And let us never forget our Captain's words, "These things I have spoken unto you, that in me ye might have peace. In the world ye shall have tribulation: but be of good cheer; I have overcome the world" (John 16:33).

Thanks be to God, there will be none missing in that day. It will be a meeting without regret. It will be a morning without clouds and tears! It will make rich amends for all we have suffered in resisting and overcoming the world.

✢ From the sermon "Victory"

Watch

Watch and pray, that ye enter not into temptation: the spirit indeed is willing, but the flesh is weak. —MATTHEW 26:41

I exhort you earnestly to watch. Watch against sin of every kind and description. Think not to say of any sin whatever, "Ah! That is one of the things that I shall never do." I tell you there is no possible sin too abominable for the very best of us all to commit! Remember David and Uriah. The spirit may sometimes be very willing, but the flesh is always very weak. You are yet in the body. Watch and pray! Watch against doubts and unbelief as to the complete acceptance of your soul if you are a believer in Christ Jesus.

Watch against inconsistency of walk and conformity to the world. Watch against sins of temper and of tongue. These are the kind of things that grieve the Spirit of God and make His witness within us faint and low. Watch and pray! Watch against the leaven of false doctrine.

Remember that Satan can transform himself into an angel of light. Remember that bad money is never marked bad, or else it would never pass. Be very jealous for the whole truth as it is in Jesus. Do not put up with a grain of error merely for the sake of a pound of truth. Do not tolerate a little false doctrine one bit more than you would a little sin. Oh, reader, remember this caution! Watch and pray!

Watch against slothfulness about the Bible and private prayer. There is nothing so spiritual but we may at last do it formally. Most backslidings begin in the closet. When a tree is snapped in two by a high wind, we generally find there had been some long-hidden decay. Oh, watch and pray! Watch against bitterness and uncharitableness toward others. A little love is more valuable than many gifts. Be eagle-eyed in seeing the good that is in your brethren and dim-sighted as the mole about the evil. Let your memory be a strongbox for their graces but a sieve for their faults. Watch against pride and self-conceit. Peter said at first, "Though all men deny You, yet I never will." And soon he fell. Pride is the high road to a fall. Oh, my believing readers, let us all watch more than we have done!

❖ From the sermon "Coming Events and Present Duties"

Doctrine of Perseverance

But he that shall endure unto the end, the same shall be saved.
—MATTHEW 24:13

When I speak of the doctrine of perseverance, I mean this. I say that the Bible teaches that true Christians shall persevere in their religion to the end of their lives. They shall never perish. They shall never be lost. They shall never be cast away. Once in Christ, they shall always be in Christ. Once made children of God by adoption and grace, they shall never cease to be His children and become children of the devil. Once endued with the saving grace of the Spirit, that grace shall never be taken from them. Once pardoned and forgiven, they shall never be deprived of their pardon. Once joined to Christ by living faith, their union shall never be broken off. Once called by God into the narrow way that leads to life, they shall never be allowed to fall into hell. In a word, every man, woman, and child on earth who receives saving grace, shall sooner or later receive eternal glory! Every soul that is once justified and washed in Christ's blood, shall be found safe at Christ's right hand in the day of judgment.

Perseverance is the peculiar privilege of real, true, spiritual Christians. It belongs to the sheep of Christ who hear His voice and follow Him. It belongs to those who are washed and justified and sanctified in the name of the Lord Jesus and by the Spirit of God. It belongs to those who repent and believe in Christ and live holy lives. It belongs to those who are fruit-bearing branches of the vine, the wise virgins, the light of the world, the salt of the earth, the heirs of the kingdom, the followers of the Lamb. These are they whom the Bible calls the saints. And it is the saints and the saints alone, of whom it is written, that they shall never perish!

✣ From the sermon "Never Perish"

Prove All Things

Prove all things; hold fast that which is good.
—1 THESSALONIANS 5:21

"Prove all things." When I say the right of private judgment, I mean that every individual Christian has a right to judge for himself by the Word of God, whether that which is put before him as religious truth, is God's truth, or is not. When I say the duty of private judgment, I mean that God requires every Christian man to use the right of which I have just spoken, to compare man's words and man's writings with God's revelation and to make sure that he is not deluded or taken in by false teaching. And when I say the necessity of private judgment, I mean this, that it is absolutely needful for every Christian who loves his soul and would not be deceived, to exercise that right, and discharge that duty to which I have referred. Seeing that experience shows that the neglect of private judgment has always been the cause of immense evils in the church of Christ!

The principle laid down is this: prove all things by the Word of God. All ministers, all teaching, all preaching, all doctrines, all sermons, all writings, all opinions, all practices—prove all by the Word of God. Measure all by the measure of the Bible. Compare all with the standard of the Bible. Weigh all in the balances of the Bible. Examine all by the light of the Bible. Test all in the crucible of the Bible. That which can abide the fire of the Bible you are to receive, hold, believe, and obey. That which cannot abide the fire of the Bible you are to reject, refuse, repudiate, and cast away. The people of God are called to test the truth, to judge between true and false, between light and darkness. God has made them the promise of His Spirit and has left unto them His Word!

❖ From the sermon "Prove All Things"

The Place of Heaven

*And there shall in no wise enter into it any thing that defileth,
neither whatsoever worketh abomination, or maketh a lie: but they
which are written in the Lamb's book of life.*
—REVELATION 21:27

The place of heaven. There is such a place as heaven. No truth is more certain in the whole of Scripture than this, there remains a rest for the people of God. This earth is not our rest, it cannot be, there breathes not a man or woman who ever found it so. O brethren, how faithful is that saying, "If in this life only we have hope in Christ, we are of all men most miserable" (1 Cor. 15:19). This life, so full of trouble and sorrow and care, of anxiety and labor and toil; this life of losses and bereavements, of partings and separations, of mourning and woe, of sickness and pain; this life of which even Elijah got so tired that he requested he might die—truly, I would be crushed to the very earth with misery if I felt that this life were all that is. If I thought there was nothing for me beyond the dark, cold, silent, lonely grave, I would indeed say, better never have been born!

Thanks be to God, this life is not all. I know and am persuaded there is a glorious rest beyond the tomb! This earth is only the training school for eternity. These graves are but the stepping-stone and halfway house to heaven. I feel assured this my poor body shall rise again; this corruptible shall yet put on incorruption, and this mortal immortality, and be with Christ forever. Yes, heaven is true, and not a fable—I do not doubt it. I am not more certain of my own existence than I am of this, there does remain a rest for the people of God!

❖ From the sermon "Heaven"

Divine Inspiration

For the prophecy came not in old time by the will of man: but holy
men of God spake as they were moved by the Holy Ghost.
—2 PETER 1:21

What is it exactly that we mean when we talk of the Scriptures as the Word of God? This is, no doubt, a difficult question. The plain truth is that inspiration is a miracle, and, like all miracles, there is much about it which we cannot fully understand. We must not confound it with intellectual power, such as great poets and authors possess. To talk of Shakespeare and Milton and Byron being inspired like Moses and St. Paul is, to my mind, almost profane. Nor must we confound it with the gifts and graces bestowed on the early Christians in the primitive church. All the apostles were enabled to preach and work miracles, but not all were inspired to write. We must rather regard it as a special supernatural gift, bestowed on about thirty people out of mankind, in order to qualify them for the special business of writing the Scriptures; and we must be content to allow that, like everything miraculous, we cannot entirely explain it, though we can believe it.

The position I take up is that while the Bible writers were not machines, as some sneeringly say, they only wrote what God taught them to write. The Holy Spirit put into their minds thoughts and ideas, and then guided their pens in writing and expressing them. Even when they made use of old records, chronicles, pedigrees, and lists of names, as they certainly did, they adopted, used, and compiled them under the direction of the Holy Spirit. When you read the Bible, you are not reading the unaided, self-taught composition of erring men like yourselves, but thoughts and words which were given by the eternal God. The men who were employed to write the Scripture "came not in old time by the will of man." They "spake as they were moved by the Holy Ghost" (2 Peter 1:21). He who holds a Bible in his hand should remember that he holds not the word of man but of God. He holds a volume which not only contains, but is, God's Word!

✤ From the sermon "Hold Fast"

Meditating on the Sufferings of Christ

*Him, being delivered by the determinate counsel and foreknowledge
of God, ye have taken, and by wicked hands have crucified and slain.*
—ACTS 2:23

I believe it is an excellent thing for us all to be continually dwelling on
the cross of Christ. It is a good thing to be often reminded how Jesus
was betrayed into the hands of wicked men—how they condemned
Him with most unjust judgment; how they spit on Him, scourged Him,
beat Him and crowned Him with thorns; how they led Him forth as a
lamb to the slaughter, without His murmuring or resisting; how they
drove the nails through His hands and feet, and set Him up on Calvary
between two thieves; how they pierced His side with a spear, mocked
Him in His sufferings, and let Him hang there naked and bleeding until
He died. Of all these things, I say, it is good to be reminded.

People seem to forget that all Christ's sufferings on the cross were
foreordained. They did not come on Him by chance or accident, they
were all planned, counseled, and determined from all eternity. The cross
was foreseen in all the provisions of the everlasting Trinity for the salvation of sinners. In the purposes of God, the cross was set up from
everlasting. Not one throb of pain did Jesus feel, not one precious drop
of blood did Jesus shed, that had not been appointed long ago. Infinite
wisdom planned that redemption should be by the cross.

People seem to forget that all Christ's sufferings on the cross were
necessary for man's salvation. He had to bear our sins, if ever they were
to be borne at all. With His stripes alone could we be healed. This was
the one payment of our debt that God would accept, this was the great
sacrifice on which our eternal life depended. If Christ had not gone to
the cross and suffered in our stead, the just for the unjust, there would
not have been a spark of hope for us. There would have been a mighty
gulf between us and God which no man ever could have passed.

✤ From the sermon "The Cross of Christ"

Assurance Produces Holiness

Now unto him that is able to keep you from falling, and to present you faultless before the presence of his glory with exceeding joy.
—JUDE 24

Assurance is to be desired because it tends to make the holiest Christians. This too sounds wonderful and amazing, and yet it is true. It is one of the paradoxes of the gospel—contrary, at first sight, to reason and common sense—and yet it is a fact. He who is freely forgiven by Christ will always do much for Christ's glory, and he who has the fullest assurance of this forgiveness will ordinarily keep up the closest walk with God. It is a faithful saying in the first epistle of John, "And every man that hath this hope in him purifieth himself, even as he is pure" (1 John 3:3).

Beloved brethren, would you have great peace? Would you like to feel the everlasting arms around you, and to hear the voice of Jesus drawing near to your soul, and saying, "I am your salvation"? Would you be useful in your day and generation? Would you be known by all as bold, firm, decided, single-eyed followers of Christ? Would you be eminently spiritually minded and holy? "Ah!" some of you will say, "These are the very things we desire; we long for them, we pant after them, but they seem far from us." Then take my advice this day. Seek an assured hope like Paul's. Seek to obtain a simple, childlike confidence in God's promises. Seek to be able to say with the apostle, "I know whom I have believed, and am persuaded that he is able to keep that which I have committed unto him against that day" (2 Tim. 1:12).

You have many of you tried the ways and methods and completely failed. Change your plan. Go upon another tack. Begin with assurance. Lay aside your doubts. Cast aside your faithless backwardness to take the Lord at His word. Come and roll yourself, your soul, and your sins upon your gracious Savior. Begin with simple believing, and all other things shall soon be added to you!

❖ From the sermon "Assurance"

Cling to Christ!

Thou shalt fear the LORD thy God; him shalt thou serve, and to him shalt thou cleave, and swear by his name.
—DEUTERONOMY 10:20

Cling to Christ, I say, and never forget your debt to Him. Sinners you were, when you were first called by the Holy Spirit, and fled to Jesus. Sinners you have been, even at your best, from the day of your conversion. Sinners, you will find yourselves to your dying hour having nothing to boast of in yourselves. Then cling to Christ. Cling to Christ, I say, and make use of His atoning blood every day. Go to Him every morning as your morning sacrifice and confess your need of His salvation. Go to Him every night, after the bustle of the day, and plead for fresh absolution. Wash in the great fountain every evening, after all the defilement of contact with the world.

Cling to Christ, I say, and show the world how you love Him. Show it by obedience to His commandments. Show it by conformity to His image. Show it by following His example. Make your Master's cause lovely and beautiful before people, by your own holiness of temper and conversation. Let all the world see that he who is much forgiven is the man who loves much, and that he who loves most is the man who does most for Christ (Luke 7:47).

Cling to Christ, I say, and have high thoughts of the atonement made by His blood upon the cross. Think highly of His incarnation and His example. Think highly of His miracles and His words. Think highly of His resurrection and intercession and coming again. But think highest of all of Christ's sacrifice, and the atoning sacrifice made by His death. Contend earnestly for the old faith concerning His atonement. See in the old doctrine that He died as a substitute for sinners, the only solution of a thousand passages in the Old Testament, and a hundred passages in the New. Never, never be ashamed to let people know that you derive all your comfort from the atoning blood of Christ and from His substitution for you on the cross!

✤ From the sermon "Where Are Your Sins?"

Always the Same!

For all the promises of God in him are yea, and in him Amen, unto the glory of God by us.
—2 CORINTHIANS 1:20

Once more Jesus Christ is always the same in His power to preserve. He will not begin the work of grace and leave it uncompleted; for it is His own word, "My sheep hear my voice, and I know them, and they follow me: And I give unto them eternal life…neither shall any man pluck them out of my hand" (John 10:27–28). It was He who raised the apostles after they had shamefully forsaken Him and fled. It was He who turned the heart of even Peter back again, though he had denied Him before His face. And what He did then, beloved, He will do now also for every believer. It shall never be said that any trusted in Jesus and were confounded, for the author and finisher of our faith never changes.

Always the same! It is this which gives such value to the Gospels in which our Lord's history is told. We are not reading there the life and sayings of one fickle and changeable like ourselves, but the life and sayings of a Redeemer who is now what He was then. We tell you confidently that all that love and gentleness and compassion and long-suffering and tenderheartedness which you may there see in your Lord and Savior's character, are placed before you that you may understand the character of Him from whom alone we receive forgiveness and to whom alone your prayer must be made. And we say this because we know He is the same yesterday, today, and forever.

Always the same! It is this which makes the gospel so excellent and precious. We do not bid you depend on anything less than the tried cornerstone, the fountain whose water shall never fail, the city of refuge whose walls shall never be broken down, the sure Rock of Ages. Churches may decay and perish; riches may make themselves wings and fly away, but he who builds his happiness on Christ crucified and union with Him by faith, that man is standing on a foundation which shall never be moved and will know something of true peace.

❖ From the sermon "The Unchanging Christ"

Neglecting of Private Prayer

And he spake a parable unto them to this end, that men ought always to pray, and not to faint.
—LUKE 18:1

We live in days of abounding religious profession. There are more places of public worship than there ever were before. There are more people attending them than there ever were before. And yet in spite of all this public religion, I believe there is a vast neglect of private prayer. It is one of those private transactions between God and our souls which no eye sees, and therefore one which people are tempted to pass over and leave undone. I believe that thousands never utter a word of prayer at all. They eat. They drink. They sleep. They rise. They go forth to their work. They return to their homes. They breathe God's air. They see God's sun. They travel on God's earth. They enjoy God's mercies. They have dying bodies. They have judgment and eternity before them. But they never speak to God. They live like the animals that perish. They behave like creatures without souls. They have not one word to say to Him in whose hand are their life and breath and all things and from whose mouth they must one day receive their everlasting sentence. How dreadful this seems, but if the secrets of men were only known, how common.

Does this surprise you? Listen to me, and I will show you that I am not speaking as I do without reason. Do you think that my assertions are extravagant and unwarrantable? Give me your attention, and I will soon show you that I am only telling you the truth. I cannot see your heart. I do not know your private history in spiritual things. But from what I see in the Bible and in the world, I am certain I cannot ask you a more necessary question than that before you: Do you pray?

❖ From the sermon "Call to Prayer"

Be Wise in Time

Redeeming the time, because the days are evil.
—EPHESIANS 5:16

O man, be wise in time. Learn to lay up treasures in heaven, think first of a house not made with hands, look to that precious friend who never fails. Away with your cold and sleeping shadow of religion. Cease to be a Christian in name and form only, become a man of God in deed and in truth. Come to your eternal Father as a little child, with confession and prayer. Take all your sins to the Savior who died upon the cross. Let nothing satisfy you until you are a living member of Jesus Christ, one with Christ and Christ with you. In Him I can warrant you a hope that never changes, a title to happiness that shall never be overthrown.

But are there any among you who have tasted of this blessed change; who have put off the old man, which is corrupt, and put on the new man, which after God is created in righteousness and true holiness; who mourn over your own daily shortcomings and sigh after more holiness, more self-denial, more mortification of the flesh with all its lusts? We bid you take comfort and remember that Christ is still the same. He called you and gave you the witness of the Spirit, and He will not forsake you. You may waver and tremble: go forward in faith, and He will still support you. There is but one more change before you, the changing of this vile body that it may be made a spiritual body, the putting off the corruptible to put on the incorruptible, the giving up what is mortal to receive what is immortal, the laying aside the earthly tabernacle, the entering on a heavenly one. Watch, then, and pray, and He who gave you the first change shall give you the second also. And then you shall go out no more, no more weariness, no more weakness, no more fainting! You shall see your Savior as He is and love Him as you ought, and like Him at last be unchanged and the same for evermore!

✤ From the sermon "The Unchanging Christ"

The Object on Which Our Eyes Are to Be Fixed

Looking unto Jesus the author and finisher of our faith.
—HEBREWS 12:2

We are to run our race "looking unto Jesus." We are to run, depending on Him for salvation; renouncing all trust in our own poor, frail exertions; counting our own performances no better than filthy rags; and resting wholly and entirely, simply and completely, upon that perfect righteousness which He worked out for us upon the cross. We need not run uncertain of the end. We need not fight in ignorance of what shall follow. We have only to behold the Lamb of God who takes away the sin of the world and believe that He has borne our griefs and carried our sorrows and will soon present us spotless and unblamable in His Father's sight.

And then we are to run, making Jesus our example, taking no lower pattern than the Son of God Himself, endeavoring to copy His meekness, His humility, His love, His zeal for souls, His self-denial, His purity, His faith, His patience, His prayerfulness. And as we look, we shall daily become more like Him! Oh, this looking unto Jesus! Here is the secret cause which kept that cloud of witnesses steadfast and unmovable in this narrow way! Here is the simple rule for all who wish to enter on the course which lands a man in paradise! Look not to earth; it is a sinful, perishable place, and they who build upon it shall find their foundation of the earth earthy. They will not stand the fire. Set not your affections upon it, or else you will perish together; the earth shall be burned up, and if you cling to it, in death you shall not be divided!

Look not to yourselves! You are by nature wretched and miserable, and poor and blind and naked; you cannot make atonement for your past transgressions, you cannot wipe out a single page in that long black list. Look simply unto Jesus, and then the weight shall fall from off your shoulders, and the course shall be clear and plain, and you shall run the race which is set before you.

❖ From the sermon "The Christian Race"

The Night Is Far Spent

The night is far spent, the day is at hand: let us therefore cast off the works of darkness, and let us put on the armour of light.
—ROMANS 13:12

The time is short. It is but a little while, and the Lord Jesus shall come in His glory. The judgment shall be set, and the books shall be opened. "Before him shall be gathered all nations" (Matt. 25:32), "that every one may receive the things done in his body, according to that he hath done, whether it be good or bad" (2 Cor. 5:10). The inmost secrets of all hearts shall be revealed. "And the kings of the earth, and the great men, and the rich men, and the chief captains, and the mighty men, and every bond-man, and every free man" will stand together on a level at the judgment, and will see each other face-to-face, and one by one will have to give account of themselves to God before the whole world (Rev. 6:15). Thus it is written, and therefore it is true and sure to come to pass.

And what does each of you intend to say in that hour? What is the defense you are prepared to set up? What is the answer you propose to give? What is the cause you mean to show as to why sentence should not be pronounced against you? Verily, beloved, I do fear that some among you do not know. Oh, what a fearful case is yours! Life is indeed uncertain; the loveliest or the strongest here may perhaps be taken next. You cannot make an agreement with death, and yet you cannot tell us what you are resting upon for comfort. You do not know how soon the last trumpet may sound, and yet you are uncertain as to the ground of your hope.

Surely these things ought not so to be.

See now how differently you act in the matter of your souls. In the great day there will be no lack of witnesses; your thoughts and words and actions will appear written in the book one after another. Your Judge is a searcher of hearts. And yet, in spite of all these facts, too many of you sleep on as if the Bible were not true. Too many of you know not how or why you are to escape God's wrath and condemnation.

✣ From the sermon "The Lord Our Righteousness"

What Is the Church?

And I say also unto thee, That thou art Peter, and upon this rock I will build my church; and the gates of hell shall not prevail against it.
—MATTHEW 16:18

The Lord Jesus Christ speaks of "my church." Now what is this church? Few inquiries can be made of more importance than this. For lack of due attention to this subject, the errors that have crept into the church, and into the world, are neither few nor small. The church of our text is no material building. It is no temple made with hands, of wood or brick or stone or marble. It is a company of men and women. It is no particular visible church on earth. It is not the Eastern Church or the Western Church. It is not the Church of England or the Church of Scotland; much less is it the Church of Rome. The church of our text is one that makes far less show in the eyes of man but is of far more importance in the eyes of God.

The church of our text is made up of all true believers in the Lord Jesus Christ. It comprehends all who have repented of sin and fled to Christ by faith and been made new creatures in Him. It comprises all God's elect, all who have received God's grace, all who have been washed in Christ's blood, all who have been clothed in Christ's righteousness, all who have been born again and sanctified by Christ's Spirit. All such—of every nation and people and tongue—compose the church of our text. This is the body of Christ. This is the flock of Christ. This is the bride. This is the Lamb's wife. This is the church on the rock.

Men and brethren, see that you hold sound doctrine on the subject of the church. A mistake here may lead to dangerous and soul-ruining errors. The church that is made up of true believers is the church for which we, who are ministers, are specially ordained to preach. The church which comprises all who repent and believe the gospel is the church to which we desire you to belong.

❖ From the sermon "The True Church"

Relationships with Unbelievers

He that walketh with wise men shall be wise:
but a companion of fools shall be destroyed.
—PROVERBS 13:20

We cannot help meeting many unconverted people as long as we live. We cannot avoid having fellowship with them, and doing business with them, unless we "go out of the world" (1 Cor. 5:10). To treat them with the utmost courtesy, kindness, and charity, whenever we do meet them, is a positive duty. But acquaintance is one thing, and intimate friendship is quite another. To seek their society without cause, to choose their company, to cultivate intimacy with them, is very dangerous to the soul.

Human nature is so constituted that we cannot be much with other people without effect on our own character. The old proverb will never fail to prove true: "Tell me with whom a man chooses to live, and I will tell you what he is." The Scripture says expressly, "He that walketh with wise men shall be wise: but a companion of fools shall be destroyed" (Prov. 13:20). If then a Christian who desires to live consistently chooses for his friends those who either do not care for their souls, or the Bible, or God, or Christ, or holiness, or regard them as of secondary importance, it seems to me impossible for him to prosper in his religion. He will soon find that their ways are not his ways, nor their thoughts his thoughts, nor their tastes his tastes; and that, unless they change, he must give up intimacy with them.

In short, there must be separation. Of course, such separation will be painful. But if we have to choose between the loss of a friend and the injury of our souls, there ought to be no doubt in our minds. If friends will not walk in the narrow way with us, we must not walk in the broad way to please them. But let us distinctly understand, that to attempt to keep up close intimacy between a converted and an unconverted person, if both are consistent with their natures, is to attempt an impossibility.

❖ From the sermon "The World"

The Ten Virgins

Then shall the kingdom of heaven be likened unto ten virgins, which took their lamps, and went forth to meet the bridegroom. And five of them were wise, and five were foolish. They that were foolish took their lamps, and took no oil with them: But the wise took oil in their vessels with their lamps. —MATTHEW 25:1–4

I can gather no other meaning from the beginning of the parable. I see wise and foolish virgins mingled in one company, virgins with oil and virgins with no oil all side by side. And I see this state of things going on until the very moment the bridegroom appears. I see all this, and I cannot avoid the conclusion that the visible church will always be a mixed body until Jesus comes again. Its members will never be all unbelievers; Christ will always have His witnesses. Its members will never be all believers; there will always be imperfection, hypocrisy, and false profession.

The wise are those who have that wisdom which the Holy Spirit alone can give. They know their sins, they know Christ, they know how to walk and please God, and they act upon their knowledge. They look on life as a season of preparation for eternity, not as an end but as a way, not as a harbor but a voyage, not as a home but a journey, not as full age but a school. Happy are those who know this! The foolish are those who are without spiritual knowledge.

They neither know God, nor Christ, nor their own hearts, nor sin, nor the world, nor heaven, nor hell, as they ought. There is no folly like soul folly. To expect wages after no work, or prosperity after no pains, or learning after no diligent reading, all this is folly. But to expect heaven without faith in Christ, or the kingdom of God without being born again, or the crown without the cross, all this is greater folly and yet more common. Until the Bridegroom comes there will always be some in the visible church who have grace, and some who have no grace. Some will stop short in the form of Christianity; others will never rest unless they have also the substance. Which are you?

❖ From the sermon "The Ten Virgins"

The World's Praises

*These things I have spoken unto you, that in me ye might have
peace. In the world ye shall have tribulation: but be of good cheer;
I have overcome the world.*　　　　　　　　　　—JOHN 16:33

Who does not know that spiritual religion never brings a man the world's
praise? It entails the world's condemnation, the world's persecution, the
world's ridicule, the world's sneers. The world will let a person go to
hell quietly and never try to stop him or her. The world will never let a
person go to heaven quietly and will do all they can to turn him or her
back. Who has not heard of nicknames in plenty bestowed on all who
faithfully follow Christ? Pietist, Methodist, saint, fanatic, enthusiast,
righteous zealot, and many more? Who does not know the petty family
persecution which often goes on in private society in our own day? Let
a young person go to every ball and theater and racecourse and utterly
neglect his soul, and no one interferes. No one says, "Spare yourself." No
one says, "Be moderate; remember your soul."

　　But let him begin to read his Bible and be diligent in prayers, let him
decline worldly amusement and be particular in his employment of time,
let him seek an evangelical ministry and live as if he had an immortal
soul—let him do this and the probability is all his relations and friends
will be up in arms. "You are going too far!" "You need not be so very
holy!" "You are taking up extreme lines!" This is the least that he will
hear. Alas, that it should be so, but so it is. These are ancient things. As it
was in the days of Cain and Abel, as it was in the days of Isaac and Ishmael, even so it is now. Those who are born after the flesh will persecute
those who are born after the Spirit. The cross of Christ will always bring
reproach with it. If a man will become a decided evangelical Christian, he
must make up his mind to lose the world's favors. He must be content to
be thought by many a total fool. Is there any dear child of God here who
is mocked and despised for the gospel's sake and feels as if he stood alone?
Take comfort; be patient: wait a little, your turn shall come!

❖ From the sermon "The Ten Virgins"

Do Not Neglect God's Word

Therefore whosoever heareth these sayings of mine, and doeth them, I will liken him unto a wise man, which built his house upon a rock.
—MATTHEW 7:24

Is the Bible the word of God? Then mind that you do not neglect it. Read it! Read it! Begin to read it this very day. What greater insult to God can a man be guilty of than to refuse to read the letter God sends him from heaven? Oh, be sure, if you will not read your Bible, you are in fearful danger of losing your soul! You are in danger, because God will reckon with you for your neglect of the Bible in the day of judgment. You will have to give an account of your use of time, strength, and money; and you will also have to give account of your use of the Word. You will not stand at that bar on the same level, in point of responsibility, with the dweller in central Africa who never heard of the Bible. Oh, no! To whom much is given, of them much will be required. Of all men's buried talents, none will weigh them down so heavily as a neglected Bible. As you deal with the Bible, so God will deal with your soul. Will you not repent and turn over a new leaf in life and read your Bible?

You are in danger because there is no degree of error in religion into which you may not fall. You are at the mercy of the first clever Jesuit, Mormonite, Socinian, Turk, or Jew who may happen to meet you. A land of unwalled villages is not more defenseless against an enemy than a man who neglects his Bible. You may go on tumbling from one step of delusion to another, until at length you are landed in the pit of hell. I say once more: Will you not repent and read your Bible?

❖ From the sermon "Inspiration"

The World's Character

And we know that we are of God, and the whole world lieth in wickedness.
—1 JOHN 5:19

Now, the testimony of Scripture upon this head is so clear and explicit that he who runs may read, "The whole world," says John, "lieth in wickedness" (1 John 5:19). Our first father, Adam, was indeed created in the image of God, pure and sinless, but in one day he fell from his high estate by eating the forbidden fruit. He broke God's express command and became at once a sinful creature. Now all we his children have inherited from him a wicked and a corrupt nature, a nature which clings to us from the moment of our birth, and which we show daily in our lives and conversation. In a word, we learn that from the hour of the fall our character has been established, that we are a sinful, a very sinful world.

Beloved, does this appear a hard saying? Do you think such a statement too strong?

Away with the flattering thought! We see it proved in Scripture, for every book of the Old Testament history tells the melancholy story of man's disobedience and man's unbelief in things pertaining to God. We read there of fearful judgments, such as the flood and the destruction of Sodom, yet men disregarded them. We read of gracious mercies, such as the calling and protection of Israel, but men soon forgot them. We read of inspired teachers and revelations from heaven, such as the law of Moses, and men did not obey them. We read of special warnings, such as the voice of the prophets, and yet men did not believe them. Yes, dear friends, whether you will receive it or not, we are indeed a sinful world. It may be a humbling truth, but Scripture says it, and experience confirms it; and therefore we tell you that the world spoken of in our text is a world that lies in wickedness, a corrupt world, a world that our great Maker and Preserver might have left to deserved destruction. And in so doing He would have acted with perfect justice because He has given us laws and they have been broken, promises and they have been despised, warnings and they have not been believed. Yes, beloved, we are a sinful world!

❖ From the sermon "Saving Faith"

Bright Shining Lights

Let your light so shine before men, that they may see your good works,
and glorify your Father which is in heaven. —MATTHEW 5:16

Believing reader, I trust I may say of you, you love the Lord Jesus Christ in sincerity.

Know then that I want you to be a bright and shining light to those around you. I want you to be such a plain epistle of Christ, that all may read something of God on the face of your conversation. I want you so to live that all may see that you are one of the people of Jesus, and thus to glorify your Father which is in heaven. Alas! I say it with shame, we many of us bring little glory to the Lord who bought us; we are far from walking worthy of our vocation. How weak is our faith! How fleeting our sorrow for sin! How faint our self-denial! How soon spent our patience! How thin and threadbare our humility! How formal our prayers! How cold our love!

We are called God's witnesses, but truly our witness is often little better than silence, it is but an uncertain sound. We are called the light of the world, but we are, many of us, poor, glimmering sparks, that can only just be seen. We are called the salt of the earth, but we scarcely do anything to make our savor felt and known. We are called pilgrims and strangers, but those who observe us might sometimes think this world was our only home. Brother or sister, what are you doing in the world? Where is the proof of your growth in grace? Are you awake, or are you asleep? Are there no tempers you might keep under more strictly? Is there no sort of besetting sin you are shamefully sparing? Is there no time you might employ more usefully? Is there no kind of selfishness you are secretly indulging? Is there no good you have the means of doing, yet leave undone? Are there no daily habits you might alter for the better? Are there no spots upon your spiritual garments which you never seek to have washed out?

Are there no friends and relations you are letting alone in their sins? Oh, that you may deal more honestly with yourself than you have done hitherto! The Lord is at hand!

✤ From the sermon "I Have Something to Say to You"

Ministers, Do Not Corrupt the Word

For we are not as many, which corrupt the word of God: but as of sincerity, but as of God, in the sight of God speak we in Christ.
—2 CORINTHIANS 2:17

It is no light matter to speak to any assembly of immortal souls about the things of God. But the most serious of all responsibilities is to speak to a gathering of ministers, such as that which I now see before me. The awful feeling will come across my mind that one single word said wrong, sinking into some heart and bearing fruit at some future time, in some pulpit, may lead to harm of which we cannot know the extent. But there are occasions when true humility is to be seen not so much in loud professions of our weakness as in forgetting ourselves altogether. I desire to forget self at this time in turning my attention to this portion of Scripture. If I say little about my own sense of insufficiency, do me the justice to believe, that it is not because I am not well aware of it.

The Greek expression, which we have translated "peddle," means either a tradesman who does his business dishonestly or a winemaker who adulterates the wine that he offers for sale. Tyndale renders it, "We are not of those who chop and change the Word of God." Another version of the Bible says, "We are not as many, who adulterate the Word of God." In our margin we read, "We are not as many, who deal deceitfully with the Word of God." In the construction of the sentence, the Holy Spirit has inspired Paul to use both the negative and the positive way of stating the truth. This mode of construction adds clearness and unmistakability to the meaning of the words, and intensity and strength to the assertion, which they contain. It will be found, therefore, that there are contained in the text both negative and positive lessons for the instruction of the ministers of Christ. Some things we ought to avoid. Others we ought to follow. It is a plain warning against corrupting or dealing deceitfully with the Word of God. We are to add nothing to it. We are to take nothing away.

❖ From the sermon "Not Corrupting the Word"

The Friend Who Never Changes

Jesus Christ the same yesterday, and to day, and for ever.
—HEBREWS 13:8

The Lord Jesus is a friend who never changes. There is no fickleness about Him. Those whom He loves, He loves unto the end! Husbands have been known to forsake their wives. Parents have been known to cast off their children. Human vows and promises of faithfulness have often been forgotten. Thousands have been neglected in their poverty and old age who were honored by all when they were rich and young. But Christ never changed His feelings toward one of His friends. He is "the same yesterday, and to day, and for ever" (Heb. 13:8).

The Lord Jesus never goes away from His friends. There is never a parting and good-bye between Him and His people. From the time that He makes His abode in the sinner's heart, He abides in it forever. The world is full of departures. Death and the lapse of time break up the most united family. Sons go forth to make their way in life; daughters are married and leave their father's house forever. Scattering, scattering, scattering, is the yearly history of the happiest home. How many we have tearfully watched as they drove away from our doors, whose pleasant faces we have never seen again! How many we have sorrowfully followed to the grave, and then come back to a cold, silent, lonely, and blank fireside! But thanks be to God, there is One who never leaves His friends! The Lord Jesus is He who has said, "I will never leave thee, nor forsake thee" (Heb. 13:5).

Look around the world, and see how failure is written on all men's schemes. Count up the partings, and separations, and disappointments, and bereavements which have happened under your own knowledge. Think what a privilege it is that there is One at least who never fails and in whom no one was ever disappointed! Never, never was there so unfailing a friend as Jesus Christ!

❖ From the sermon "The Best Friend"

The Great Separation

Whose fan is in his hand, and he will throughly purge his floor, and gather his wheat into the garner; but he will burn up the chaff with unquenchable fire.
—MATTHEW 3:12

Wheat or chaff? You see my question, for whom do you think it is meant? Is it for corn merchants and farmers only, and for none else? If you think so, then you are much mistaken. It is meant for every man, woman, and child in the world. And among others, it is meant for you. The question is drawn from the verse of Scripture which is now before your eyes. The words of that verse were spoken by John the Baptist. They are a prophecy about our Lord Jesus Christ, and a prophecy which has not yet been fulfilled. They are a prophecy which we shall all see fulfilled one day, and God alone knows how soon.

Reader, dear reader, see now what cause there is for self-inquiry! Are you among the wheat or among the chaff? Neutrality is impossible. Either you are in one class or in the other. Which is it of the two? Have you been born again? Are you a new creature? Have you put off the old man and put on the new? Have you ever felt your sins, and repented of them? Are you looking only to Christ for pardon and eternal life? Do you love Christ? Do you serve Christ? Do you loathe heart sins and fight against them? Do you long for perfect holiness and follow hard after it? Have you come out from the world? Do you delight in the Bible? Do you wrestle in prayer? Do you love Christ's people? Do you try to do good to the world? Are you vile in your own eyes and willing to take the lowest place? Are you a Christian in business and on weekdays and by your own fireside? Oh, think, think, think on these things, and then perhaps you will be better able to tell the state of your soul!

Reader, remember my question. Begin to meditate on it this very day. Are you wheat or chaff?

❖ From the sermon "The Great Separation"

The Foundation of Christianity

*All scripture is given by inspiration of God, and is profitable for
doctrine, for reproof, for correction, for instruction in righteousness.*
—2 TIMOTHY 3:16

How was the Bible written? Whence is it from? From heaven or from
men? Had the writers of the Bible any special or peculiar help in doing
their work? Is there anything in the Bible that makes it unlike all other
books and therefore demands our respectful attention? These are questions of vast importance. I believe the Bible to have been written by
inspiration of God, and I want others to be of the same belief. The subject is always important.

Inspiration, in short, is the very keel and foundation of Christianity.
If Christians have no divine book to turn to as the warrant of their doctrine and practice, they have no solid ground for present peace or hope
and no right to claim the attention of mankind. They are building on
quicksand, and their faith is vain. We ought to be able to say boldly, "We
are what we are, and we do what we do because we have here a book
which we believe to be the word of God."

The subject is one of peculiar importance in the present day. Infidelity and skepticism abound everywhere. In one form or another they are
to be found in every rank and class of society. Thousands of Englishmen
are not ashamed to say that they regard the Bible as an old, obsolete
Jewish book which has no special claim on our faith and obedience, and
that it contains many inaccuracies and defects. Myriads who will not go
so far as this are wavering and shaken in their belief and show plainly by
their lives that they are not quite sure that the Bible is true. In a day like
this the true Christian should be able to set his foot down firmly and
render a reason of his confidence in God's Word. He should be able by
sound arguments to meet and silence the gainsayer if he cannot convince
him. He should be able to show good cause why he thinks the Bible is
from heaven and not of men!

❖ From the sermon "Inspiration"

Beware the Leaven

Then Jesus said unto them, Take heed and beware of the leaven of the Pharisees and of the Sadducees. —MATTHEW 16:6

The words which our Lord used were always the wisest and the best that could be used. He might have said, "Be careful and be on your guard against the doctrine, or of the teaching, or of the opinions of the Pharisees and of the Sadducees." But He does not say so. He uses a word of a peculiar nature. He says, "Be careful and be on your guard against the leaven of the Pharisees and of the Sadducees." Now we all know what is the true meaning of the word "leaven." The leaven is added to the lump of dough in making a loaf of bread. This leaven bears but a small proportion to the lump into which it is mixed. Just so, our Lord would have us know, the first beginning of false doctrine is but small, compared to the body of Christianity. It works quietly and silently. Just so, our Lord would have us know, false doctrine works secretly in the heart in which it is once planted. It insensibly changes the character of the whole mass with which it is mingled. Just so, our Lord would have us know, the doctrines of the Pharisees and Sadducees turn everything upside down, when once admitted into a church or into a man's heart.

Let us be on our guard against supposing that we at any rate are not in danger. Our views are sound; our feet stand firm. Others may fall away, but we are safe! Hundreds have thought the same and have come to a dreadful end. In their self-confidence they tampered with little temptations and little forms of false doctrine. In their self-conceit they went near the brink of danger; and now they seem lost forever! Very striking is the vision in *Pilgrim's Progress*, which describes the hill Error as "very steep on the farthest side" and "when Christian and Hopeful looked down they saw at the bottom, several men dashed all to pieces by a fall they had from the top." Never, never let us forget the caution to beware of leaven. And if we think we stand, let us be careful that we don't fall!

❖ From the sermon "Pharisees and Sadducees"

Foundational Truths

For I delivered unto you first of all that which I also received, how that Christ died for our sins according to the scriptures; and that he was buried, and that he rose again the third day according to the scriptures. —1 CORINTHIANS 15:3–4

The text that heads this devotional is taken from a passage of Scripture with which most Englishmen are only too well acquainted. The starting point of the whole argument of this chapter will be found in the two verses which form the text. The apostle opens by reminding the Corinthians that "among the first things" which he delivered to them when he commenced his teaching were two great facts about Christ: one was His death, the other was His resurrection. Why did Paul lay so much stress upon Christ's death rather than His life? Because, he tells the Corinthians, He "died for our sins." For that death of Christ was not the involuntary death of a martyr or a mere example of self-sacrifice. It was the voluntary death of a divine substitute for the guilty sinners! It was a death of such mighty influence on the position of sinful man before God that it provided complete redemption from the consequences of the fall.

The other great fact about Christ that Paul placed in the front part of his teaching was His resurrection from the dead. He boldly told the Corinthians that the same Jesus who died and was buried came forth alive from the grave on the third day after His death and was seen, touched, handled, and talked to in the body by many competent witnesses. By this amazing miracle He proved, as He had frequently said He would, that He was the promised and long-expected Savior foretold in prophecy; that the satisfaction for sin He had made by His death was accepted by God the Father; that the work of our redemption was completed; and that death, as well as sin, was a conquered enemy.

In short, the apostle taught that the greatest of miracles had been wrought and that with such a founder of the new faith that He came to proclaim, first dying for our sins and then rising again for our justification, nothing was impossible and nothing lacking for the salvation of the human soul!

✢ From the sermon "Foundational Truths"

The Heart Is the Seat of True Religion

For as he thinketh in his heart, so is he: Eat and drink, saith he to thee; but his heart is not with thee.   —PROVERBS 23:7

The heart is the real test of a man's character. It is not what he says or what he does, by which the man may be always known. He may say and do things that are right from false and unworthy motives, while his heart is altogether wrong. The heart is the man! "For as he thinketh in his heart, so is he" (Prov. 23:7). The heart is the right test of a man's religion. It is not enough that a man holds a correct creed of doctrine and maintains a proper outward form of godliness. What is his heart? That is the grand question. The heart is the place where saving religion must begin. It is naturally irreligious and must be renewed by the Holy Spirit. "A new heart also will I give you." It is naturally hard and must be made tender and broken. "And I will take away the stony heart out of your flesh, and I will give you an heart of flesh" (Ezek. 36:26). "The sacrifices of God are a broken spirit: a broken and a contrite heart, O God, thou wilt not despise" (Ps. 51:17). It is naturally closed and shut against God, and must be opened. The Lord "opened" the heart of Lydia (Acts 16:14).

The heart is the seat of true saving faith. "For with the heart man believeth unto righteousness; and with the mouth confession is made unto salvation" (Rom. 10:10). A man may believe that Jesus is the Christ, as the devils do, and yet remain in his sins. He may believe that he is a sinner, and that Christ is the only Savior, and feel occasional, lazy wishes that he was a better man. But no one ever lays hold on Christ, and receives pardon and peace, until he believes with the heart. It is heart faith that justifies!

❖ From the sermon "The Heart"

Repentance

I tell you, Nay: but, except ye repent,
ye shall all likewise perish.
—LUKE 13:3

The text that heads this page, at first sight, looks stern and severe: "Except ye repent, ye shall all likewise perish." I can fancy someone saying, "Is this the gospel? Are these the glad tidings? Are these the good news of which ministers speak?" "This is an hard saying; who can hear it?" (John 6:60). But from whose lips did these words come? They came from the lips of One who loves us with a love that passes knowledge, even Jesus Christ, the Son of God.

They were spoken by One who so loved us that He left heaven for our sakes; came down to earth for our sakes; lived a poor, humble life for three and thirty years on earth for our sakes; went to the cross for us; went to the grave for us; and died for our sins. The words that come from lips like these must surely be words of love.

And, after all, what greater proof of love can be given than to warn a friend of coming danger? The father who sees his son tottering toward the brink of a precipice and as he sees him cries out sharply, "Stop, stop!"—does not that father love his son? The tender mother who sees her infant on the point of eating some poisonous berry, and cries out sharply, "Stop, stop! put it down!"—does not that mother love that child? It is indifference that lets people alone and allows them to go on each in their own way. It is love, tender love, that warns and raises the cry of alarm. The cry of "Fire, fire!" at midnight may sometimes startle a man out of his sleep rudely, harshly, unpleasantly. But who would complain if that cry was the means of saving his life? The words, "Except ye repent, ye shall all likewise perish," may seem at first sight stern and severe. But they are words of love and may be the means of delivering precious souls from hell!

❖ From the sermon "Repentance"

Assured Hope!

I laid me down and slept; I awaked; for the LORD sustained me.
—PSALM 3:5

He who has assured hope can sing in prison, like Paul and Silas at Philippi. Assurance can give songs in the night. He can sleep with the full prospect of execution on the next day, like Peter in Herod's dungeon. Assurance says, "I will both lay me down in peace, and sleep: for thou, LORD, only makest me dwell in safety" (Ps. 4:8). He can rejoice to suffer shame for Christ's sake, as the apostles did. Assurance says, "Rejoice and be exceeding glad, there is a far more exceeding and eternal weight of glory." He can meet a violent and painful death without fear, as Stephen did in olden time and Cranmer, Ridley, Latimer, and Taylor in our own land. Assurance says, "Fear not those who kill the body and after that have no more they can do. Lord Jesus, into Your hand I commend my spirit."

Ah, brethren, the comfort assurance can give in the hour of death is a great point, depend upon it, and never will you think it so great as when your turn comes to die. In that solemn hour there are few believers who do not find out the value and privilege of assurance, whatever they may have thought about it in their lives; general hopes and trusts are all very well to live upon, but when you come to die you will want to be able to say, "I know and I feel." Believe me, Jordan is a cold stream to cross alone. The last enemy, even death, is a strong foe. When our souls are in departing, there is no cordial like the strong wine of assurance. There is a beautiful expression in the Prayer Book's "Visitation of the Sick." "The Almighty Lord, who is a most strong tower to all those who put their trust in Him, be now and evermore your defense, and make you know and feel that there is no other name under heaven through whom you may receive health and salvation, but only the name of our Lord Jesus Christ." The compilers showed great wisdom there; they saw that when the eyes grow dim and the heart grows faint, there must be knowing and feeling what Christ has done for us if there is to be perfect peace.

❖ From the sermon "Ready to Be Offered"

We Live in a World of Troubles

Then Simon Peter answered him, Lord, to whom shall we go? thou hast the words of eternal life. —JOHN 6:68

When we think of the age when Peter lived, we cannot help feeling that he had abundant cause to ask that question. In his days, at the end of four thousand years, "the world by wisdom knew not God" (1 Cor. 1:21). Egypt, Assyria, Greece, and Rome, the very nations that attained the highest excellence in secular things, in the things of religion were sunk in gross darkness. The fellow countrymen of matchless historians, tragedians, poets, orators, and architects, worshiped idols, and bowed down to the work of their own hands. The ablest philosophers of Greece and Rome groped after truth like blind men and wearied themselves in vain to find the door. The whole earth was defiled with spiritual ignorance and immorality, and the wisest men could only confess their need of light, like the Greek philosopher Plato, and groan and sigh for a deliverer. Peter might well cry, "Lord, if we leave You, to whom shall we go?"

But the question Peter asked is one that true Christians may always ask boldly when they are tempted to go away from Christ. At this very day, when men tell us that Christianity is an effete and worn-out thing, we may safely challenge them to show us anything better. To whom, indeed, shall we go for help, strength, and comfort, if we turn our backs on Christ? We live in a world of troubles, whether we like it or not. You can no more stave off and prevent them than King Canute could prevent the tide rising and rudely swelling round the royal chair. Our bodies are liable to a thousand ailments, and our hearts to a thousand sorrows. No creature on earth is so vulnerable and so capable of intense physical as well as mental suffering as man. Sickness and death and funerals and partings and separations and losses and failures and disappointments and private family trials, which no mortal eye sees, will break in upon us from time to time; and we desperately need help to meet them! Alas, where will thirsty, wailing hearts find such help if we leave Christ?

✤ From the sermon "To Whom?"

Observe Festus

And as he thus spake for himself, Festus said with a loud voice, Paul, thou art beside thyself; much learning doth make thee mad.
—ACTS 26:24

Let us look at Festus the Roman governor. This is the man who abruptly broke in upon Paul's address, exclaiming, "Paul, thou art beside thyself; much learning doth make thee mad." Festus, no doubt, was a heathen, ignorant of any religion except the idolatrous temple worship which in the time of the apostles overspread the civilized world. From the language he addressed to Agrippa in a preceding chapter, he seems to have been profoundly ignorant both of Judaism and Christianity. He spoke of "questions against him of their own superstition, and of one Jesus, which was dead, whom Paul affirmed to be alive" (Acts 25:19). Most probably, like many a proud Roman in the declining age of the Roman Empire, he regarded all religions with secret contempt, as all equally false, or equally true, and all alike unworthy of the notice of a great man.

Now, are there many among us like Festus? Yes! I fear there are tens of thousands. They are to be found in every rank and class of society. They walk in our streets. They travel with us in railway carriages. They meet us in our daily interaction with the world. They fill the various relations of life respectably. They are often good men of business, and eminent in the professions they have chosen. They discharge the various duties of their positions with credit and leave a good name behind them, when their place is empty. But, like Festus, they have no religion! These are they who seem to live as if they had no souls. From January to December, they appear neither to think nor feel nor see nor know anything about a life to come. It forms no part of their schemes and plans and calculations. They live as if they had nothing to attend to but the body, nothing to do but to eat and drink and sleep and dress and get money and spend money, and no world to provide for except the world that we see with our eyes!

❖ From the sermon "Portraits"

Observe King Agrippa

Then Agrippa said unto Paul, Almost thou persuadest me to be a Christian.

—ACTS 26:28

Let us look at King Agrippa. This is the man who was so much struck by Paul's address that he said, "Almost thou persuadest me to be a Christian!" Agrippa, whose picture now demands our attention, knew and believed the prophets. He must have understood many things in Paul's address, which were mere "words and names" and raving fancies to his companion in the place of hearing. He had a secret inward conviction that the man before him had truth on his side. He saw and felt and was moved and affected and conscience-stricken and had inward wishes and longing desires. But he could get no further. He saw, but he had not courage to act. He felt, but he had not the will to move. He was not far from the kingdom of God, but he halted outside. He neither condemned nor ridiculed Christianity but, like a man who is paralyzed, he could only look at it and examine it, and had not strength of mind to lay hold on it and receive it into his heart.

Now, are there many professing Christians like Agrippa? I fear there is only one answer to that question. They are an exceeding great army, a multitude which it is difficult to number. They are to be found in our churches and are pretty regular attendants on all means of grace. They have no doubt of the truth of the Bible. They have not the slightest objection to the doctrines of the gospel. They know the difference between sound and unsound teaching. They admire the lives of holy people. They read good books and give money to good objects. But, unhappily, they never seem to get beyond a certain point in their religion. They never come out boldly on Christ's side, never take up the cross, never confess Christ before men, never give up petty inconsistencies. They cannot cut off the right hand or pluck out the right eye, and so they cannot become disciples. Alas for these excuses! Weighed in the balance, they are worthless and vain. Alas for those who rest in them! Except they awake, and cast off their chains, they will make shipwreck forever!

❖ From the sermon "Portraits"

Ryle's Thoughts on Church

And I say also unto thee, That thou art Peter, and upon this rock I will build my church; and the gates of hell shall not prevail against it.
—MATTHEW 16:18

Which is the best visible church upon earth? That is the best visible church which adds most members to the one true church; which most promotes repentance toward God, faith toward the Lord Jesus Christ; and good works among its members. These are the true tests and tokens of a really good and flourishing church. Give me that church which has evidence of this kind to show. Which is the worst visible church on earth? That is the worst visible church, which has the fewest members of the one true church to show in its ranks. Such a church may possess excellent forms, learned ministers, venerable customs, and ancient institutions. But if it cannot point to faith, repentance, and holiness of heart and life among its members, it is a poor church indeed. By their fruits the churches upon earth must be judged, as well as individual Christians.

We shall do well to remember these things. On the one side, a visible professing church is a true thing, and a thing according to the mind of God. It is not, as some would tell us in these days, a more human device, a thing which God does not speak of in the Word. It is amazing to my mind that anyone can read the New Testament and then say that visible churches are not authorized in the Bible. On the other side, something more is needed than merely belonging to this visible church or to that visible church to take a man to heaven. Are we born again? Have we repented of our sins? Have we laid hold of Christ by faith? Are we holy in life and conversation? These are the grand points that a man must seek to ascertain. Without these things, the highest, the strictest, and the most regular member of a visible church will be a lost churchman in the last great day!

✣ From the sermon "The Church"

Believing in Christ

And they said, Believe on the Lord Jesus Christ, and thou shalt be saved, and thy house.

— ACTS 16:31

True belief in Christ is so immensely important, that the Holy Spirit has graciously used many figures in the Bible in describing it. The Lord God knows the slowness of man to comprehend spiritual things. He has therefore multiplied forms of expression in order to set true faith fully before us. The man who cannot understand believing in one form of words will perhaps understand it in another. Three points:

1. Believing is the soul's coming to Christ. The Lord Jesus says, "He that cometh to me shall never hunger" (John 6:35). "Come unto me, all ye that labour and are heavy laden, and I will give you rest" (Matt. 11:28). Christ is that almighty friend, advocate, and physician to whom all sinners needing help are commanded to apply. The believer comes to Him by faith and is relieved.

2. Believing is the soul's receiving Christ. Paul says, "As ye have therefore received Christ Jesus the Lord, so walk ye in him" (Col. 2:6). Christ offers to come into man's heart with pardon, mercy, and grace and to dwell there as its peacemaker and king. He says, "Behold, I stand at the door, and knock" (Rev. 3:20). The believer hears His voice, opens the door, and admits Christ as his teacher, priest, and king.

3. Believing is the soul's laying hold on Christ. Paul says, "Who have fled for refuge to lay hold upon the hope set before us" (Heb. 6:18). Christ is that true city of refuge to which the man fleeing from the avenger of blood runs and in which he is safe. Christ is that altar which provided a sanctuary to him who laid hold on its horns. Christ is that almighty hand of mercy that God holds out from heaven to lost and drowning sinners. The believer lays hold on this hand by faith and is delivered from the pit of hell!

✤ From the sermon "Do You Believe?"

True Spiritual Worship

God is a Spirit: and they that worship him must worship him in spirit and in truth.
—JOHN 4:24

This is a point of vast importance and one that every professing Christian should look fairly in the face. Too many are apt to cut the knot of all difficulties about the subject before us by referring to their own feelings. They will tell us that they are not theologians, that they do not pretend to understand the difference between one school of divinity and another. But they do know that the worship in which they take part makes them feel so much better, that they cannot doubt it is all right. Some thoughts:

1. True spiritual worship will affect a man's heart and conscience. It will make him feel more keenly the sinfulness of sin, and his own particular personal corruption. It will deepen his humility. It will render him more jealously careful over his inward life. False public worship, like liquor drinking and opium eating, will every year produce weaker impressions. True spiritual worship, like wholesome food, will strengthen him who uses it, and make him grow inwardly every year.

2. True spiritual worship will draw a man into close communion with Jesus Christ Himself. It will lift him far above churches and ordinances and ministers. It will make him hunger and thirst after a sight of the King. The more he sincerely hears and reads and prays and praises the more he will feel that nothing but Christ Himself will feed the life of his soul and that heart communion with Him is food indeed and drink indeed.

3. True spiritual worship will continually increase the holiness of a man's life. It will make him every year more watchful over tongue and temper and time and behavior in every relation of life. The true worshiper's conscience becomes annually more tender. The false worshiper's becomes annually more seared and more hard.

This is the worship that comes down from heaven and has the stamp and seal and superscription of God.

❖ From the sermon "Worship"

Hope That Is Felt Inwardly in the Heart

And hope maketh not ashamed; because the love of God is shed abroad in our hearts by the Holy Ghost which is given unto us.
—ROMANS 5:5

The man who has a good hope is conscious of it. He feels within him something that another man does not, he is conscious of possessing a well-grounded expectation of good things to come. This consciousness may vary exceedingly in different people. In one it may be strong and well-defined; in another it may be feeble and indistinct. It may vary exceedingly in different stages of the same person's experience. At one time he may be full of "joy and peace in believing" (Rom. 15:13); at another he may be depressed and cast down. But in all people who have a good hope, in a greater or less degree, this consciousness does exist.

I am aware that this truth is one which has been fearfully abused and perverted. It has been brought into great disrepute by the fanaticism, enthusiasm, and extravagance of some professing Christians. Mere animal excitement has been mistaken for the work of the Holy Spirit. The overwrought feelings of weak and nervous people have been prematurely and rashly supposed to be the result of grace. Men and women have been hastily pronounced converted who have soon gone back to the world and proved utterly unconverted and dead in sins. And then has come in the devil. Contempt has been poured on religious feelings of every description. Their very existence has been denied and scouted, and the result is that the very name of feelings in religion is in many quarters dreaded and disliked.

But the abuse and perversion of a truth must never be allowed to rob us of the use of it. When all has been said that can be said against fanaticism and enthusiasm, it is still undeniable that religious feelings are plainly spoken of and described in Scripture. The Word of God tells us that the true Christian has peace and rest and joy and confidence. Let us beware of a hope that is not felt and a Christianity that is destitute of any inward experience.

❖ From the sermon "Our Hope"

Love Like Christ

A new commandment I give unto you, That ye love one another;
as I have loved you, that ye also love one another. By this shall all
men know that ye are my disciples, if ye have love one to another.
—JOHN 13:34–35

Would we like to know where the true pattern of love like this can be found? We have only to look at the life of our Lord Jesus Christ as described in the Gospels and we shall see it perfectly exemplified. Love shone forth in all His doings. His daily life was an incessant going about doing good. Love shone forth in all His bearing. He was continually hated, persecuted, slandered, misrepresented. But He patiently endured it all. The law of kindness was ever on His lips. Among weak and ignorant disciples, among sick and sorrowful petitioners for help and relief, among publicans and sinners, among Pharisees and Sadducees, He was always one and the same, kind and patient to all.

And yet, be it remembered, our blessed Master never flattered sinners or connived at sin. He never shrank from exposing wickedness in its true colors, or from rebuking those who would cleave to it. He never hesitated to denounce false doctrine, by whoever it might be held, or to exhibit false practice in its true colors, and the certain end to which it tends. He called things by their right names. He spoke as freely of hell and the fire that is never quenched as of heaven and the kingdom of glory. He has left on record an everlasting proof that perfect love does not require us to approve everybody's life or opinions, and that it is quite possible to condemn false doctrine and wicked practice, and yet to be full of love at the same time!

❖ From the sermon "Christian Love"

What Is the Grace of God?

We then, as workers together with him, beseech you also that ye receive not the grace of God in vain. —2 CORINTHIANS 6:1

What is this grace of God, which the apostle here speaks of? It is an expression which has different meanings in Scripture. Sometimes it signifies the free favor of God, as when we read, "By grace are you saved... not of works" (Eph. 2:8–9). Sometimes it means the operation of the Holy Spirit in a man's conversion, as when Paul tells the Galatians, it was "God, who...called me by his grace" (Gal. 1:15). But in our text, I conceive it has a wider, broader signification. I take it to mean that gracious offer of free salvation for the worst of sinners which is commonly called the gospel, and so called because it is in every way good tidings—that free gift of righteousness, peace, and pardon that is provided for all who will believe in the Lord Jesus.

Now, what is it that makes this offer so important and so precious? It is simply this: that we are all by nature sinful and corrupt. We are born into the world with a disposition inclined to evil and not to good. We show it in our angry tempers, by jealousy and by selfishness. We show it in our youth by deceit, by idleness, by unwillingness to learn, by disobedience to parents, by lack of gratitude, by self-conceit. And when we come to adulthood, we show it in a hundred fashions: by giving way to our lusts and passions whenever we dare, by loving pleasure more than God, by Sabbath breaking and swearing and drinking and fornication, by uncharitable conduct to our neighbors, by pride and vanity, by neglecting God's Bible, by staying away from His church, by despising His sacraments, by dishonoring His ministers, by worldly mindedness, by living on from year to year without a spark of love to Him who gave us life and breath and all things that we enjoy. This is the manner in which we naturally like to pass our time, and thus it is that one way or another we prove our hearts to be "deceitful above all things, and desperately wicked" (Jer. 17:9).

✣ From the sermon "The Grace of God in Vain"

The Blood of Christ

But if we walk in the light, as he is in the light, we have fellowship one with another, and the blood of Jesus Christ his Son cleanseth us from all sin.
—1 JOHN 1:7

The blood of Christ is that lifeblood which the Lord Jesus shed when He died for sinners upon the cross. It is the blood that flowed so freely from His head pierced with thorns and His hands and feet pierced with nails and His side pierced with a spear in the day when He was crucified and slain. The quantity of that blood may very likely have been small; the appearance of that blood was doubtless like that of our own. But never since the day when Adam was first formed out of the dust of the ground has any blood been shed of such deep importance to the whole family of mankind.

It was blood that had been long covenanted and promised. In the day when sin came into the world, God mercifully engaged that the Seed of the woman should bruise the serpent's head (Gen. 3:15). One born of woman would appear one day and deliver the children of Adam from Satan's power. That Seed of the woman was our Lord Jesus Christ. In the day that He suffered on the cross, He triumphed over Satan and accomplished redemption for mankind. When Jesus shed His lifeblood on the cross, the head of the serpent was bruised and the ancient promise was fulfilled.

This wondrous blood of Christ, applied to your conscience, can cleanse you from all sin. From sins of youth and sins of age, from sins of ignorance and sins of knowledge, from sins of open profligacy and sins of secret vice, from sins against law and sins against gospel, from sins of head and heart and tongue and thought and imagination, from sins against each and all of the Ten Commandments—from all these the blood of Christ can set us free. To this end was it appointed; for this cause was it shed; for this purpose it is still a fountain open to all mankind. That thing which you cannot do for yourself can be done in a moment by this precious fountain. You can have all your sins cleansed away.

❖ From the sermon "Where Are Your Sins?"

The Nature of True Saving Faith

Whosoever believeth that Jesus is the Christ is born of God: and every one that loveth him that begat loveth him also that is begotten of him.

—1 JOHN 5:1

Faith. It is constantly spoken of as the distinguishing characteristic of New Testament Christians. They are called believers. In the single gospel of John, believing is mentioned eighty or ninety times. There is hardly any subject about which so many mistakes are made. There is none about which mistakes are so injurious to the soul. The darkness of many a sincere inquirer may be traced up to confused views about faith. Let us try to get a distinct idea of its real nature.

True saving faith is not the possession of everybody. The opinion that all who are called Christians are, as a matter of course, believers is a most mischievous delusion. A man may be baptized, like Simon Magus, and yet have "neither part nor lot" (Acts 8:21) in Christ. The visible church contains unbelievers as well as believers. "All men have not faith" (2 Thess. 3:2). True saving faith is not a mere matter of feeling. A man may have many good feelings and desires in his mind toward Christ, and yet they may all prove as temporary and short-lived as the morning cloud and the early dew. Many are like the stony-ground hearers and receive the word "with joy" (Matt. 13:20). Many will say under momentary excitement, "I will follow thee whithersoever thou goest," and yet return to the world (Matt. 8:19).

True saving faith is an act of the whole inner man. It is an act of the head, heart, and will, all united and combined. It is an act of the soul in which, seeing his own guilt, danger, and hopelessness and seeing at the same time Christ offering to save him, a man ventures on Christ, flees to Christ, receives Christ as his only hope, and becomes a willing dependent on Him for salvation. It is an act which becomes at once the parent of a habit. He who has it may not always be equally sensible of his own faith; but in the main he lives by faith and walks by faith.

❖ From the sermon "Justification"

Are You Asleep?

Wherefore he saith, Awake thou that sleepest, and arise from the
dead, and Christ shall give thee light. —EPHESIANS 5:14

I put before you now a simple question. "Are you asleep about your soul?" There are many who have the name of Christians but not the character that should go with the name. God is not king of their hearts. They mind earthly things. Such people are often quick and clever about the affairs of this life. These people do not see the sinfulness of sin and their own lost condition by nature. They appear to make light of breaking God's commandments and to care little whether they live according to His law or not. Yet God says that sin is the transgression of the law, that His commandment is exceeding broad; that every imagination of the natural heart is evil; that sin is the thing He cannot bear, He hates it; that the wages of sin is death; and the soul that sins shall die. Surely they are asleep.

If conscience pricks you and tells you that you are yet asleep, what can I say to arouse you? Your soul is in awful peril. Without a mighty change it will be lost. When shall that change once be? You are dying and not ready to depart. You are going to be judged and are not prepared to meet God. Your sins are not forgiven, your person is not justified, your heart is not renewed. Heaven itself would be no happiness to you if you got there, for the Lord of heaven is not your friend.

I speak strongly because I feel deeply. Time is too short, life is too uncertain, to allow of relying on religious ceremonies. At the risk of offending, I use great plainness of speech. I cannot bear the thought of hearing you condemned in the great day of judgment; of seeing your face in the crowd on God's left hand among those who are helpless, hopeless, and beyond the reach of mercy. I cannot bear such thoughts; they grieve me to the heart. Before the day of grace is past and the day of vengeance begins, I call upon you to open your eyes and repent. Oh, consider your ways and be wise. Awake, awake! Why will you die!

✤ From the sermon "Are You Asleep?"

Evidences of Sonship

For as many as are led by the Spirit of God, they are the sons of God.
—ROMANS 8:14

How shall a man make sure work of his own sonship? How shall he find out whether he is one that has come to Christ by faith and been born again? What are the marks and signs, and tokens, by which the sons of God may be known? This is a question which all who love eternal life ought to ask. This is a question to which the verses of Scripture I am asking you to consider, like many others, supply an answer.

The sons of God, for one thing, are all led by His Spirit. What says the Scripture that heads this paper? "For as many as are led by the Spirit of God, they are the sons of God" (Rom. 8:14). They are all under the leading and teaching of a power that is almighty, though unseen, even the power of the Holy Spirit. They no longer turn every man to his own way and walk every man in the light of his own eyes and follow every man his own natural heart's desire. The Spirit leads them. The Spirit guides them. There is a movement in their hearts, lives, and affections that they feel though they may not be able to explain and a movement that is always more or less in the same direction.

This is the road by which the Spirit leads God's children. Those whom God adopts as His children, He teaches and trains. He shows them their own hearts. He makes them weary of their own ways. He makes them long for inward peace. Settle this down in your heart and do not let it go. The sons of God are a people "led by the Spirit of God" and always led more or less in the same way. Their experience will tally wonderfully when they compare notes in heaven. This is one mark of sonship.

❖ From the sermon "Heirs of God"

Contentment in the Will of God

I know both how to be abased, and I know how to abound: every where and in all things I am instructed both to be full and to be hungry, both to abound and to suffer need. —PHILIPPIANS 4:12

To be content is to be rich and well-off. He is the rich man who has no wants and requires no more. I ask not what his income may be. A man may be rich in a cottage and poor in a palace. To be content is to be independent. He is the independent man who hangs on no created things for comfort and has God for his portion. Such a man is the only one who is always happy. Nothing can come amiss or go wrong with such a man. Afflictions will not shake him, and sickness will not disturb his peace. He can gather grapes from thorns, and figs from thistles, for he can get good out of evil. Like Paul and Silas, he will sing in prison with his feet fast in the stocks. Like Peter, he will sleep quietly in prospect of death the very night before his execution. Like Job, he will bless the Lord even when stripped of all his comforts.

You may say, perhaps, that you have such crosses and trials and troubles, that it is impossible to be content. I answer that you would do well to remember your ignorance. Do you know best what is good for you, or does God? Are you wiser than He? The things you want might ruin your soul. The things you have lost might have poisoned you. Let these things sink down into your heart. If you would be truly happy, who does not want this, seek it where alone it can be found. Seek it in having a will in perfect harmony with the will of God!

✤ From the sermon "Be Content"

Christ's Sheep

My sheep hear my voice, and I know them, and they follow me: and I give unto them eternal life; and they shall never perish, neither shall any man pluck them out of my hand. My Father, which gave them me, is greater than all; and no man is able to pluck them out of my Father's hand. —JOHN 10:27–29

Let me, then, remind you what the text says of their character. "My sheep hear my voice, and I know them, and they follow me" (John 10:27). Four points:

1. God's children, His real believing people, are compared to sheep because they are gentle, quiet, harmless and inoffensive; because they are useful and do good to all around them; because they love to be together, and dislike separation; and, last, because they are very helpless and wandering and liable to stray.

2. Jesus calls them "My sheep," as if they were His peculiar property. "Mine," He would have us know, by election; "Mine" by purchase; and "Mine" by adoption.

3. Christ's sheep hear His voice; they listen humbly to His teaching; they take His word for their rule and guide.

4. Christ's sheep follow Him; they walk in the narrow path He has marked out; they do not refuse because it is sometimes steep and narrow, but wherever the line of duty lies they go forward without doubting.

It only remains for us now to consider the other part of my text, which respects the blessings and privileges that Jesus the Good Shepherd bestows upon His people. The Lord grant that none of you may take to yourselves promises which do not belong to you, that none may take liberty from God's exceeding mercy to continue sleeping in sin. Glorious and comfortable things are written in this passage, but remember they are given to Christ's flock only. I fence it out against all that are unbelieving and impenitent and profane. I warn you plainly: except you will hear the voice of Christ and follow Him, you have no right or portion in this blessed fountain of consolations.

❖ From the sermon "The Privileges of the True Christian"

Being Made Spiritually Alive

And you, being dead in your sins and the uncircumcision of your flesh,
hath he quickened together with him, having forgiven you all trespasses.
—COLOSSIANS 2:13

Life is the mightiest of all possessions. From death to life is the mightiest of all changes.

And no change short of this will ever avail to fit man's soul for heaven. Yes! It is not a little mending and alteration, a little cleansing and purifying, a little painting and patching, a little whitewashing and varnishing, a little turning over a new leaf and putting on a new outside that is needed. It is the bringing in of something altogether new, the planting within us of a new nature, a new being, a new principle, a new mind. This alone, and nothing less than this, will ever meet the necessities of man's soul. We need not merely new skin, but a new heart.

I know well this is a hard saying. I know the children of this world dislike to hear that they must be born again. It pricks their consciences; it makes them feel they are further off from heaven than they are willing to allow. It seems like a narrow door which they have not yet stooped to enter, and they would gladly make the door wider, or climb in some other way. But I dare not give place by subjection in this matter. I will not foster a delusion, and tell people they only need repent a little, and stir up a gift they have within them, in order to become real Christians. I dare not use any other language than that of the Bible; and I say, echoing the words which are written for our learning, we all need to be born again, we are all naturally dead, and must be made alive (Eph. 2:1).

Oh, you that have passed from death to life, you have reason indeed to be thankful!

Remember what you once were by nature—dead. Think what you are now by grace—alive! Look at the dry bones thrown up from the graves. Such were you; and who has made you to differ? Go and fall low before the footstool of your God. Bless Him for His grace, His free, distinguishing grace!

❖ From the sermon "Alive or Dead"

What Is Zeal in Religion?

Who gave himself for us, that he might redeem us from all iniquity,
and purify unto himself a peculiar people, zealous of good works.
—TITUS 2:14

Zeal in religion is a burning desire to please God, to do His will, and to advance His glory in the world in every possible way. It is a desire which no human feels by nature, which the Spirit puts into the heart of every believer when he or she is converted, but which some believers feel so much more strongly than others, that they alone deserve to be called zealous Christians. This desire is so strong when it really reigns in believers that it impels them to make any sacrifice, to go through any trouble, to self-deny to any amount, to suffer, to work, to labor, to toil, to spend and be spent, and even to die, if only they can please God and honor Christ.

A zealous man is preeminently a man of one thing. It is not enough to say that he is earnest, hearty, uncompromising, thoroughgoing, wholehearted, fervent in spirit. He sees only one thing, he cares for one thing, he lives for one thing, he is swallowed up in one thing—and that one thing is to please God. Whether he lives or dies, whether he has health or sickness, whether he is rich or poor; whether he pleases man or gives offense; whether he is thought wise or foolish; whether he gets blame or praise; whether he gets honor or shame—for all this the zealous man cares nothing at all. He burns for one thing, and that one thing is to please God and to advance God's glory. If he is consumed in the very burning, he is not worried; he is content.

✣ From the sermon "Be Zealous"

Great Ministers May Make Great Mistakes

But when Peter was come to Antioch, I withstood him to the face, because he was to be blamed. —GALATIANS 2:11

What clearer proof can we have than that which is set before us in this place? Peter, without doubt, was one of the greatest in the company of the apostles. He was an old disciple. He was a disciple who had had peculiar advantages and privileges. He had been a constant companion of the Lord Jesus. He had heard the Lord preach, seen the Lord work miracles, enjoyed the benefit of the Lord's private teaching, been numbered among the Lord's intimate friends, and gone out and come in with Him all the time He ministered upon earth. He was the apostle to whom the keys of the kingdom of heaven were given and by whose hand those keys were first used. He was the first who opened the door of faith to the Jews, by preaching to them on the day of Pentecost. And yet here this very Peter, this same apostle, plainly falls into a great mistake!

It is all meant to teach us that even the apostles themselves, when not writing under the inspiration of the Holy Spirit, were at times liable to err. It is meant to teach us that the best men are weak and fallible so long as they are in the body. Unless the grace of God holds them up, any one of them may go astray at any time. It is very humbling but it is very true. All these things speak with a loud voice. They all lift up a beacon to the church of Christ. They all say, "Do not trust man; call no man master; call no man father on earth; let no man glory in man." "He who glories, let him glory in the Lord." They all cry, "No infallibility!" The lesson is one that we all need. We are all naturally inclined to lean upon man whom we can see rather than upon God whom we cannot see. We naturally love to lean upon the ministers of the visible church rather than upon the Lord Jesus Christ, the Great Shepherd and High Priest, who is invisible. We need to be continually warned and set on our guard.

❖ From the sermon "The Fallibility of Ministers"

Victorious Soldiers

I have fought a good fight,
I have finished my course,
I have kept the faith.
—2 TIMOTHY 4:7

The one point I want to impress on your soul just now is this: that if you want to be saved you must be not only a soldier but a victorious soldier. You must not only profess to fight on Christ's side against sin, the world, and the devil, but you must actually fight and overcome. Now this is one grand distinguishing mark of true Christians. Other people perhaps like to be numbered in the ranks of Christ's army. Other people may have lazy wishes and languid desires after the crown of glory, but it is the true Christian alone who does the work of a soldier, who fairly meets the enemies of his or her soul, really fights with them, and in that fight overcomes them.

Reader, one great lesson I wish you to learn this day is this, that if you would prove you are born again and going to heaven, you must be a victorious soldier of Christ. If you would make it clear that you have any title to Christ's precious promises, you must fight the good fight in Christ's cause, and in that fight you must conquer.

Victory is the only satisfactory evidence that you have a saving religion. You like good sermons, perhaps. You respect the Bible, and read it occasionally. You say your prayers night and morning. You have family prayers and give to religious societies. I thank God for this; it is all very good. But how goes the battle? How does the great conflict go on all this time? Are you overcoming the love of the world and the fear of man? Are you overcoming the passions, tempers, and lusts of your own heart? Are you resisting the devil, and making him flee from you? How is it in this matter? My dear brother or sister, you must either rule or serve sin and the devil and the world. There is no middle course. You must either conquer or be lost. Sin, the world, and the devil must be actually mortified, resisted, and overcome.

❖ From the sermon "The Great Battle"

Hell Is behind You

But he that shall endure unto the end, the same shall be saved.
—MATTHEW 24:13

Men and brethren, we who preach the gospel can hold out to all who come to Christ exceeding great and precious promises. We can offer boldly to you in our Master's name the peace of God which passes all understanding. Mercy, free grace, and full salvation are offered to everyone who will come to Christ and believe on Him. But we promise you no peace with the world or with the devil. We warn you, on the contrary, that there must be warfare, so long as you are in the body. We would not keep you back or deter you from Christ's service. But we would have you count the cost and fully understand what Christ's service entails. Hell is behind you. Heaven is before you. Home lies on the other side of a troubled sea.

Thousands, tens of thousands, have crossed these stormy waters, and in spite of all opposition have reached the haven where they would be. Hell has assailed them but has not prevailed. Go forward, beloved brethren, and fear not the adversary. Only abide in Christ and the victory is sure. Marvel not at the hatred of the gates of hell. "If ye were of the world, the world would love his own" (John 15:19). So long as the world is the world and the devil the devil, there must be warfare, and believers in Christ must be soldiers! The world hated Christ and the world will hate true Christians as long as the earth stands.

Be prepared for the hostility of the gates of hell. Put on the whole armor of God. The weapons of our warfare have been tried by millions of poor sinners like us and have never been found to fail. Be patient under the bitterness of the gates of hell. It is all working together for your good. It tends to sanctify. It keeps you awake. It makes you humble. It drives you nearer to the Lord Jesus Christ. It weans you from the world. It helps to make you pray more. Above all, it makes you long for heaven and say with heart as well as lips, "Come, Lord Jesus."

✤ From the sermon "The True Church"

Resting in Christ

There remaineth therefore a rest to the people of God. For he that is entered into his rest, he also hath ceased from his own works, as God did from his. Let us labour therefore to enter into that rest, lest any man fall after the same example of unbelief. —HEBREWS 4:9–11

The rest that Christ gives is an inward thing. It is rest of heart, rest of conscience, rest of mind, rest of affection, rest of will. It is rest from a comfortable sense of sins being all forgiven and guilt all put away; it is rest from a solid hope of good things to come, laid up beyond the reach of disease, and death, and the grave. It is rest from the well-grounded feeling that the great business of life is settled, its great end provided for; that in time all is well done; and in eternity heaven will be our home.

Rest such as this the Lord Jesus gives to those who come to Him by showing them His own finished work on the cross, by clothing them in His own perfect righteousness, and washing them in His own precious blood. When a man begins to see that the Son of God actually died for his sins, his soul begins to taste something of inward quiet and peace. Rest such as this the Lord Jesus gives to those who come to Him by revealing Himself as their ever-living High Priest in heaven, and God reconciled to them through Him. When a man begins to see that the Son of God actually lives to intercede for him, he will begin to feel something of inward quiet and peace.

Rest such as this the Lord Jesus gives to those who come to Him by implanting His Spirit in their hearts and witnessing with their spirits that they are God's children. When a man begins to feel an inward drawing toward God as a father and a sense of being an adopted and forgiven child, his soul begins to feel something of quiet and peace!

❖ From the tract *Come*

Motivations for Being Holy

But as he which hath called you is holy, so be ye holy in all manner of conversation; because it is written, Be ye holy; for I am holy.
—1 PETER 1:15–16

Would I find strong reasons for being a holy man? Where shall I turn for them? Shall I listen to the Ten Commandments merely? Shall I study the examples given me in the Bible of what grace can do? Shall I meditate on the rewards of heaven and the punishments of hell? Is there no stronger motive still? Yes! I will look at the cross of Christ! There I see the love of Christ constraining me to live not unto myself, but unto Him (2 Cor. 5:15) There I see that I am not my own now, I am "bought with a price" (1 Cor. 6:20). I am bound by the most solemn obligations to glorify Jesus with body and spirit, which are His. There I see that Jesus gave Himself for me, not only to redeem me from all iniquity but also to purify me and to make me one of a "peculiar people, zealous of good works" (Titus 2:14). He bore my sins in His own body on the tree, "that [I] being dead to sin should live unto righteousness" (1 Peter 2:24). There is nothing so sanctifying as a clear view of the cross of Christ! It crucifies the world unto us, and us unto the world. How can we love sin when we remember that because of our sins Jesus died? Surely none ought to be so holy as the disciples of a crucified Lord.

Are you a believer who longs to be more holy? Do you find your heart too ready to love earthly things? To you also I say, "Behold the cross of Christ." Look at the cross, think of the cross, meditate on the cross, and then go and set affections on the world if you can. I believe that holiness is nowhere learned so well as on Calvary. I believe you cannot look much at the cross without feeling your will sanctified and your tastes made more spiritual!

✢ From the sermon "The Cross of Christ"

The Good Shepherd

I am the good shepherd, and know my sheep, and am known of mine. As the Father knoweth me, even so know I the Father: and I lay down my life for the sheep. —JOHN 10:14–15

Sheep of all animals are most helpless, most ready to stray, most likely to lose themselves and wander out of their pasture; and so it is with Christ's people. They are far too ready to turn aside and go in ways that are not good. In vain they are warned and advised to be watchful and take heed to their path. They often get into a drowsy, sleepy frame and imagine there is no danger, and so they wander down some bypath and are only wakened by some merciful chastisement or heavy fall. They imagine that they are strong enough to get on without this constant vigilance, and so they take their eye off the Chief Shepherd and wander on from this field to that after their own desires, until they find themselves at last in darkness and doubt. And Christ's sheep, too, like other sheep, do seldom return to the fold without some damage and loss, for it is far easier to get out of the right way when you are in, than to get into it when you are out.

There are some people who imagine Christians are perfect and faultless creatures, but this is indeed an opinion far wide of the truth. No doubt they aim at perfection, but the very best come far short of it. They would tell you that in many things they offend daily, that they are continually erring and straying and backsliding, that the most fitting prayer they could offer up would be this: "Lord, we are no better than wandering sheep. God be merciful to us unworthy sinners!" Finally, our Lord does not simply call His people sheep, but He says also "My sheep." It is as though Jesus would have us understand He looks upon them as His property. They are, as it were, stamped and sealed and marked as the possession of the Lord Jesus Christ Himself!

❖ From the sermon "The Character of the True Christian"

False Professions

Not every one that saith unto me, Lord, Lord, shall enter into the kingdom of heaven; but he that doeth the will of my Father which is in heaven.
— MATTHEW 7:21

Millions of people profess and call themselves Christians whom the apostle would not have called Christians at all. Millions are annually baptized—added to the rolls and registers of churches—who have little or no real religion. Many of them live and die without ever attending a place of worship and live very ungodly lives. Many more only go to a church or chapel occasionally or once on Sunday at the most. Many others pass through life without ever becoming communicants and live and die in the habitual neglect of that holy sacrament which the Lord commanded to be received. Most of these people are reckoned Christians while they live and are buried with Christian burial when they die. But what would Paul have said of them? I fear there can be no doubt about the answer. He would have said they did not deserve to be reckoned members of any church at all! He would not have addressed them as saints and faithful brethren in Christ Jesus. He would not have called upon them to hold fast their profession (Heb. 4:14). He would have told them they had no profession to hold fast, and that they were "who were dead in trespasses and sins" (Eph. 2:1). All this is sorrowful and painful, but it is only too true. Let those deny it who dare.

I do not deny that there are many hypocrites in religion. There always were, and there always will be as long as the world stands. It is one of Satan's favorite devices in order to bring discredit on Christianity, to persuade some unhappy people to profess what they do not really believe. He tries to damage the cause of our Lord Jesus Christ in the world by sending out wolves in sheep's clothing and by raising up men and women who talk the language of Canaan and wear the coat of God's children while they are inwardly rotten at heart.

❖ From the sermon "Our Profession"

The Path of Happiness

Therefore being justified by faith, we have peace with God through our Lord Jesus Christ.
—ROMANS 5:1

The true Christian is the only happy man because his conscience is at peace. That mysterious witness for God that is so mercifully placed within us is fully satisfied and at rest. It sees in the blood of Christ a complete cleansing away of all its guilt. It sees in the priesthood and mediation of Christ a complete answer to all its fears. It sees that through the sacrifice and death of Christ, God can now be just and yet be the justifier of the ungodly. It no longer bites and stings and makes its possessor afraid of himself. The Lord Jesus Christ has amply met all its requirements. Conscience is no longer the enemy of the true Christian but his friend and adviser. Therefore, he is happy.

The true Christian is the only happy man because he can sit down quietly and think about his soul. He can look behind him and before him, he can look within him and around him and feel, "All is well!" He can think calmly on his past life, however many and great his sins, and take comfort in the thought that they are all forgiven. The righteousness of Christ covers all, as Noah's flood overtopped the highest hills. The true Christian is the only happy person because he or she has sources of happiness entirely independent of this world—something which cannot be affected by sickness and by deaths, by private losses and by public calamities—the "peace of God, which passeth all understanding" (Phil. 4:7). He or she has a hope laid up in heaven, a treasure which moth and rust cannot corrupt, a house which can never be taken down!

✣ From the sermon "Happiness"

The Holy Spirit's Work in Salvation

But ye are not in the flesh, but in the Spirit, if so be that the Spirit of God dwell in you. Now if any man have not the Spirit of Christ, he is none of his.
—ROMANS 8:9

The necessity of the work of the Holy Spirit arises from the total corruption of human nature. We are all by nature "dead in…sins" (Eph. 2:1). However shrewd and clever and wise in the things of this world, we are all dead toward God. The eyes of our understanding are blinded. We see nothing aright. Our wills, affections, and inclinations are alienated from Him who made us. "Because the carnal mind is enmity against God: for it is not subject to the law of God, neither indeed can be" (Rom. 8:7). We have naturally neither faith nor fear nor love nor holiness. In short, left to ourselves, we would never be saved.

Without the Holy Spirit no man ever turns to God, repents, believes, and obeys.

Intellectual training and secular education alone make no true Christians. Acquaintance with fine arts and science leads no one to heaven. Pictures and statues never brought one soul to God. The "tender strokes of art" never prepared any man or woman for the judgment day. They bind up no broken heart; they heal no wounded conscience. The most zealous efforts of ministers alone cannot make people Christians. The ablest scriptural reasoning has no effect on the mind; the most fervent pulpit eloquence will not move the heart; the naked truth alone will not lead the will.

What is it then that man needs? We need to be born again, and this new birth we must receive of the Holy Spirit. The Spirit of life must quicken us. The Spirit must renew us. The Spirit must take away from us the heart of stone. The Spirit must put in us the heart of flesh. A new act of creation must take place. A new being must be called into existence. Without all this we cannot be saved!

❖ From the sermon "Having the Spirit"

Making Your Election Sure

Wherefore the rather, brethren, give diligence to make your calling and election sure: for if ye do these things, ye shall never fall.
—2 PETER 1:10

Surer in the sight of God than your election has been from all eternity, you cannot make it. With Him there is no uncertainty. Nothing that God does for His people is left to chance, or liable to change. But surer and more evident to yourself and to the church, your election can be made; and this is the point that I wish to press on your attention. Strive to obtain such well-grounded assurance of hope that, as John says, we may "know that we know [Christ]" (1 John 2:3). Strive so to live and walk in this world that all may take knowledge of you as one of God's children and feel no doubt that you are going to heaven.

Strive, then, with all diligence, to make your calling and election sure. "Let us lay aside every weight, and the sin which doth so easily beset us and let us run with patience the race that is set before us" (Heb. 12:1). Be ready to cut off the right hand and pluck out the right eye, if need be. Settle it firmly in your mind that it is the highest privilege on this side the grave to know that you are one of the children of God.

Those who contend for place and office in this world are sure to be disappointed. When they have done all and succeeded to the uttermost, their honors are thoroughly unsatisfying and their rewards are short-lived. Seats in Parliament and places in cabinets must all be vacated one day. At best they can only be held for a few years. But he who is one of God's elect has a treasure that can never be taken from him and a place from which he can never be removed. Blessed is that man who sets his heart on this election. There is no election like the election of God!

✤ From the sermon "Election"

All Kinds of Strange Teachings

Be not carried about with divers and strange doctrines. For it is a
good thing that the heart be established with grace; not with meats,
which have not profited them that have been occupied therein.
—HEBREWS 13:9

The text that heads this paper is an apostolic caution against false doctrine. It forms part of a warning that Paul addressed to Hebrew Christians. It is a caution just as much needed now as it was eighteen hundred years ago. Never, I think, was it so important for Christian ministers to cry aloud continually, "Do not be carried away by all kinds of strange teachings!" That old enemy of mankind, the devil, has no more subtle instrument for ruining souls, than that of spreading false doctrine. He was a murderer and a liar from the beginning! Be careful! Watch out for attacks from the devil, your great enemy. He prowls around like a roaring lion looking for some victim to devour!

Outside the church, he is ever persuading men to maintain sinful lives and destructive superstitions. Human sacrifice to idols; gross, revolting, cruel worship of disgusting and abominable false deities; persecution, slavery, cannibalism, child murder, devastating religious wars—all these are a part of Satan's handiwork and the fruit of his suggestions! Like a pirate, his object is to sink, burn, and destroy! Inside the church he is ever laboring to sow heresies, to propagate errors, to foster departures from the faith. If he cannot prevent the waters flowing from the fountain of life, he tries hard to poison them. If he cannot destroy the remedy of the gospel, he strives to adulterate and corrupt it. No wonder that he is called Apollyon, the destroyer.

The divine Comforter of the church, the Holy Spirit, has always employed one great weapon to oppose Satan's plans. That weapon is the Word of God: the Word expounded and unfolded, the Word explained and opened up, the Word made clear to the head and applied to the heart. The Word is the chosen weapon by which the devil must be confronted and confounded. The Word is the sword that His ministers must use in the present day if they would successfully resist the devil. The Bible, faithfully and freely expounded, is the safeguard of Christ's true church.

❖ From the sermon "All Kinds of Strange Teaching"

Need for Missions Giving

But to do good and to communicate forget not: for with such sacrifices God is well pleased. —HEBREWS 13:16

There is needed among us more liberality in giving money. I am not at all ashamed to speak of this matter. After the most solemn chapter in the epistles to the Corinthians, I mean the chapter about the resurrection, Paul goes on to say, "Now concerning the collection" (1 Cor. 16:1). God generally works by means. He might convert the heathen in a day if He thought fit, but He does not do so. He is pleased to use means. So long as He does use our money and contributions, we should count it a privilege to be fellow workers with God. Means, doubtless, can do nothing without God, but they are not therefore to be despised. It is one thing to put our trust in means, but it is quite another thing to use them in humble dependence on God's blessing. Money is one great means of setting forward the work of missions.

Missionaries must live, and they cannot live without money. Their wives and children must be supported and educated; they cannot feed on air. And this is one grand reason why I say money is needed.

Now the hands of the Church Missionary Society are positively tied and her strength crippled for lack of more money. There are many stations where there are two or three missionaries laboring and there ought to be fifty. There are places where there is a great opening for sending missionaries and we cannot afford to do anything at all. There are vast fields of heathenism entirely untouched simply because we are not able to send workers.

The plain truth is that there is not enough giving to the cause of missions. I find no fault with the poor; they generally give according to their ability and even beyond. If all people gave in proportion to their income as the poor do, then our society would have millions at her command instead of thousands. But many members of our church who have money give nothing at all to missions. I lay these facts before you for your own consideration. I declare, I think our small contributions to the missionary cause are a positive disgrace to the nation!

❖ From the sermon "Work to Be Done"

Christianity That Turns the World Upside Down

These that have turned the world upside down are come hither also.
—ACTS 17:6

The Christianity which I call fruit-bearing, which shows its divine origin by its blessed effects on mankind—the Christianity which you may safely defy infidels to explain away—that Christianity is a very different thing. Too often and in too many parts of Christendom, there has been so little of it that Christ's religion has seemed extinct and has fallen into utter contempt! This is the Christianity that, in the days of the apostles, "turned the world upside down" (Acts 17:6). It was this that emptied the idol temples of their worshipers, routed the Greek and Roman philosophers, and obliged even heathen writers to confess that the followers of the "new superstition," as they called it, were people who loved one another and lived very pure and holy lives!

This is the Christianity that, after dreary centuries of ignorance, priestcraft, and superstition, produced the Protestant Reformation and changed the history of Europe. The leading doctrines that were preached by Luther and Zwingli on the Continent and by Latimer and his companions in England were precisely those which I have briefly described. That they bore rich fruit, in an immense increase of general morality and holiness, is a simple fact which no historian has ever denied.

This is the Christianity that, in the middle of last century, delivered our own church from the state of deadness and darkness into which she had fallen. The main truths on which Whitefield and Wesley and Romaine and Venn and their companions continually insisted were the truth about sin, Christ, the Holy Spirit, and holiness. And the results were the same as they were in the primitive days and at the era of the Reformation. Men persecuted and hated all who taught these truths. But no one could say that they did not make men live and die well.

✣ From the sermon "Tried by Its Fruits"

To Whom Shall We Go?

Then Simon Peter answered him, Lord, to whom shall we go? thou hast the words of eternal life. —JOHN 6:68

What made this fiery, impulsive disciple cry out, "To whom shall we go?" The verses which precede our text supply an answer. "From that time many…went back, and walked no more with him. Then Jesus said unto the twelve, Will ye also go away?" (John 6:66–67). There you have recorded a melancholy and most instructive fact. Even from Christ Himself, who "spoke as never any man spoke," did works of matchless power, lived as no one ever lived, holy, harmless, undefiled, and separate from sinners—even from Christ many, after following Him for a time, went away. Yes! Many, not a few. Many in the noontide blaze of miracles and sermons such as earth had never seen or heard before, many turned away from Christ, left Him, deserted Him, gave up His blessed service, and went back—some to Judaism, some to the world, and some, we may fear, to their sins. "For if they do these things in a green tree, what shall be done in the dry?" (Luke 23:31). If men could forsake Christ then, we have no right to be surprised if His erring, weak ministers are forsaken also in these last days.

But why did these men go back? Some of them probably went back because they had not counted the cost, and when tribulation or persecution arose because of the word they were offended. Some of them went back because they had totally misunderstood the nature of our Lord's kingdom and had dreamed only of temporal advantages and rewards. Most of them, however, it is very clear, went back because they could not receive the deep doctrine that had just been proclaimed; I mean the doctrine that eating Christ's flesh and drinking Christ's blood are absolutely necessary to salvation. It is the old story. As it was in the beginning, so it will be to the end. There is nothing that the dark, natural heart of man dislikes so much as the so-called blood theology. Cain turned away in his proud ignorance from the idea of vicarious sacrifice, and the Jews who fell away from our Lord went back when they heard that they must eat the flesh and drink the blood of the Son of Man (John 6:54–58).

❖ From the sermon "To Whom?"

Where Are the Good Samaritans Today?

But a certain Samaritan, as he journeyed, came where he was: and when he saw him, he had compassion on him, and went to him, and bound up his wounds, pouring in oil and wine, and set him on his own beast, and brought him to an inn, and took care of him. And on the morrow when he departed, he took out two pence, and gave them to the host, and said unto him, Take care of him; and whatsoever thou spendest more, when I come again, I will repay thee. Which now of these three, thinkest thou, was neighbour unto him that fell among the thieves? And he said, He that shewed mercy on him. Then said Jesus unto him, Go, and do thou likewise. —LUKE 10:33–37

Where are the Samaritans, we may well ask, in this land of Bibles and New Testaments?

Where are the men who love their neighbors and will help to provide for dying bodies and souls? Where are the people always ready and willing to give unasked and without asking how much others have given? Millions are annually spent on hunting and yachting and racing and gambling and balls and theaters and dressing and pictures and furniture and recreation.

Little—comparatively, ridiculously little—is given or done for the cause of Christ.

The very first principles of Christian giving seem lost and forgotten in many quarters.

Where, after all to come to the root of the matter, where is that brotherly love which used to be the distinguishing mark of the primitive Christians? Where is that love by which our Lord declared all men should know His disciples and which John said was the distinction between the children of God and the children of the devil? Where is it indeed? It is no pleasure to me to write these things, and I can truly say that I have handled them with pain. It is high time to awaken out of sleep and amend our ways, lest we be given over to judicial blindness and be forsaken by God. A church in which Pharisees and formalists are many and good Samaritans are few is in a most unhealthy condition. God grant we may "strengthen the things which remain" (Rev. 3:2) before it is too late, lest our candlestick be taken away!

✣ From the sermon "The Parable of the Good Samaritan"

A Growing Christian

With all lowliness and meekness, with longsuffering, forbearing one another in love.
—EPHESIANS 4:2

If we want to grow in grace and have more hope, we must seek more holiness in life and conversation. This is a humbling lesson to dwell upon, but one that cannot be dwelled upon too much. There is an inseparable connection between a close walk with God and comfort in our religion. Let this never be forgotten. Truly, many of the vessels in the Lord's house are very dull and dingy. When I look around, I see many things missing among us that Jesus loves. I miss the meekness and gentleness of our Master. Many of us are harsh, rough-tempered, and censorious, and we flatter ourselves that we are faithful. I miss real boldness in confessing Christ before men. We often think much more of the time to be silent than the time to speak.

I miss real humility. Not many of us like to take the lowest place and esteem everyone better than ourselves and consider our own strength perfect weakness. I miss real charity. Few of us have that unselfish spirit which seeks not its own. There are few who are not more taken up with their own feelings and their own happiness than that of others. I miss real thankfulness of spirit. We complain and murmur and fret and brood over the things we have not, and forget the things we have. We are seldom content; there is generally a Mordecai at our gate. I miss decided separation from the world. The line of distinction is often rubbed out. Many of us, like the chameleon, are always taking the color of our company; we become so like the ungodly that it strains a man's eyes to see the difference. Reader, these things ought not so to be. If we want more hope, let us be zealous of good works. This is the way to be useful Christians. The world knows little of Christ beyond what it sees of Him in His people. Oh, what plain clearly written epistles they ought to be! A holy believer is a walking sermon. He preaches far more than a minister does, for he preaches all the week round! Oh, the value and the power of a growing Christian! The Lord make you and me such!

✤ From the sermon "Where Are You?"

As in the Days of Lot and Noah

But the same day that Lot went out of Sodom it rained fire and brimstone from heaven, and destroyed them all. Even thus shall it be in the day when the Son of man is revealed. —LUKE 17:29–30

But as the days of Noah were, so shall also the coming of the Son of man be. —MATTHEW 24:37

Our Lord Jesus Christ Himself uses two most striking comparisons when dwelling on this point. He says in one that as it was in the days of Lot, so shall it be in the days when the Son of Man is revealed. Do you remember how it was? In the days when Lot went out of Sodom the men of Sodom were eating and drinking, planting and building, marrying and giving in marriage. The sun rose as usual. They thought of nothing but worldly things; they saw no sign of danger. But all at once the fire of God fell upon them and destroyed them!

He says in another place, "As it was in the days of Noah, so shall it be also in the days of the Son of man" (Luke 17:26). Do you remember how it was in the days of Noah? Stay a little and let me remind you. When the flood came on the earth, there was no appearance beforehand of anything so awful being near. The sun rose and set as usual; the day and night followed each other in regular succession. The grass and trees and crops were growing; the business of the world was going on; and though Noah preached continually and warned men of coming danger, no one believed him. But, at last, one day the rain began and did not cease; the waters ran and did not stop. The flood came and the flood swelled; the flood went on and covered one thing after another, and all were drowned who were not in the ark. Everything in which was the breath of life perished. Now, as the flood took the world by surprise, just so will the coming of the Son of Man. It will come on men like a thunderclap. In the midst of the world's business, when everything is going on just as usual, in such an hour as this the Lord Jesus Christ will return!

❖ From the sermon "The Ten Virgins"

Prayer and Fruitfulness

*But grow in grace, and in the knowledge of our Lord and Saviour
Jesus Christ. To him be glory both now and for ever. Amen.*
—2 PETER 3:18

Without controversy there is a vast difference among true Christians.
There is an immense interval between the foremost and the hindermost
in the army of God. They are all fighting the same good fight, but how
much more valiantly some fight than others. They are all doing the Lord's
work, but how much more some do than others. They are all light in the
Lord, but how much more brightly some shine than others. They are all
running the same race, but how much faster some get on than others.
They all love the same Lord and Savior, but how much more some love
Him than others. I ask any true Christian whether this is not the case.

Are these things not so?

There are some of the Lord's people who seem never able to get
on from the time of their conversion. They are born again, but they
remain babies all their lives. You hear from them the same old experience. You remark in them the same lack of spiritual appetite, the same
lack of interest in anything beyond their own little circle, which you
remarked ten years ago. There are others of the Lord's people who seem
to be always advancing. They are ever adding grace to grace, and faith to
faith, and strength to strength. Every time you meet them, their hearts
seems larger, and their spiritual stature taller and stronger. Now how can
you account for the difference which I have just described? What is the
reason that some believers are so much brighter and holier than others? I believe the difference, in nineteen cases out of twenty, arises from
different habits about private prayer. I believe that those who are not
eminently holy pray little, and those who are eminently holy pray much!

❖ From the sermon "Call to Prayer"

The Danger of Formal Religion

Having a form of godliness, but denying the power thereof.
—2 TIMOTHY 3:5

What do I mean when I speak of formal religion? This is a point that must be made clear. Thousands, I suspect, know nothing about it. Without a distinct understanding of this point, my whole paper will be useless. My first step shall be to paint, describe, and define. When a person is a Christian in name only, and not in reality; in outward things only, and not in the inward feelings; in profession only, and not in practice—when his or her Christianity, in short, is a mere matter of form or fashion or custom, without any influence on his heart or life, in such a case as this the person has what I call a "formal religion." He or she possesses indeed the form, or husk, or skin of religion but does not possess its substance or its power.

Look, for example, at those thousands of people whose whole religion seems to consist in keeping religious ceremonies and ordinances. They attend regularly on public worship. They go regularly to the Lord's Table. But they never get any further. They know nothing of experimental Christianity. They are not familiar with the Scriptures and take no delight in reading them. They do not separate themselves from the ways of the world. They draw no distinction between godliness and ungodliness in their friendships, or matrimonial alliances.

They care little or nothing about the distinctive doctrines of the gospel. They appear utterly indifferent as to what they hear preached. You may be in their company for weeks and for anything you may hear or see, you might suppose they were infidels! What can be said about these people? They are Christians undoubtedly, by profession; and yet there is neither heart nor life in their Christianity. There is but one thing to be said about them: They are formal Christians, their religion is a mere form! They are formal Christians, their religion is an empty form! Are you such a Christian? Examine yourself!

❖ From the sermon "Formal Religion"

Thoughts on Immortality

While we look not at the things which are seen, but at the things which are not seen: for the things which are seen are temporal; but the things which are not seen are eternal. —2 CORINTHIANS 4:18

A subject stands out on the face of this text that is one of the most solemn and heart searching in the Bible. That subject is eternity, or immortality. The subject is one of which the wisest man can only take in a little. We have no eyes to see it fully, no line to fathom it, no mind to grasp it; and yet we must not refuse to consider it. There are star depths in the heavens above us which the most powerful telescope cannot pierce. Yet it is well to look into them and learn something, if we cannot learn everything. There are heights and depths about the subject of eternity that mortal man can never comprehend. But God has spoken of it, and we have no right to turn away from it altogether.

The subject is one that we must never approach without the Bible in our hands. The moment we depart from God's written word in considering eternity and the future state of man, we are likely to fall into error. In examining points like these, we have nothing to do with preconceived notions as to what is God's character and what we think God ought to be, or ought to do with man after death.

Let us all settle it firmly in our minds that the only way to pass through things seen with comfort and look forward to things unseen without fear is to have Christ for our Savior and friend, to lay hold on Christ by faith, to become one with Christ and Christ in us, "and the life which I now live in the flesh I live by the faith of the Son of God, who loved me, and gave himself for me" (Gal. 2:20). How vast is the difference between the state of him who has faith in Christ and the state of him who has none!

✣ From the sermon "Thoughts on Immortality"

I Will Build My Church

And I say also unto thee, That thou art Peter, and upon this rock I will build my church; and the gates of hell shall not prevail against it.
—MATTHEW 16:18

The Lord Jesus Christ declares, "I will build my church." The true church of Christ is tenderly cared for by all the three persons of the blessed Trinity. In the economy of redemption, beyond all doubt, God the Father chooses and God the Holy Spirit sanctifies every member of Christ's mystical body. God the Father, God the Son, and God the Holy Spirit—three persons in one God—cooperate for the salvation of every saved soul.

In building the true church, the Lord Jesus condescends to use many subordinate instruments. The ministry of the gospel, the circulation of the Scriptures, the friendly rebuke, the word spoken in season, the drawing influence of afflictions—all, all are means and methods by which His work is carried on. But Christ is the great superintending architect, ordering, guiding, directing all that is done. What the sun is to the whole solar system, that Christ is to all the members of the true church. Paul may plant, and Apollos water, but God gives the increase. Ministers may preach and writers may write, but the Lord Jesus Christ alone can build. And except He builds, the work stands still.

In short, God was pleased to have all His fullness dwell in Christ (see Col. 1:19). He is the author and finisher of faith. From Him every joint and member of the mystical body of Christians is supplied. Through Him they are strengthened for duty. By Him they are kept from falling. He shall preserve them to the end and present them faultless before the Father's throne with exceeding great joy. He is all things, and all in all to believers. Forever let us thank God, my beloved brethren, that the building of the one true church is laid on the shoulders of One who is mighty. Let us bless God that it does not rest upon man. Christ will never fail. That which He has undertaken He will certainly accomplish!

❖ From the sermon "The True Church"

The Bible's Effects on Nations

Blessed is the nation whose God is the LORD; and the people whom
he hath chosen for his own inheritance. —PSALM 33:12

The Bible has had a most extraordinary effect on the condition of those nations in which it has been known, taught, and read. I invite any honest-minded reader to look at a map of the world and see what a story that map tells. Which are the countries on the face of the globe at this moment where there is the greatest amount of idolatry or cruelty or tyranny or impurity or misgovernment or disregard of life and liberty and truth? Precisely those countries where the Bible is not known. Which are the countries where the greatest quantity of ignorance, superstition, and corruption is to be found at this very moment? The countries in which the Bible is a forbidden or neglected book, such countries as Spain and the South American states. Which are the countries where liberty and public and private morality have attained the highest pitch? The countries where the Bible is free to all, like England, Scotland, Germany, and the United States. Yes! When you know how a nation deals with the Bible, you may generally know what a nation is!

But this is not all. Let us look nearer home. Which are the cities on earth where the fewest soldiers and police are required to keep order? London, Manchester, Liverpool, New York, Philadelphia—cities where Bibles abound. Which are the countries in Europe where there are the fewest murders and illegitimate births? The Protestant countries, where the Bible is freely read. Which are the churches and religious bodies on earth that are producing the greatest results by spreading light and dispelling darkness? Those that make much of the Bible, teaching and preaching it as God's word. According to poet William Wordsworth, "The Bible is the fountain of all true patriotism and loyalty in states, it is the source of all true wisdom and sound policy. It is the spring of all true discipline and obedience, and of all valor and chivalry, in armies and fleets, in the battle-field and on the wide sea. It is the pure, unsullied fountain of all love and peace, happiness, quietness and joy, in families and households. Wherever it is duly obeyed it makes the 'desert' to rejoice and blossom as the rose."

❖ From the sermon "Inspiration"

Perfect Rest and Peace in Heaven

But as it is written, Eye hath not seen, nor ear heard, neither have entered into the heart of man, the things which God hath prepared for them that love him.
—1 CORINTHIANS 2:9

Heaven shall be a place of perfect rest and peace. Those who dwell there have no more conflict with the world, the flesh, and the devil. Their warfare is finished, and their fight is fought. At length they lay aside the armor of God, at last they may say to their spiritual weapons, "Rest and be still." They watch no longer, for they have no spiritual enemies to fear. They fast and mortify the flesh no longer, for they have no vile earthy body to keep under subjection. They pray no more, for they have no evil to pray against. There the wicked must cease from troubling! There sin and temptation are forever shut out! The gates are better barred than those of Eden, and the devil shall enter in no more.

O Christian brethren, rouse you and take comfort; surely this shall be indeed a blessed rest. There shall be no need of means of grace, for we shall have the end to which they are meant to lead. There shall be no need of ordinances, we shall have the substance they are appointed to keep in mind. There faith shall be swallowed up in sight, and hope in certainty, and prayer in praise, and sorrow in joy! Now in this present world is the school time, the season of the "lesson and the rod"; then will be the eternal holiday.

Now we are tossed upon a stormy sea, then we shall be safe in harbor! Now we have to plow and sow; there we shall reap the harvest! Now we have the labor, but then the wages!

Now we have the battle, but then the victory and reward! Now we must bear the cross, but then we shall receive the crown! Now we are journeying through the wilderness, but then we shall be at home!

❖ From the sermon "Heaven"

A Word about Our Bodies

For ye are bought with a price: therefore glorify God in your body,
and in your spirit, which are God's. —1 CORINTHIANS 6:20

This body of ours—which takes up so much of our thoughts and time to warm it, dress it, feed it, and make it comfortable—this body alone is not all the man. It is but the lodging of a noble tenant, and that tenant is the immortal soul! The death that each of us has one day to die does not make an end of the man. All is not over when the last breath is drawn and the doctor's last visit has been paid, when the coffin is screwed down and the funeral preparations are made, when "ashes to ashes and dust to dust" has been pronounced over the grave, when our place in the world is filled up, and the gap made by our absence from society is no longer noticed. No, all is not over then! Everyone has within him an undying soul!

When we are alone on the bed of sickness and the world is shut out, when we watch by the deathbed of a friend, when we see those whom we love lowered into the grave, at times like these, who does not know the feelings that come across men's minds? Who does not know that in hours like these, something rises in the heart, telling us that there is a life to come, and that all, from the highest to the lowest, have undying souls?

I do ask every reader to keep it ever before his mind. Perhaps your lot is cast in the midst of some busy city. You see around you an end-less struggle for temporal things. Hurry, bustle, and business hem you in on every side. I can well believe you are sometimes tempted to think that this world is everything, and the body is all that is worth caring for. But resist the temptation and cast it behind you. Say to yourself every morning when you rise and every night when you lie down, "This world is passing away. The life that I now live is not all. There is something besides business and money and pleasure and commerce and trade. There is a life to come!"

❖ From the sermon "Our Souls"

Many Have Gone before Us

Wherefore seeing we also are compassed about with so great a cloud of witnesses, let us lay aside every weight, and the sin which doth so easily beset us, and let us run with patience the race that is set before us.
—HEBREWS 12:1

Many have gone before us. "We also are compassed about with so great a cloud of witnesses." The witnesses here spoken of are those patriarchs and prophets who are mentioned in the eleventh chapter, and the apostle calls upon us to remember them and their troubles and take courage. Are we frail earthen vessels? So were they. Are we weak and encompassed with infirmities? So were they. Are we exposed to temptation and burdened with this body of corruption? So were they. Are we afflicted? So were they. Are we alone in our generation, the scorn of all our neighbors? So were they. Have we trials of cruel mockings? So had they. What can we possibly be called upon to suffer which they have not endured?

Some men were tortured, not accepting release, so that they might gain a better resurrection, and others experienced mocking and scourings, as well as bonds and imprisonment. They were stoned, they were sawed in two, they died by the sword, they wandered about in sheepskins, in goatskins, destitute, afflicted, and mistreated. But grace exceedingly abounded, and all fought a good fight and finished their course and kept the faith, and to God Almighty every one of them appeared in Zion. Take courage, fainting Christians; you are encompassed with a great cloud of witnesses! The race that you are running has been run by millions before. You think that no one ever had such trials as yourself, but every step that you are journeying has been safely trod by others. The valley of the shadow of death has been securely passed by a multitude of trembling, doubting ones like yourself. They had their fears and anxieties, like you, but they were not cast away. The world, the flesh, and the devil can never overwhelm the weakest man or woman who will set his or her face toward God. These millions journeyed on in bitterness and tears like your own, and yet not one perished; they all reached their eternal home.

❖ From the sermon "The Christian Race"

The Apostle Paul's Convictions

But thou hast fully known my doctrine, manner of life, purpose,
faith, longsuffering, charity, patience, persecutions, afflictions, which
came unto me at Antioch, at Iconium, at Lystra; what persecutions
I endured: but out of them all the Lord delivered me.
—2 TIMOTHY 3:10–11

Paul was altogether convinced of the truth of the facts of Christianity. That the Lord Jesus Christ was actually God "manifest in the flesh" (1 Tim. 3:16); that He had proved His divinity by doing miracles that could not be denied; that He had, finally, risen from the grave and ascended up into heaven and was sitting at God's right hand as man's Savior—on all these points he had thoroughly made up his mind and had not the slightest doubt of their credibility. On behalf of them he was willing to die. Paul was altogether convinced of the truth of the doctrines of Christianity. That we are all guilty sinners and in danger of eternal ruin, that the grand object of Christ coming into the world was to make atonement for our sins and to purchase redemption by suffering in our stead on the cross, that all who repent and believe on Christ crucified are completely forgiven all sins and that there is no other way to peace with God and heaven after death but faith in Christ—all this he most steadfastly believed. To teach these doctrines was his one object from his conversion until his martyrdom.

Last, but not least, Paul was altogether convinced of the reality of a world to come. The praise or favor of man, the rewards or punishments of this present world, were all as dross to him. He had before his eyes continually an inheritance incorruptible, and a crown of glory that would never fade away (Phil. 3:8; 2 Tim. 4:8). Of that crown he knew that nothing could deprive him. Now, are there many in the present day like Paul? I do not, of course, mean are there many inspired apostles? But I do mean is it common to meet Christians who are as thorough, as unhesitating, as full of assurance as he was?

❖ From the sermon "Portraits"

The Reward of the Redeemed

Therefore are they before the throne of God, and serve him day and night in his temple: and he that sitteth on the throne shall dwell among them. —REVELATION 7:15

You have heard of tribulation, but it leads, you see, to comfort. You have heard of the cross, but the end is indeed a crown. Now we can tell you something of the affliction of God's children, for we are able to speak that we know, but when we have to treat of the glory which shall be revealed, we are on ground which human eye has not seen and we must be careful not to go beyond what is written.

The saints shall "serve him day and night." There shall be no weariness in heaven; there shall be no earthly labors to distract our attention. Here, in this present world, alas! The cares of the world are continually breaking in, and these poor frail bodies of ours do often bind us down to the earth by their weakness, even when the spirit is willing. We may be on the mount for a short season sometimes, but our powers are soon exhausted. But there we shall have no wandering thoughts, no distractions, no bodily wants, we shall never faint!

It is a pleasant thing to have the company of those we love; our very earthly happiness is incomplete while those who have the keys of our affection—the husband, the wife, the brother, the sister, the friends who are as our own souls—are far away. But there shall be no such incompleteness in heaven. There we shall have the presence of our glorious Lord before our eyes, who loved us and gave Himself for us and paid the price of our salvation, even His own blood, and the Scripture shall be fulfilled which says, "In thy presence is fulness of joy; at thy right hand there are pleasures for evermore" (Ps. 16:11)!

❖ From the sermon "The Blood of the Lamb"

Importance of the Heart in Religion

Keep thy heart with all diligence;
for out of it are the issues of life.
—PROVERBS 4:23

The Bible teaches that the heart is that part of us on which the state of our soul depends. Out of it are "the issues of life" (Prov. 4:23). The reason, the understanding, the conscience, the affections are all second in importance to the heart. The heart is the person. It is the seat of all spiritual life and health and strength and growth. It is the hinge and turning point in the condition of the human soul. If the heart is alive to God and quickened by the Spirit, the individual is a living Christian. If the heart is dead and has not the Spirit, the individual is dead before God. The heart is the person! Tell me not merely what someone says and professes, and where he or she goes on Sunday, and what money he or she puts in the collecting plate. Tell me rather what someone's heart is, and I will tell you what he or she is. "For as he thinketh in his heart, so is he" (Prov. 23:7).

For another thing, the Bible teaches that the heart is that part of us at which God especially looks. "Man looketh on the outward appearance, but the LORD looketh on the heart" (1 Sam. 16:7). "Every way of a man is right in his own eyes: but the LORD pondereth the hearts" (Prov. 21:2). Man is naturally content with the outward part of religion, with outward morality, outward correctness, outward regular attendance on means of grace. But the eyes of the Lord look much further. He regards our motives. He "weigheth the spirits" (Prov. 16:2). He says Himself, "I the LORD search the heart, I try the reins, even to give every man according to his ways, and according to the fruit of his doings" (Jer. 17:10).

What is the heart in man's body? It is the principal and most important organ in the whole frame. A man may live many years in spite of fevers, wounds, and loss of limbs. But a man cannot live if you injure his heart. Just so it is with the heart in religion. It is the fountain of life to the soul.

✣ From the sermon "The Heart"

The Way of Forgiveness

Let the wicked forsake his way, and the unrighteous man his thoughts: and let him return unto the LORD, and he will have mercy upon him; and to our God, for he will abundantly pardon.
—ISAIAH 55:7

Simply trust in the Lord Jesus Christ as your Savior. It is to cast your soul, with all its sins, unreservedly on Christ, to cease completely from any dependence on your own works or doings, either in whole or in part, and to rest on no other work but Christ's work, no other righteousness but Christ's righteousness, no other merit but Christ's merit, as your ground of hope. Take this course and you are a pardoned soul.

The Lord Jesus Christ, in great love and compassion, has made a full and complete satisfaction for sin, by suffering death in our place upon the cross. There He offered Himself as a sacrifice for us and allowed the wrath of God, which we deserved, to fall on His own head. For our sins, as our substitute, He gave Himself, suffered, and died—the just for the unjust, the innocent for the guilty—that He might deliver us from the curse of a broken law and provide a complete pardon for all who are willing to receive it. And by so doing, as Isaiah says, He has borne our sins (Isa. 53:11). As John the Baptist says, He has taken away sin (John 1:29). As Paul says, He has purged our sins and put away sin (Heb. 1:3; 9:26). And as Daniel says, He has made an end of sin and finished transgression (Dan. 9:24).

Christ, in one word, has purchased a full forgiveness, if we are only willing to receive it. He has done all, paid all, suffered all that was needful to reconcile us to God. He has provided a garment of righteousness to clothe us. He has opened a fountain of living waters to cleanse us. He has removed every barrier between us and God the Father, taken every obstacle out of the way, and made a road by which the vilest may return. All things are now ready, and the sinner has only to believe and be saved, to eat and be satisfied, to ask and receive, to wash and be clean.

✣ From the sermon "Forgiveness"

Seven Steps to Die Daily

I die daily. —1 CORINTHIANS 15:31

What then are the best means of preserving in a believer's heart that lively sense of justification which is so precious to the soul that knows it? I offer a few hints to believers. I lay no claim to infallibility in setting down these hints, for I am only a man. But such as they are I offer them.

1. To keep up a lively sense of peace, there must be constant looking to Jesus. As the pilot keeps his eye on the mark by which he steers, so must we keep our eye on Christ.

2. There must be constant communion with Jesus. We must use Him daily as our soul's physician and high priest. There must be daily conference, daily confession, and daily absolution.

3. There must be constant watchfulness against the enemies of your soul. He who would have peace must always be prepared for war.

4. There must be constant following after holiness in every relation of life, in our tempers, in our tongues, abroad and at home. A small speck on the lens of a telescope is enough to prevent our seeing distant objects clearly. A little dust will soon make a watch go incorrectly.

5. There must be a constant laboring after humility. Pride goes before a fall. Self-confidence is often the mother of sloth, of hurried Bible reading, and sleepy prayers. Peter first said he would never forsake his Lord, though all others did; then he slept when he should have prayed; then he denied Him three times and found wisdom only after bitter weeping.

6. There must be constant boldness in confessing our Lord before people. Those who honor Christ, Christ will honor with much of His company. When the disciples forsook our Lord, they were wretched and miserable. When they confessed Him before the council, they were filled with joy and the Holy Spirit.

7. Last, there must be constant jealousy over our own souls and frequent self-examination. We must be careful to distinguish between justification and sanctification. We must beware that we do not make a christ of holiness.

❖ From the sermon "Justification"

Christ's Intercession!

Wherefore he is able also to save them to the uttermost that come unto God by him, seeing he ever liveth to make intercession for them.
—HEBREWS 7:25

There is one subject in religion about which we can never know too much. That subject is Jesus Christ the Lord. This is the mighty subject which the text that heads this page unfolds, Jesus Christ and Jesus Christ's intercession. There is no end to all the riches that are treasured up in Him, in His person, in His work, in His offices, in His words, in His deeds, in His life, in His death, in His resurrection. I take up only one branch of the great subject this day. I am going to consider the intercession and priestly office of our Lord Jesus Christ.

It is the intercession of our Lord and Savior Jesus Christ whereby the true Christian knows his prayers are made acceptable and received in the court of heaven. What is the believer's prayer in itself? A poor, weak thing, unfit to rise above the ground. I know nothing it is more like than a banknote without the signature at the bottom. What is the value of that banknote without the signature? Nothing at all. Once get a very few letters traced in ink upon the bottom of that banknote, and that which was a piece of wastepaper a few moments before becomes worth, it may be, many hundred pounds, through the signature being attached to it. So it is with the intercession of Christ. He signs, endorses, and presents the believer's petitions. And through His all-prevailing intercession, they are heard on high and bring down blessings upon the Christian's soul.

Would you know the secret of daily comfort in all the toil and business and distractions we have to go through? Lay hold upon the intercession of Jesus Christ. Grasp the great thought that Christ not merely died for you but rose again and still lives for you.

✤ From the sermon "Christ's Power to Save"

Christians Generous in Giving

But this I say, He which soweth sparingly shall reap also sparingly;
and he which soweth bountifully shall reap also bountifully.
—2 CORINTHIANS 9:6

I entreat all professing Christians to encourage themselves in habits of liberality toward causes of charity and mercy. Remember that you are God's stewards and give money liberally, freely, and without grudging whenever you have an opportunity. You cannot keep your money forever. You must give an account one day of the manner in which it has been expended. Oh, lay it out with an eye to eternity while you can!

I do not ask rich men to leave their situations in life and go into the workhouse. I ask no man to neglect his worldly calling and to omit to provide for his family. Diligence in business is a positive Christian duty; provision for those dependent on us is proper Christian prudence.

But I ask all to look around continually as they journey on and to remember the poor, the poor in body and the poor in soul. We are here for a few short years. How can we do most good with our money while we are here? How can we spend it so as to leave the world somewhat happier and somewhat holier when we are gone? Might we not abridge some of our luxuries? Might we not lay out less upon ourselves and give more to Christ's cause and Christ's poor? Is there none we can do good to? Are there no sick, no poor, no needy whose sorrows we might lessen and whose comforts we might increase?

I believe that in giving to support works of charity and mercy, we are doing that which is according to Christ's mind, and I ask readers of these pages to begin the habit of giving, if they never began it before, and to go on with it increasingly if they have begun. I believe that in offering a warning against covetousness, I have done no more than bring forward a warning specially called for by the times, and I ask God to bless the consideration of these pages to many souls!

✣ From the sermon "Riches and Poverty"

The Great Gathering

Now we beseech you, brethren, by the coming of our Lord Jesus Christ, and by our gathering together unto him. —2 THESSALONIANS 2:1

That expression is "our gathering together." The gathering I speak of shall take place at the end of the world, in the day when Christ returns to earth the second time. As surely as He came the first time, so surely shall He come the second time. In the clouds of heaven He went away, and in the clouds of heaven He shall return. And the very first thing that Christ will do will be to "gather together" His people. "And he shall send his angels with a great sound of a trumpet, and they shall gather together his elect from the four winds, from one end of heaven to the other" (Matt. 24:31).

The object of this "gathering together" is as clearly revealed in Scripture as its manner. It is partly for the final reward of Christ's people that they may receive the unfading crown of glory (1 Peter 5:4) and the kingdom prepared before the foundation of the world (Matt. 25:34) that they may be admitted publicly into the joy of their Lord! This gathering will be a great one. All children of God who have ever lived, from Abel, the first saint, down to the last born in the day that our Lord comes, all of every age and nation and church and people and tongue, all shall be assembled together. Not one shall be overlooked or forgotten. The weakest and feeblest shall not be left behind. Now, when scattered, true Christians seem a little flock; then, when gathered, they shall be found a multitude which no man can number.

This mighty, wonderful "gathering together" is the gathering that ought to be often in men's thoughts. It deserves consideration; it demands attention. Gatherings of other kinds are incessantly occupying our minds—political gatherings, scientific gatherings, gatherings for pleasure, gatherings for gain. But the hour comes, and will soon be here, when gatherings of this kind will be completely forgotten! One thought alone will swallow up men's minds. That thought will be, "Shall I be gathered with Christ's people into a place of safety and honor, or be left behind to everlasting woe?" Let us take care that we are not left behind.

✢ From the sermon "The Great Gathering"

Widespread Skepticism of the Times, Part 1

*The fool hath said in his heart, There is no God. They are corrupt,
they have done abominable works, there is none that doeth good.*
—PSALM 14:1

In reviews, magazines, newspapers, lectures, essays, novels, and sometimes
even in sermons, scores of clever writers are incessantly waging war against
the very foundations of Christianity. Reason, science, geology, anthropol-
ogy, modern discoveries, free thought are all boldly asserted to be on their
side. No educated person, we are constantly told nowadays, can really
believe supernatural religion or the plenary inspiration of the Bible or the
possibility of miracles. Such ancient doctrines as the Trinity, the divinity of
Christ, the personality of the Holy Spirit, the atonement, the obligation of
the Sabbath, the necessity and efficacy of prayer, the existence of the devil,
and the reality of future punishment are quietly put on the shelf by many
professing leaders of modern thought as useless old almanacs or contemptuously thrown overboard as lumber! And all this is done so cleverly, and
with such an appearance of candor and liberality, and with such compli-
ments to the capacity and nobility of human nature that multitudes of
unstable Christians are carried away as by a flood and become partially
unsettled if they do not make complete shipwreck of faith.

I tell you not to be surprised at the widespread skepticism of the
times, so also I must urge you not to be shaken in mind by it or moved
from your steadfastness. There is no real cause for alarm. The ark of
God is not in danger, though the oxen seem to shake it. Christianity has
survived the attacks of Hume and Hobbes and Tindal; of Collins and
Woolston and Bolingbroke and Chubb; of Voltaire and Paine and Holy-
oake. These men made a great noise in their day and frightened weak
people. But they produced no more real effect than idle travelers produce by scratching their names on the Great Pyramid of Egypt. Depend
on it, Christianity in like manner will survive the attacks of the clever
writers of these times. The startling novelty of many modern objections
to revelation, no doubt, makes them seem weightier than they really are!

❖ From the sermon "Hold Fast"

Widespread Skepticism of the Times, Part 2

*Verily, verily, I say unto thee, We speak that we do know, and testify
that we have seen; and ye receive not our witness.* —JOHN 3:11

When skeptics and infidels have said all they can, we must not forget
that there are three great broad facts which they have never explained
away; and I am convinced they never can and never will. Let me tell you
briefly what they are. They are very simple facts, and any plain man can
understand them.

The first fact is Jesus Christ Himself. If Christianity is a mere invention of man and the Bible is not from God, how can infidels explain
Jesus Christ? His existence in history they cannot deny. How is it that
without force or bribery, without arms or money, without flattering
man's pride of reason, without granting any indulgence to man's lusts
and passions He has made such an immensely deep mark on the world?
Who was He? What was He? Where did He come from? How is it that
there has never been one like Him, neither before nor after, since the
beginning of time? They cannot explain it. Nothing can explain it but
the great foundation principle of revealed religion, that Jesus Christ is
truly God and that His gospel is all true.

The second fact is the Bible itself. If Christianity is a mere invention
of man and the Bible is of no more authority than any other uninspired
volume, how is it that the book is what it is? How is it that a book written by a few Jews in a remote part of the earth, written at distant and
various periods without concert or collusion among the writers; written
by members of a nation that, compared to Greece and Rome, did nothing for literature; how is it that this book stands entirely alone, and that
there is nothing that even approaches it, for high views of God, for true
views of man, for solemnity of thought, for grandeur of doctrine, and
for purity of morality? What account can the infidel give of this book,
so deep, so simple, so wise, so free from defects? He cannot explain its
existence and its nature on his principles. We only can do that who hold
that the book is supernatural and is the book of God!

❖ From the sermon "Hold Fast"

Widespread Skepticism of the Times, Part 3

The fool hath said in his heart, There is no God. Corrupt are they, and have done abominable iniquity: there is none that doeth good.
—PSALM 53:1

When skeptics and infidels have said all they can, we must not forget that there are three great broad facts which they have never explained away; and I am convinced they never can and never will. Let me tell you briefly what they are. They are very simple facts, and any plain man can understand them.

The third fact is the effect that Christianity has produced on the world. If Christianity is a mere invention of man and not a supernatural, divine revelation, how is it that it has wrought such a complete alteration in the state of mankind? Any well-read person knows that the moral difference between the condition of the world before Christianity was planted and since Christianity took root is the difference between night and day; the difference between the kingdom of heaven and the kingdom of the devil. At this very moment I defy anyone to look at the map of the world and compare the countries where men are Christians with those where men are not Christians, and to deny that these countries are as different as light and darkness, black and white. How can any infidel explain this on his principles? He cannot do it. We only can who believe that Christianity came down from God and is the only divine religion in the world.

Whenever you are tempted to be alarmed at the progress of infidelity, look at the three facts that I have just mentioned and cast your fears away! Take up your position boldly behind the ramparts of these three facts, and you may safely defy the utmost efforts of modern skeptics. They may often ask you a hundred questions you cannot answer and start clever problems about geology, or the origin of man, or the age of the world that you cannot solve. They may vex and irritate you with wild speculations and theories of which at the time you cannot prove the fallacy though you feel it. But be calm and fear not. Remember the three great facts I have named, and boldly challenge them to explain them away!

✥ From the sermon "Hold Fast"

The Way in Which People Obtain the Benefit of God's Love and Christ's Salvation

That whosoever believeth in him
should not perish, but have eternal life.
—JOHN 3:15

God has loved the world. God has given His Son "to be the Saviour of the world" (1 John 4:14). And yet we learn from Scripture that many people in the world never reach heaven! Here at any rate is limitation. Here the gate is strait and the way narrow. Only a small remnant out of mankind obtains eternal benefit from Christ. Who then, and what are they? Christ and His benefits are only available to those who believe. To believe, in the language of the New Testament, is simply to trust. Trusting and believing are the same thing. This is a doctrine repeatedly laid down in Scripture, in plain and unmistakable language. Those who will not trust or believe in Him have no part in Him. Without believing there is no salvation. It is vain to suppose that any will be saved merely because Christ was incarnate or because Christ is in heaven or because they belong to Christ's church or because they are baptized or because they have received the Lord's Supper. All this is entirely useless to any man except he believes. Without faith, or trust, on his part, all these things together will not save his soul. We must have personal faith in Christ, personal dealings with Christ, personal transactions with Christ or we are lost for evermore.

It is utterly false and unscriptural to say that Christ is in every man. Christ no doubt is for everyone, but Christ is not in everyone. He dwells only in those hearts which have faith; and all, unhappily, have not faith. He who believes not in the Son of God is yet in his sins; "the wrath of God abideth on him" (John 3:36). "He that believeth not," says our Lord Jesus Christ in words of fearful distinctness, "shall be damned" (Mark 16:16).

❖ From the sermon "Faith"

Have We Troubles?

For we have not an high priest which cannot be touched with the feeling of our infirmities; but was in all points tempted like as we are, yet without sin.
—HEBREWS 4:15

And now, have we troubles? Where is the man or woman on earth who can say, "I have none"? Let us take them all to the Lord Jesus Christ. None can comfort like Him. He who died on the cross to purchase forgiveness for our sins is sitting at the right hand of God with a heart full of love and sympathy. He knows what sorrow is, for He lived thirty-three years in this sinful world and suffered Himself being tempted and saw suffering every day. And He has not forgotten it. When He ascended into heaven, to sit at the right hand of the Father, He took a perfect human heart with Him.

Have we troubles? Let us never forget the everlasting covenant to which old David clung to the end of his days. It is still in full force. It is not canceled. It is the property of every believer in Jesus, whether rich or poor, just as much as it was the property of the son of Jesse. Let us never give way to a fretting, murmuring, complaining spirit. Let us firmly believe at the worst of times that every step in our lives is ordered by the Lord, with perfect wisdom and perfect love, and that we shall see it all at last. Let us not doubt that He is always doing all things well. He is good in giving and equally good in taking away.

Finally, have we troubles? Let us never forget that one of the best remedies and most soothing medicines is to try to do good to others and to be useful. Let us lay ourselves out to make the sorrow less and the joy greater in this sin-burdened world. There is always some good to be done within a few yards of our own doors. Let every Christian strive to do it and to relieve either bodies or minds!

❖ From the sermon "Without Clouds"

Why Should You Be Afraid?

Yea, though I walk through the valley of the shadow of death, I will fear no evil: for thou art with me; thy rod and thy staff they comfort me.
—PSALM 23:4

Why should you be afraid? What should make you fear? What should make you suppose that you shall ever be allowed to fall away, while Jesus Christ lives at the right hand of God to make intercession for you? All the power of the Lord Jesus Christ is pledged upon your behalf. He has undertaken to care for all the flock that God the Father has committed into His hand. He will care for it. He has cared for it. He went to the cross for it. He died for it. He is ever at the right hand of God and has not ceased to care for it.

Every member of that flock—the weakest, the feeblest sheep or lamb—is equally dear to the Lord and Savior, and none shall pluck the least of Christ's sheep out of God's hand. Can you stop the tides of the sea and make them not rise at your command? Can you make the waters stop when the tide begins to come? Can you prevent the sun in heaven going down in the west or prevent the same sun from rising tomorrow morning in the east? You cannot do it; these things are impossible. And all the power of devils, all the power of the world, and all the enemies of the Christian shall not be able to pluck out of the hand of Jesus Christ one single soul who has been brought by the Spirit's teaching to true union with Christ and for whom Jesus Christ intercedes. The days of Christ's weakness have passed away. He was "crucified through weakness" and was weak on our account when He went to the cross (2 Cor. 13:4). The days of His weakness are over; the days of His power have begun. Pilate shall no more condemn Him; He shall come to condemn Pilate. All power is His in heaven and earth, and all that power is engaged on behalf of His believing people.

❖ From the sermon "Christ's Power to Save"

The Duties of Parents

Train up a child in the way he should go, and when he is old, he will not depart from it.
—PROVERBS 22:6

I believe that most professing Christians are acquainted with our sermon text. The sound of it is probably very familiar to your ears, like an old tune. It is likely that you have heard it or read it, talked of it, or quoted it many times. Is that not true? But despite it being a well-known Bible verse, how little do we regard its truth! The doctrine it contains appears scarcely known; the duty it puts before us is seldom put into practice. My friends, am I not speaking the truth? It cannot be said that the subject is a new one. We live in days when there is a mighty zeal for education. We hear of new schools rising up everywhere. We are told of new systems and new books for the young of every sort and description. And still for all of this, the vast majority of children are clearly not trained in the way they should go, for when they grow up, they do not walk with God.

It is also a subject on which all concerned are in great danger of falling short of their duty. This is notably a point in which men can see the faults of their neighbors more clearly than their own. They will often raise their children in the very path which they have denounced to their friends as unsafe. They will see little problems in other people's families and overlook major ones in their own.

As a minister, I cannot help remarking that there is hardly any subject about which people seem so stubborn as they are about their own children. I have sometimes been absolutely astonished at the slowness of sensible Christian parents to accept the fact that their own children are at fault or deserve blame. There are many people to whom I would much rather speak about their own sins than to tell them that their children had done anything wrong!

❖ From the book *The Duties of Parents*

Flashy Church Services

For the time will come when they will not endure sound doctrine;
but after their own lusts shall they heap to themselves teachers, having
itching ears.   —2 TIMOTHY 4:3

We must not be content with what men call bright and hearty services.
We must remember that these things do not constitute the whole of
religion and that no Christianity is valuable in the sight of God which
does not influence the hearts, the consciences, and the lives of those who
profess it. It is not always the church and congregation in which there is
the best music and singing and from which young people return saying
how beautiful it was in which God takes most pleasure. It is the church
in which there is most of the presence of Jesus Christ and the Holy Spirit
and the congregation in which there are most broken hearts and contrite
spirits. If our eyes were only opened to see invisible things, like the eyes
of Elisha's servant, we might discover to our amazement that there is
more presence of the King of Kings, and consequently more blessing,
in some humble, unadorned mission room where the gospel is faithfully
preached than in some of the grandest churches in the land.

The preaching of the pure Word of God is the first mark of a healthy
church. It is sound doctrine taught and preached, and not ritual, which
in every age the Holy Spirit has used for awakening sleeping human consciences, building up the cause of Christ, and saving souls. The dens and
caves and upper rooms in which the primitive Christians used to meet
were doubtless very rough and unadorned. They had no carved wood or
stone, no stained glass, no costly vestments, no organs, and no surpliced
choirs. But these primitive worshipers were the men who "turned the
world upside down" (Acts 17:6), and I doubt not that their places of
worship were far more honorable in God's sight. It was well and truly
said in those ancient days that "the church had wooden Communion
vessels, but golden ministers," and it was this which gave the primitive
church its power. And when religion began to decay, it was said that
the conditions were reversed; the ministers became wooden, and the
Communion plate golden! I long to have everywhere golden ministers,
golden worship, golden preaching, golden praying, and golden praise!

❖ From the sermon "Signs of the Times"

Christ Laid Down His Life

But God commendeth his love toward us, in that, while we were yet sinners, Christ died for us.
—ROMANS 5:8

People seem to forget that all Christ's sufferings were endured voluntarily and of His own free will. He was under no compulsion. Of His own choice He laid down His life; of His own choice He went to the cross in order to finish the work He came to do. He might easily have summoned legions of angels with a word and scattered Pilate and Herod and all their armies, like chaff before the wind. But He was a willing sufferer. His heart was set on the salvation of sinners. He was resolved to open "a fountain...for all sin and uncleanness," by shedding His own blood (Zech. 13:1).

When I think of all this, I see nothing painful or disagreeable in the subject of Christ's cross. On the contrary, I see in it wisdom and power, peace and hope, joy and gladness, comfort and consolation. The more I keep the cross in my mind's eye, the more fullness I seem to discern in it. The longer I dwell on the cross in my thoughts, the more I am satisfied that there is more to be learned at the foot of the cross than anywhere else in the world.

Would I know the length and breadth of God the Father's love toward a sinful world? Where shall I see it most displayed? Shall I look at His glorious sun, shining down daily on the unthankful and evil? Shall I look at seedtime and harvest, returning in regular yearly succession? Oh, no! I can find a stronger proof of love than anything of this sort. I look at the cross of Christ. I see in it not the cause of the Father's love, but the effect. There I see that God so loved this wicked world, "that he gave his only begotten Son, that whosoever believeth in him should not perish, but have everlasting life" (John 3:16).

✤ From the sermon "The Cross of Christ"

Saints in Death

For to me to live is Christ, and to die is gain.
—PHILIPPIANS 1:21

Consider how it is with the most holy and eminent saints when dying. Did you ever see or hear any boasting of their own works and performances? They may, and do own to the praise of His grace, what they have been made to be, what they have been helped to do or allow for Christ's sake. But when they draw near to the solemn tribunal, what else is in their eye and heart, but only free grace, ransoming blood, and a well-ordered covenant in Christ the surety? They cannot bear to have any make mention to them of their holiness, their own grace, and attainments.

Would anyone like to know what kind of deathbeds a minister of the gospel finds comfort in attending? Would you know what closing scenes are cheering to us and leave favorable impressions on our minds? We like to see dying people making much of Christ. So long as they can only talk of the Almighty and providence and God and mercy, we must stand in doubt. Dying in this state, they give no satisfactory sign. Give us the men and women who feel their sins deeply and cling to Jesus, who think much of His dying love, who like to hear of His atoning blood, who return again and again for the story of His cross. These are the deathbeds which leave good evidence behind them. For my part I had rather hear the name of Jesus come heartily from a dying relative's lips than see him die without a word about Christ and then be told by an angel that he was saved.

The dying words of Mr. Ash, the Puritan, are well deserving of notice. He said, "When I consider my best duties, I sink, I die, I despair. But when I think of Christ, I have enough. He is all and in all."

❖ From the sermon "Our Hope"

What Is It to Think Rightly of Christ?

He saith unto them, But whom say ye that I am?
—MATTHEW 16:15

We must think of Him as perfect man, of like nature with ourselves in everything, sin only excepted. If Christ had not been man He could not have suffered the punishment of our iniquities by dying on the cross. If He had not taken on Him a body and a nature liable to temptation like our own, He could never have fulfilled the law for us and in our stead. And we could not have looked upon Him with a brotherly confidence, as one who can be touched with the feeling of our infirmities.

We must think of Him as the great Redeemer and Savior, who by the voluntary sacrifice and death of Himself made atonement for the sins of the whole world and provided a means of reconciliation between His Father and mankind. We must think of Him as a King. He is the great head of a spiritual dominion over the heart of all whom He chooses and calls out of the world; the chief of a spiritual kingdom that confers peculiar blessings and privileges on all who become subjects of it; a kingdom that is unseen, invisible at present, but shall be known and acknowledged by all at Christ's second coming.

We must think of Him as the Great High Priest, who, like the Jewish high priest of old, has gone alone before us into the holy of holies—that is, heaven—to make satisfaction for the sin of His people with blood, even the blood of Himself, who ever stands at the right hand of God to make intercession for them and can always feel for and pity them because as man He was tempted like as they are. We must think of Him as the Prophet who would come, who has shown to mankind the way of salvation, who has clearly explained how God's mercy and God's justice can be reconciled when sinners are accounted righteous. Last, we must think of Him as the great example, who has left men a pattern that they should walk in His steps; who has given them, in His own person and behavior, a model of conduct in nearly every department of life that they cannot strive too much to imitate.

❖ From the sermon "What Do You Think about Christ?"

Contending for the Truth

Beloved, when I gave all diligence to write unto you of the common salvation, it was needful for me to write unto you, and exhort you that ye should earnestly contend for the faith which was once delivered unto the saints.
—JUDE 3

We have no right to expect anything but the pure gospel of Christ, unmixed and unadulterated, the same gospel that was taught by the apostles to do good to the souls of men. I believe that to maintain this pure truth in the church, men should be ready to make any sacrifice, to hazard peace, to risk dissension, and run the chance of division. They should no more tolerate false doctrine than they would tolerate sin. They should withstand any adding to or taking away from the simple message of the gospel of Christ.

Yes! Peace without truth is a false peace. It is the very peace of the devil. Unity without the gospel is a worthless unity. It is the very unity of hell. Let us never be ensnared by those who speak kindly of it. Never let us be guilty of sacrificing any portion of truth, on the altar of peace. Let us rather be like the Jews, who, if they found any manuscript copy of the Old Testament Scriptures incorrect in a single letter, burned the whole copy rather than run the risk of losing one jot or tittle of the word of God. Let us be content with nothing short of the whole gospel of Christ.

I am quite aware that the things I have said are exceedingly distasteful to many minds. I believe many are content with teaching that is not the whole truth and fancy it will be all the same in the end. I am sorry for them. I am convinced that nothing but the whole truth is likely, as a general rule, to do good to souls. I am satisfied that those who willfully put up with anything short of the whole truth will find at last that their souls have received much damage. There are three things that men never ought to trifle with: a little poison, a little false doctrine, and a little sin. They are the truest friends of the church who labor most for the preservation of truth.

❖ From the sermon "The Fallibility of Ministers"

Strive to Bear Much Fruit

Abide in me, and I in you. As the branch cannot bear fruit of itself,
except it abide in the vine; no more can ye, except ye abide in me.
—JOHN 15:4

We must not be content with a low measure of holiness. We must not rest satisfied with a little sanctification. We must not think it is enough because we have attained a small degree of grace and are just one step better than the world. No! Indeed, we must go forward from strength to strength. We must shine more and more unto the perfect day. We must strive to bear much fruit. Christ did not give Himself to us that we should be a sleeping generation, trees that grow not, always standing still. He would have us be a peculiar people, zealous of good works, valiant for the truth, fervent in spirit, living not unto ourselves, but unto Him. Freely saved, we should freely and willingly labor. Freely forgiven, we should freely and cheerfully work. Our lives should be books of evidence. Our acts should tell out whose we are. "Ye are my friends," said Jesus, "if ye do whatsoever I command you" (John 15:14).

Brother or sister, look within. Take heed lest a deceitful heart and an ensnaring world and a busy devil turn you out of the way. Study a tender conscience. Beware of indolence under the cloak of false humility. Make not the old Adam and the devil an excuse for little sins. Remember the apostle's advice: "Watch ye, stand fast in the faith, quit you like men, be strong" (1 Cor. 16:13). Those who follow the Lord fully are those that follow Him most comfortably. Be zealous though the world may sleep. Brother or sister, I give you this word of quickening in love. I would not have you be the least in the kingdom of heaven. I would not like you to be the palest and dimmest among the stars in glory. I want you not only to be scarcely saved, and so as by fire, but to receive a full reward. Then lay these things well to heart!

❖ From the sermon "The Lord Our Righteousness"

The Simple Doctrine of Christ

Jesus answered them, and said,
My doctrine is not mine, but his that sent me.
—JOHN 7:16

The simple doctrine and rule of Christ then—nothing added, nothing taken away, nothing substituted—this is the mark at which we ought to aim. This is the point from which departure ought to be dreaded. Can we improve on His teaching? Are we wiser than He? Can we suppose that He left anything of real vital importance unwritten or liable to the vague reports of human traditions? Shall we take on ourselves to say that we can mend or change for the better any ordinance of His appointment? Can we doubt that in matters about which He is silent we have need to act very cautiously, very gently, very moderately and must beware of pressing them on those who do not see with our eyes? Above all, we must beware of asserting anything to be needful to salvation of which Christ has said nothing at all. I only see one answer to such questions as these. We must beware of anything which has even the appearance of departure from the "simplicity that is in Christ" (2 Cor. 11:3).

The plain truth is that we cannot sufficiently exalt the Lord Jesus Christ as the great head of the church and Lord of all ordinances, no less than as the Savior of sinners. I take it we all fail here. We do not realize how high and great and glorious a king the Son of God is and what undivided loyalty we owe to one who has not delegated any of His offices or given His glory to another. He is the Alpha and Omega, the first and the last, the founder and finisher of our salvation. Oh, blessed Jesus, how much better it would be not to exist than to exist without You! Never to be born than not to die in You! A thousand hells are nothing compared to eternally without Jesus Christ!" This witness is true.

❖ From the sermon "Apostolic Fears"

Your Portion in Christ

The LORD is my portion, saith my soul;
therefore will I hope in him.
—LAMENTATIONS 3:24

I want you to know the length and breadth of your portion in Christ. I want you to understand the full amount of treasure to which faith in Jesus entitles you. You have found out that you are a great sinner. Thank God for that. You have fled to Christ for pardon and peace with God. Thank God for that. You have committed yourself to Jesus for time and eternity. Thank God for that. You have no hope but in Christ's blood, Christ's righteousness, Christ's mediation, Christ's daily all-persevering intercession. Thank God for that. Your heart's desire and prayer is to be holy in all of life. Thank God for that. But oh, lay hold upon the glorious truth, that believing on Jesus you shall never perish, you shall never be cast away, you shall never fall away! It is written for you as well as the apostles, "My sheep shall never perish." Yes! Reader, Jesus has spoken it, and Jesus meant it to be believed. Jesus has spoken it, who never broke His promises. Jesus has spoken it, who cannot lie. Jesus has spoken it, who has power in heaven and earth to keep His word. Jesus has spoken it for the least and lowest believers: "My sheep shall never perish."

Would you have perfect peace in life? Then lay hold on to this doctrine of perseverance. Your trials may be many and great. Your cross may be very heavy. But the business of your soul is all conducted according to an everlasting covenant, ordered in all things and sure. All things are working together for your good. Your sorrows are only purifying your soul for glory. Your bereavements are only fashioning you as a polished stone for the temple above, made without hands. From whatever quarter the storms blow, they only drive you nearer to heaven! Whatever weather you may go through it is only ripening you for the garner of God. Your best things are quite safe. Come what will, you shall never perish!

✣ From the sermon "Never Perish"

Fill Your Mind with God's Word

Blessed is the man that walketh not in the counsel of the ungodly, nor standeth in the way of sinners, nor sitteth in the seat of the scornful. But his delight is in the law of the LORD; and in his law doth he meditate day and night. And he shall be like a tree planted by the rivers of water, that bringeth forth his fruit in his season; his leaf also shall not wither; and whatsoever he doeth shall prosper.
—PSALM 1:1–3

You and I have trouble and sorrow before us; it needs no prophetic eye to see that. Sicknesses, deaths, partings, separations, disappointments are sure to come. What is to sustain us in the days of darkness, which are many? Nothing is so able to do it as texts out of the Bible. You and I, in all probability, may lie for months on a bed of sickness. Heavy days and weary nights, an aching body, and an enfeebled mind may make life a burden. And what will support us? Nothing is likely to cheer and sustain us so much as verses out of the Bible. You and I have death to look forward to. There will be friends to be left, home to be given up, the grave to be visited, an unknown world to be entered, and the last judgment after all. And what will sustain and comfort us when our last moments draw near? Nothing, I firmly believe, is so able to help our heart in that solemn hour as texts out of the Bible.

I want men to fill their minds with passages of Scripture while they are well and strong, that they may have sure help in the day of need. I want them to be diligent in studying their Bibles and becoming familiar with their contents in order that the grand old book may stand by them and talk with them when all earthly friends fail. Build your foundation on the rock of Jesus Christ!

❖ From the sermon "Be Content"

Believers Are an Enclosed Garden

A garden inclosed is my sister, my spouse;
a spring shut up, a fountain sealed.
—SONG OF SOLOMON 4:12

There is an enclosure around believers, or else they never would be saved. This is the secret of their safety. It is not their faithfulness, their strength, or their love; it is the wall around them that prevents their being lost. They are a "garden enclosed." They are enclosed by God the Father's everlasting election. Long before they were born, long before the foundations of the world, God knew them, chose them, and appointed them to obtain salvation by Jesus Christ. The children of this world do not like to hear this doctrine proclaimed. It humbles man and leaves him no room to boast. But whether it is abused or not, the doctrine of election is true. It is the cornerstone of the believer's foundation, that he was chosen in Christ before the world began. Who can rightly estimate the strength of this enclosure?

They are enclosed by the special love of God the Son. The Lord Jesus is the Savior of all men, but He is specially the Savior of those who believe. He has power over all flesh, but He gives eternal life to those who are specially given to Him in a way that He does to none others. He shed His blood on the cross for all, but He washes only those who have part in Him. He invites all, but He quickens whom He will and brings them to glory. He prays for them. He prays not for the world. He intercedes for them, that they may be kept from evil, that they may be sanctified by the truth, that their faith fail not. Who can fully describe the blessedness of this enclosure?

Who can tell the comfort of this threefold wall of enclosure! Believers are enclosed by election, enclosed by washing and intercession, enclosed by calling and regeneration. Great is the consolation of these threefold bands of love around us, the love of God the Father, the love of God the Son, the love of God the Holy Spirit!

✤ From the sermon "The Lord's Garden"

The Need for Zealous Christians

Who gave himself for us, that he might redeem us from all iniquity,
and purify unto himself a peculiar people, zealous of good works.
—TITUS 2:14

Let everyone who professes to be a Christian beware of checking zeal. Seek it. Cultivate it. Try to blow up the fire in your own heart and the hearts of others, but never, never check it. Beware of throwing cold water on zealous souls whenever you meet with them. Beware of nipping in the bud this precious grace when first it shoots. If you are a parent, beware of checking it in your children. If you are a husband, beware of checking it in your wife. If you are a brother, beware of checking it in your sisters. If you are a minister, beware of checking it in the members of your congregation. It is a shoot of heaven's own planting. Beware of crushing it, for Christ's sake.

Zeal may make mistakes. Zeal may need directing. Zeal may need guiding, controlling, and advising. Like the elephants on ancient fields of battle, it may sometimes do injury to its own side. But zeal does not need damping in a wretched, cold, corrupt, miserable world like this! There is little danger of there ever being too much zeal for the glory of God. God forgive those who think there is! You know little of human nature. You forget that sickness is far more contagious than health and that it is much easier to catch a cold than impart a glow. Depend upon it, the church seldom needs a bridle but often needs a spur. It seldom needs to be checked; it often needs to be urged on. Such zeal will make a man hate everything that God hates, such as drunkenness, slavery, or infanticide, and long to sweep it from the face of the earth. It will make him jealous of God's honor and glory and look on everything that robs Him of it as an offense!

✣ From the sermon "Christian Zeal"

Benefits of the Lord's Supper

And he took bread, and gave thanks, and brake it, and gave unto them, saying, This is my body which is given for you: this do in remembrance of me.

—LUKE 22:19

He who eats the bread and drinks the wine in a right spirit will find himself drawn into closer communion with Christ and will feel to know Him more and understand Him better.

Three points:

1. Right reception of the Lord's Supper has a humbling effect on the soul. The sight of the bread and wine as emblems of Christ's body and blood reminds us how sinful sin must be if nothing less than the death of God's own Son could make satisfaction for it or redeem us from its guilt.

2. Right reception of the Lord's Supper has a cheering effect on the soul. The sight of the bread broken and the wine poured out reminds us how full, perfect, and complete is our salvation! Those vivid emblems remind us what an enormous price has been paid for our redemption. They press on us the mighty truth that believing on Christ, we have nothing to fear because a sufficient payment has been made for our debt. The precious blood of Christ answers every charge that can be brought against us. God can be "just, and the justifier of him which believeth in Jesus" (Rom. 3:26).

3. Right reception of the Lord's Supper has a sanctifying effect on the soul. The bread and wine remind us how great is our debt of gratitude to our Lord and how thoroughly we are bound to live for Him who died for our sins. They seem to say to us, "Remember what Christ has done for you, and ask yourself whether there is anything too great to do for Him!"

Such is a brief account of the benefits that a right-hearted communicant may expect to receive from the Lord's Supper. In eating that bread and drinking that cup, such a man will have his repentance deepened, his faith increased, his knowledge enlarged, his habit of holy living strengthened.

❖ From the sermon "The Lord's Supper"

I Cannot Think Little of Sin

For Christ also hath once suffered for sins, the just for the unjust, that he might bring us to God, being put to death in the flesh, but quickened by the Spirit.
—1 PETER 3:18

Would I know how exceedingly sinful and abominable sin is in the sight of God? Where shall I see that most fully brought out? Shall I turn to the history of the flood, and read how sin drowned the world? Shall I go to the shore of the Dead Sea, and mark what sin brought on Sodom and Gomorrah? Shall I turn to the wandering Jews, and observe how sin has scattered them over the face of the earth? No! I can find a clearer proof still! I look at the cross of Christ. There I see that sin is so black and damnable that nothing but the blood of God's own Son can wash it away. There I see that sin has so separated me from my holy Maker that all the angels in heaven could never have made peace between us. Nothing could reconcile us, short of the death of Christ. If I listened to the wretched talk of proud people, I might sometimes fancy sin was not so very sinful! But I cannot think little of sin when I look at the cross of Christ!

There I see that a full payment has been made for all my enormous debts. The curse of that law which I have broken has come down on One who there suffered in my stead. The demands of that law are all satisfied. Payment has been made for me, even to the uttermost farthing. It will not be required twice over. Ah, I might sometimes imagine I was too bad to be forgiven! My own heart sometimes whispers that I am too wicked to be saved. But I know in my better moments this is all my foolish unbelief. I read an answer to my doubts in the blood shed on Calvary. I feel sure that there is a way to heaven for the very vilest of people when I look at the cross!

✤ From the sermon "The Cross of Christ"

The Cross Is the Power of Missions

For I am not ashamed of the gospel of Christ: for it is the power of God unto salvation to every one that believeth; to the Jew first, and also to the Greek.
—ROMANS 1:16

The cross is the secret of all missionary success. Nothing but this has ever moved the hearts of the heathen. Just according as this has been lifted up, missions have prospered. This is the weapon that has won victories over hearts of every kind, in every quarter of the globe. Greenlanders, Africans, South Sea Islanders, Hindus, Chinese—all have alike felt its power. Just as that huge iron tube that crosses the Menai Straits is more affected and bent by half an hour's sunshine than by all the dead weight that can be placed in it, so in like manner the hearts of savages have melted before the cross when every other argument seemed to move them no more than stones.

"Brethren," said a North American Indian after his conversion, I have been a heathen. I know how heathens think. Once a preacher came and began to explain to us that there was a God; but we told him to return to the place from whence he came. Another preacher came and told us not to lie, nor steal, nor drink; but we did not heed him. At last another came into my hut one day and said, "I am come to you in the name of the Lord of heaven and earth. He sends to let you know that He will make you happy and deliver you from misery. For this end He became a man, gave His life a ransom, and shed His blood for sinners." I could not forget his words. I told them to the other Indians, and an awakening began among us.

I say, therefore, preach the sufferings and death of Christ, our Savior, if you wish your words to gain entrance among the heathen. Never indeed did the devil triumph so thoroughly as when he persuaded the Jesuit missionaries in China to keep back the story of the cross!

❖ From the sermon "The Cross of Christ"

Our Profession

Seeing then that we have a great high priest, that is passed into the heavens, Jesus the Son of God, let us hold fast our profession.
—HEBREWS 4:14

When Paul uses this expression ["our profession"], there can be little doubt about his meaning. He meant that public profession of faith in Christ and obedience to Him that every person made when he became a member of the Christian church. In the days of the apostle, when a man or woman left Judaism or heathenism and received Christ as a Savior, he declared himself a Christian by certain acts. He did it by being publicly baptized, by joining the company of those who had been baptized already, by publicly promising to give up idolatry and wickedness of all kinds, and by habitually taking part with the followers of Jesus of Nazareth in all their religious assemblies, their ways, and their practices. This is what Paul had in view when he wrote the words "Let us hold fast our profession."

Profession in those days was a very serious matter and entailed very serious consequences. It often brought on a man persecution, loss of property, imprisonment, and even death. The consequence was that few people ever made a Christian profession in the early church unless they were thoroughly in earnest, truly converted, and really believers. No doubt there were some exceptions. People like Ananias and Sapphira, and Simon Magus, and Demas crept in and joined themselves to the disciples. But these were exceptional cases. As a general rule, it was not worthwhile for a man to profess Christianity if his heart was not entirely in his profession. It cost much. It brought on a man the risk of a vast amount of trouble and brought in very little gain. The whole result was that the proportion of sincere, right-hearted, and converted people in the church of the apostle's days was far greater than it ever has been at any other period in the last eighteen centuries. There was a very deep meaning in Paul's words when he said, "Let us hold fast our profession."

✣ From the sermon "Our Profession"

Are You Ready for Christ's Second Coming?

Therefore be ye also ready: for in such an hour as ye think not the
Son of man cometh.   —MATTHEW 24:44

Are you ready for the second coming of Christ? He will come again to this world one day. As surely as He came the first time, eighteen hundred years ago, so surely will He come the second time. He will come to reward all His saints who have believed in Him and confessed Him on earth. He will come to judge all His enemies—the careless, the ungodly, the impenitent, and the unbelieving. He will come very suddenly at an hour when no man thinks, as a thief in the night. He will come in terrible majesty, in the glory of His Father, with the holy angels. A flaming fire shall burn before Him. The dead shall be raised. The judgment shall be set. The books shall be opened. Some shall be exalted into heaven. Many, very many, shall be cast down to hell. The time for repentance shall be past. Many shall cry, "Lord, Lord, open to us," but find the door of mercy shut forever. After this there will be no change. Reader, if Christ should come the second time this year, are you ready? Oh! Reader, these are solemn questions. They ought to make you examine yourself. They ought to make you think. It would be a terrible thing to be taken by surprise.

But shall I leave you here? I will not do so. Shall I raise searchings of heart, and not set before you the way of life? I will not do so. Hear me for a few moments, while I try to show you the man who is ready. He who is ready has a ready Savior. He has Jesus ever ready to help him. He has found out his own sinfulness and fled to Christ for peace. If those whom he loves are taken away, he remembers that Jesus is a friend who sticks closer than a brother and a husband who never dies. If the Lord should come again, he knows that he has nothing to fear. The Judge of all will be that very Jesus who has washed his sins away!

❖ From the sermon "Are You Ready?"

Fire! Fire!

And whosoever was not found written in the book of life was cast into the lake of fire.   —REVELATION 20:15

When a house is on fire, what ought to be done first? We ought to give the alarm and wake the inhabitants. This is true love to our neighbor. This is true charity. Reader, I love your soul and want it to be saved. I am therefore going to tell you something about hell. There is such a place as hell. Let no one deceive you with vain words. What men do not like they try hard not to believe. When the Lord Jesus Christ comes to judge the world, He will punish all who are not His disciples with a fearful punishment.

The punishment of hell shall be most severe. There is no pain like that of burning. Put your finger in the candle for a moment if you doubt this and try. Fire is the most destructive and devouring of all elements. Look into the mouth of a blast furnace and think what it would be to be there. Fire is of all elements most opposed to life. Creatures can live in air, and earth, and water; but nothing can live in fire. Yet fire is the portion to which the Christless and unbelieving will come. They will be "cast into the lake of fire." The punishment of hell will be eternal. Millions of ages will pass away, and the fire will never burn low or become dim. The fuel of that fire will never waste away and be consumed. It is unquenchable fire. O reader, these are the sad and painful things to speak of. I have no pleasure in dwelling on them. I could rather say with the apostle Paul, "I have great…sorrow" (Rom. 9:2). But they are things written for our learning, and it is good to consider them. They are part of that Scripture which is all profitable, and they ought to be heard. Painful as the subject of hell is, it is one about which I dare not, cannot, and must not be silent.

❖ From the sermon "Fire! Fire!"

Suffering with Christ

The Spirit itself beareth witness with our spirit, that we are the children of God: And if children, then heirs; heirs of God, and joint-heirs with Christ; if so be that we suffer with him, that we may be also glorified together. —ROMANS 8:16–17

All the children of God have a cross to carry. They have trials, troubles, and afflictions to go through for the gospel's sake. They have trials from the world, trials from the flesh, and trials from the devil. They have trials of feeling from relations and friends, hard words, hard conduct, and hard judgment. They have trials in the matter of character, slander, misrepresentation, mockery, insinuation of false motives, all these often rain thick upon them. They have trials in the matter of worldly interest. They have often to choose whether they will please man and lose glory or gain glory and offend man. They have trials from their own hearts.

Some of them suffer more and some less. Some of them suffer in one way and some in another. God measures out their portions like a wise physician and cannot err. But never, I believe, was there one child of God who reached paradise without a cross. Suffering is the diet of the Lord's family. "For whom the Lord loveth he chasteneth" (Heb. 12:6). "But if ye be without chastisement, whereof all are partakers, then are ye bastards, and not sons" (Heb. 12:8). "Through much tribulation enter into the kingdom of God" (Acts 14:22). When Bishop Hugh Latimer was told by his landlord that he had never had a trouble, "then," said he, "God cannot be here."

Suffering is a part of the process by which the sons of God are sanctified. They are chastened to wean them from the world and make them partakers of God's holiness. The Captain of their salvation was made perfect through sufferings, and so are they. There never yet was a great saint who faced neither great afflictions or great corruptions. Well said Philip Melancthon, "Where there are no cares, there will generally be no prayers."

❖ From the sermon "Heirs of God"

Your Soul Is the Greatest Treasure You Have

The LORD shall preserve thee from all evil:
he shall preserve thy soul.
—PSALM 121:7

I ask every reader to realize the dignity and responsibility of having a soul. Yes, realize the fact that in your soul you have the greatest treasure which God has committed to your charge. Know that in your soul you have a pearl above all price, compared to which all earthly possessions are trifles light as air. The horse that wins the derby or the leger attracts the attention of thousands. Painters paint it and engravers engrave it and vast sums of money turn on its achievements. Yet the weakest infant in a working man's family is far more important in God's sight than that horse. The spirit of the animal goes downward, but that infant has an immortal soul.

You may be poor in this world, but you have a soul. You may be sickly and weak in body, but you have a soul. You may not be a king or a queen or a duke or an earl, yet you have a soul. The soul is the part of us that God chiefly regards. The soul is the man. The soul that is in man is the most important thing about him.

I do not stop to prove that men have souls, but I do ask all men to live as if they believed it. Live as if you really believed that we were not sent into the world merely to spin cotton and grow corn and hoard up gold but to "glorify God and to enjoy Him forever." Read your Bible and become acquainted with its contents. Seek the Lord in prayer and pour out your heart before Him. Go to a place of worship regularly and hear the gospel preached. And if any ask you the reason why, if wife, or child, or companion say, "What are you about?" answer them boldly, like a man, and say, "I do these things because I have a soul!"

✤ From the sermon "Our Souls"

What Shall It Profit?

For what shall it profit a man, if he shall gain the whole world,
and lose his own soul?
— MARK 8:36

It is a sad proof, beloved, of our evil and corrupt nature that our Lord Jesus Christ should have thought it necessary to use such language and to ask such a question. He was preaching to His own people, to the children of Abraham, Isaac, and Jacob, to the nation that for fifteen hundred years had alone enjoyed the privilege of knowing the true God. He was not instructing ignorant heathen, but Israelites to whom pertained the adoption and the glory and the covenant and the giving of the law and the service of God and the promises. And yet behold, He deals with them as if they had still to learn the first principles of religious knowledge: "For what shall it profit a man, if he shall gain the whole world, and lose his own soul?"

But it is far more sad, beloved, and far more deplorable, that at the present hour, eighteen hundred years after Jesus died for men, it should still be necessary for a minister of the gospel to urge upon you the very same words. Who, indeed, would have thought it possible that we should be obliged to remind you that the care of the soul is the one thing needful for all: for the rich, because of their temptations; for the poor, because of their trials; for the old, because death is close at hand; for the young, because life with all its intoxicating follies is before them. And they can never have a more convenient season to remind you that, although men have different abilities and fill different stations here on earth, they have one thing at least in common; they have all immortal souls, they must all give account of themselves at the day of judgment. And yet, "Hear, O heavens, and give ear, O earth" (Isa. 1:2) we are obliged to tell you, professing Christians, all this!

✤ From the sermon "Profit and Loss"

Would You Know the Secret?

The secret things belong unto the LORD our God: but those things which are revealed belong unto us and to our children for ever, that we may do all the words of this law. —DEUTERONOMY 29:29

Would you know the secret of the believer's boldness in prayer? It is a marvel how a man that feels his sin so deeply as the believer does can speak with the confidence the believer frequently does. How one that acknowledges he is "wretched, and miserable, and poor, and blind, and naked" (Rev. 3:17), ruined, undone, who often does what he ought not to do and leaves undone what he ought to do and finds no spiritual health in him, how such a one as this can go before God with confidence, pour out his heart before Him freely, ask from Him what he requires day after day and not feel afraid, this is wonderful indeed. What is the secret of it? It is the intercession of our Lord and Savior Jesus Christ, whereby the true Christian knows his prayers are made acceptable and received in the court of heaven.

Would you know the secret of comfort in looking forward to that heaven whereunto every believer desires to go? I believe there are few children of God who do not sometimes feel anxious, troubled, and cast down when they think quietly about the eternal habitation toward which they are traveling. The nature of it, the manner of it, the employments of it, their own apparent unfitness for it will sometimes perplex their minds. These thoughts will sometimes come across the believer's mind, especially in times of sickness, filling him with heaviness and making his heart sink. Now I know no remedy against these thoughts to be compared to the recollection of the continual intercession of the Lord and Savior Jesus Christ. Christ is gone into heaven to be the forerunner of a people who are to follow after Him. He is gone "to prepare a place" for them (John 14:2), and the place whereto He goes is the place whereto His people are to go by and by. When they go there, they will find all things made ready, a place for everyone, and a fitting and proper place, too, through the intercession of their Lord and Savior.

✥ From the sermon "Christ's Power to Save"

What Is Christ Doing Now?

But this man, after he had offered one sacrifice for sins for ever, sat down on the right hand of God; From henceforth expecting till his enemies be made his footstool. —HEBREWS 10:12–13

Reader, what is that special thing Christ is doing now? Give me your attention. This is no light and speculative matter. It lies near the foundation of all comfortable Christianity. Come and see. Christ is now carrying on in heaven the work of a priest that He began upon earth. He took our nature on Him in the fullness of time and became a man that He might be perfectly fitted to be the priest that our case required. As a priest He offered up His body and soul as a sacrifice for sin upon the cross and made a complete atonement for us with His own blood. As a priest He ascended up on high, passed within the veil, and entered into the presence of God. As a priest He is now sitting on our behalf at the right hand of God; and what He began actively on earth, He is carrying on actively in heaven. This is what Christ is doing.

How and in what manner does Christ now exercise His priestly office? This is a deep subject, and one about which it is easy to make rash statements. The action of one of the persons of the blessed Trinity in heaven is a high thing and surpasses man's understanding. The place whereon we stand is holy ground. The thing we are handling must be touched with reverence, like the ark of God. Nevertheless, there are some things about Christ's priestly office which even our weak eyes may boldly look at, and God has caused them to be written plainly for our learning. "The secret things belong unto the LORD our God: but those things which are revealed belong unto us and to our children for ever, that we may do all the words of this law" (Deut. 29:29).

✤ From the sermon "Do You Have a Priest?"

Our Hope!

For we are saved by hope: but hope that is seen is not hope: for what a man seeth, why doth he yet hope for? —ROMANS 8:24

"I hope" is a very common expression. Everybody can say, "I hope." About no subject is the expression used so commonly as it is about religion. Nothing is more common than to hear people turn off some home thrust at conscience by this convenient form of words "I hope." "I hope it will be all right at last." "I hope I shall be a better man someday." "I hope I shall get to heaven at last." But why do they hope? On what is their hope built? Too often they cannot tell you! Too often it is a mere excuse for avoiding a disagreeable subject. Hoping, they live on. Hoping, they grow old. Hoping, they die at last and find too often that they are lost forever in hell!

I ask the serious attention of all who read this. The subject is one of the deepest importance, "We are saved by hope" (Rom. 8:24). Let us, then, make sure that our hope is sound. Have we a hope that our sins are pardoned, our hearts renewed, and our souls at peace with God? Then let us see to it that our hope is good, and living, and one that makes not ashamed (see 2 Thess. 2:16; 1 Peter 1:3; Rom. 5:5). Let us consider our ways. Let us not shrink from honest, searching inquiry into the condition of our souls. If our hope is good, examination will do it no harm. If our hope is bad, it is high time to know it, and to seek a better one.

Christ Himself is the only true foundation of a good hope. "He is the Rock, his work is perfect" (Deut. 32:4). He is the stone, the sure stone, the tried cornerstone (Isa. 28:16). He is able to bear all the weight that we can lay upon Him. He only that builds and "believeth on him shall not be confounded" (1 Peter 2:6).

✤ From the sermon "Our Hope"

Rivers of Living Water Flowing Through You

He that believeth on me, as the scripture hath said, out of his belly shall flow rivers of living water.
—JOHN 7:38

I doubt if there will be a believer who will not have been to someone or other a river of living water, a channel through whom the Spirit has conveyed saving grace. Even the penitent thief, short as his time was after he repented, has been a source of blessing to thousands of souls. Some believers are "rivers of living water" while they live. Their words, their conversation, their preaching, their teaching are all means by which the water of life has flowed into the hearts of their fellow men. Such, for example, were the apostles, who wrote no epistles and preached only the word. Such were Luther and Whitefield and Wesley and Berridge and Rowlands, and thousands of others of whom I cannot now speak particularly.

Some believers are "rivers of living water" when they die. Their courage in facing the king of terrors, their boldness in the most painful sufferings, their unswerving faithfulness to Christ's truth even at the stake, their manifest peace on the edge of the grave, all this has set thousands thinking and led hundreds to repent and believe. Such, for example, were the primitive martyrs, whom the Roman emperors persecuted. Such were John Huss and Jerome of Prague. Such were Cranmer, Ridley, Latimer, Hooper, and the noble army of Marian martyrs. The work that they did at their deaths, like Samson, was far greater than the work done in their lives.

I charge every reader of this paper to lay hold on this view of our Lord's promise and never forget it. Think not for a moment that your own soul is the only soul that will be saved if you come to Christ by faith and follow Him. Think of the blessedness of being a river of living water to others. Who can tell that you may not be the means of bringing many others to Christ? Live and act and speak and pray and work, keeping this continually in view.

❖ From the sermon "Let Any Man Come"

Are You Alive in Christ?

For as in Adam all die, even so in Christ shall all be made alive.
—1 CORINTHIANS 15:22

Are you alive? Then see that you prove it by your actions. Be a consistent witness. Let your words and works and ways and tempers all tell the same story. Be an epistle of Christ so clearly written, penned in such large, bold characters, that he who runs may read it. Let your Christianity be so unmistakable, your eye so single, your heart so whole, your walk so straightforward that all who see you may have no doubt whose you are and whom you serve. If we are quickened by the Spirit, no one ought to be able to doubt it. Our conversation should declare plainly that we "seek a country" (Heb. 11:14). It ought not to be necessary to tell people, as in the case of a badly painted picture, "This is a Christian." We ought not to be so sluggish and still that people shall be obliged to come close and look hard and say, "Is he dead or alive?"

Are you alive? Then see that you prove it by your growth. Let the great change within become every year more evident. Let your light be an increasing light. Let the image of your Lord, wherein you are renewed, grow clearer and sharper every month. Let it not be like the image and superscription on a coin, more indistinct and defaced the longer it is used. Let it rather become more plain the older it is and let the likeness of your King stand out more fully and sharply.

Awake to know your privileges, awake and sleep no longer. Tell me not of spiritual hunger and thirst and poverty so long as the throne of grace is before you. Say, rather, that you are proud and will not come to it as poor sinners. Say, rather, you are slothful and will not take pains to get more. While we live, may we live unto the Lord. When we die, may we die the death of the righteous. And when the Lord Jesus comes, may we be found ready and "not be ashamed before him at his coming" (1 John 2:28).

✢ From the sermon "Alive or Dead"

The Key to Happiness

In the last day, that great day of the feast, Jesus stood and cried, saying, If any man thirst, let him come unto me, and drink.
—JOHN 7:37

The keys of the way to happiness are in the hands of the Lord Jesus Christ. He is sealed and appointed by God the Father to give the bread of life to those who hunger and to give the water of life to those who thirst. The door that riches and rank and learning have so often tried to open, and tried in vain, is now ready to open to every humble, praying believer. Oh, if you want to be happy, come to Christ! Come to Him, confessing that you are weary of your own ways and want rest; that you find you have no power and might to make yourself holy or happy or fit for heaven; and have no hope but in Him. Tell Him this unreservedly. This is coming to Christ.

Come to Him, imploring Him to show you His mercy and grant you His salvation, to wash you in His own atoning blood and take your sins away, to speak peace to your conscience and heal your troubled soul. Tell Him all this unreservedly. This is coming to Christ. You have everything to encourage you. The Lord Jesus Himself invites you. He proclaims to you as well as to others, "Come unto me, all ye that labour and are heavy laden, and I will give you rest. Take my yoke upon you, and learn of me; for I am meek and lowly in heart: and ye shall find rest unto your souls. For my yoke is easy, and my burden is light" (Matt. 11:28–30). Wait for nothing. You may feel unworthy. You may feel as if you did not repent enough. But wait no longer. Come to Christ!

✤ From the sermon "Happiness"

Our Particular Besetting Sins

The night is far spent, the day is at hand: let us therefore cast off the works of darkness, and let us put on the armour of light.
—ROMANS 13:12

There are particular besetting sins of which each separate Christian can alone furnish an account. Each single one of us has some weak point; each one has got a thin, weak spot in his wall of defense against the devil; each one has a traitor in his camp ready to open the gates to Satan, and he who is wise will never rest until he has discovered where this weak point is.

This is that special sin that you are here exhorted to watch against, to overcome, to cast forth, to spare no means in bringing it into subjection, that it may not entangle you in your race toward Zion. One man is beset with lust, another with a love of drinking, another with evil temper, another with malice, another with covetousness, another with worldly-mindedness, another with idleness, but each of us has got about him some besetting infirmity that is able to hinder him far more than others and with which he must keep an unceasing warfare, or else he will never so run as to obtain the prize.

Oh, these bitter besetting sins! How many have fallen in their full course and given occasion to God's enemies to blaspheme from thinking lightly of them, from not continually guarding against them, from a vain notion that they were altogether cut off! They have been overconfident and presumptuous. But what was the simple cause? They disregarded some besetting sin. Go, child of God, and search the chambers of your heart! See whether you can find there some seed of evil, some darling thing that you have tenderly spared hitherto because it was a little one. Away with it! There must be no mercy, no compromise, no reserve! It must be laid aside, plucked up, torn up by the roots, or it will one day trip you up and prevent you running your race toward Zion. The gates of heaven are broad enough to receive the worst of sinners but too narrow to admit the smallest grain of unforsaken sin!

❖ From the sermon "The Christian Race"

Hearing Christ's Voice

My sheep hear my voice, and I know them, and they follow me.
—JOHN 10:27

This hearing of Christ's voice, what is it? It cannot be the mere hearing of the ears, for many do that who die in their sins. It must be the hearing with the heart, the listening with attention, the believing what is heard, the acting manfully on what is believed. And where may Christ's voice be heard? It sometimes whispers in a sinner's conscience, saying, "Oh, do not these abominable things: turn, turn, why will you die?" It sometimes speaks solemnly in a visitation of providence, as a sickness or an accident or an affliction or a death, saying slowly but clearly, "Stop and think; consider your ways. Are you ready to die and be judged?" But it generally is to be heard in the reading of Scripture or the preaching of the gospel; then the voice of the Lord Jesus may be heard plain and distinct. One day it is sharp and piercing: "Except you repent, you shall all likewise perish." "You must be born again." "Awake, you who sleep, and arise from the dead." Another day it is gentle, winning, entreating: "Come unto me, O weary and heavy-laden one, and I will give you rest." "If any man thirsts, let him come unto Me and drink." "Whoever will, let him take the water of life freely." In all these ways and manners the voice of Jesus may be heard.

And here comes the distinction between the converted and the unconverted. Those who are converted hear Christ's voice, but they that are unconverted hear it not. The true sheep of Christ were once foolish and disobedient, serving divers lusts and pleasures, dead in trespasses and sins, but they heard their Redeemer's voice at last, and when they heard they lived. They knew not at first who called them, but they heard a voice they could not disobey, and now they can tell you they are sure it was the Lord's. They heard His voice, they listened to His invitation, they believed His promises, they confessed themselves sinners, and in Him they found peace.

✢ From the sermon "The Character of the True Christian"

Practical Holiness

Having therefore these promises, dearly beloved, let us cleanse our-
selves from all filthiness of the flesh and spirit, perfecting holiness in
the fear of God. —2 CORINTHIANS 7:1

I have had a deep conviction for many years that practical holiness and
entire self-consecration to God are not sufficiently attended to by modern Christians in this country. Politics or controversy or party spirit or
worldliness have eaten out the heart of lively piety in too many of us.
The subject of personal godliness has fallen sadly into the background.
The standard of living has become painfully low in many quarters. The
immense importance of "adorn[ing] the doctrine of God our Saviour"
(Titus 2:10) and making it lovely and beautiful by our daily habits and
tempers has been far too much overlooked. Worldly people sometimes
complain with reason that religious persons, so called, are not as ami-
able and unselfish and good-natured as others who make no profession
of religion. Yet sanctification, in its place and proportion, is quite as
important as justification. Sound Protestant and evangelical doctrine is
useless if it is not accompanied by a holy life. It is worse than useless; it
does positive harm. It is despised by keen-sighted and shrewd men of the
world as an unreal and hollow thing and brings religion into contempt.

It is, however, of great importance that the whole subject should
be placed on right foundations and that the movement about it should
not be damaged by crude, disproportioned, and one-sided statements.
If such statements abound, we must not be surprised. Satan knows well
the power of true holiness, and the immense injury that increased attention to it will do to his kingdom. It is his interest, therefore, to promote
strife and controversy about this part of God's truth. Just as in time
past he has succeeded in mystifying and confusing men's minds about
justification, so he is laboring in the present day to make men "darken
counsel by words without knowledge" about sanctification. May the
Lord rebuke him!

❖ From the book *Holiness*

Are You Looking unto Jesus?

Looking unto Jesus the author and finisher of our faith; who for the joy that was set before him endured the cross, despising the shame, and is set down at the right hand of the throne of God.
—HEBREWS 12:2

The question that heads this page may seem an odd one at first sight. To whom or to what does it apply? The words of Paul, below it, supply the key to its meaning. It is an inquiry concerning your soul and the Lord Jesus Christ. It means neither more nor less than this: "Are you looking unto Jesus?"

"Looking unto Jesus" is a very simple expression. It is soon spoken and soon written; it contains no words hard to be understood. But it is an expression rich in contents and filled to the brim with food for thought. Here is a brief account of the Christian's character: he is one who looks to Jesus. Here is the secret of running successfully the race that leads toward heaven: we must be ever looking to Jesus. Here is the photograph of patriarchs and prophets, of apostles and martyrs, of holy fathers and holy reformers, of holy saints in every land and age; they were all men who looked to Jesus. Here is the marrow of all creeds and articles and confessions of guilt: to look to Jesus. Reader, if you and I wish to be saved, let us begin by asking ourselves the simple question, Am I looking to Jesus?

Reader, there is but one answer to this question. You must look to Jesus by faith. True believing with the heart is the looking of which Paul makes mention to the Hebrew Christians. Faith is the eye of the Christian's soul. As Moses lifted up the brazen serpent in the wilderness and the suffering Israelite who looked at it was immediately healed, so must you look at Jesus Christ with trust, confidence, reliance, and expectation. This is what Paul meant when he talked of "looking unto Jesus"!

✤ From the sermon "Are You Looking?"

Yet a Little While

For I reckon that the sufferings of this present time are not worthy to be compared with the glory which shall be revealed in us.
—ROMANS 8:18

Yet a little while, and believers shall part forever with sickness and disease! The sick and wearied ones who have mourned over their seeming uselessness to the church; the weak and infirm who have had the will to labor but not the power; the feeble and bedridden who have waited long-drawn years in quiet chambers until their eyes know every crack and speck on their walls—all, all shall be set free! They shall each have a glorious body like their Lord's. Yet a little while, and mourning believers shall part forever with their tears! Every wound in their heart shall be completely healed. They shall find that those who have died in the Lord were not lost but gone before. They shall see that infinite wisdom arranged every bereavement by which one was taken and another left. They shall magnify the Lord together with those who were once their companions in tribulation and acknowledge that He did all things well and led them by a right way!

Yet a little while, and believers shall no more feel that they are alone. They shall no longer be scattered over the earth, a few in one place and a few in another. They shall no longer lament that they see so few to speak to, as a man speaks with his friend; so few who are of one mind and travel with them in the one narrow way. They shall be united to the general assembly and church of the firstborn. They shall join the blessed company of all the believers of every name and people and tongue! They shall see a multitude of saints that none can number, with not one wicked person among them! Yet a little while, and working believers shall find that their labor was not in vain. The ministers who have preached and seemed to reap no fruit, the missionaries who testified of the gospel and none seemed to believe, the teachers who poured into children's minds line upon line and none seemed to attend—all, all shall discover that they have not spent their strength for nothing! They shall find that the seed sown can spring up after many days, and that sooner or later in all labor there is profit!

❖ From the sermon "Coming Events and Present Duties"

Guard against Deception

But I fear, lest by any means, as the serpent beguiled Eve through his subtilty, so your minds should be corrupted from the simplicity that is in Christ.
—2 CORINTHIANS 11:3

I charge every loyal member of the church to open his eyes to the peril in which his own church stands, and to beware lest it is damaged through apathy and a morbid love of peace. Controversy is an odious thing, but there are days when it is a positive element. Peace is an excellent thing, but, like gold, it may be gotten too dear. Unity is a mighty blessing, but it is worthless if it is purchased at the cost of truth. Once more I say, open your eyes and be on your guard!

I denounce, from the bottom of my heart, despondency or coward-ice at this crisis. All I say is, let us exercise a godly fear. I do not see the slightest necessity for forsaking the old ship and giving it up for lost. Bad as things look inside our ark, they are not one bit better outside. But I do protest against that careless spirit of slumber which seems to seal the eyes of many Christians and to blind them to the enormous peril in which we are placed by the rise and progress of false doctrine in these days. I protest against the common notion so often proclaimed by men in high places, that unity is of more importance than sound doctrine, and peace more valuable than truth. I call on every reader who really loves the church to recognize the dangers of the times and to do his duty, courageously and energetically, in resisting them by united action and by prayer. Let us not forget Paul's words, "Watch ye, stand fast in the faith, quit you like men, be strong" (1 Cor. 16:13). Our noble Reformers bought the truth at the price of their own blood and handed it down to us. Let us be careful that we do not cheaply sell it for some bread and stew, under the seeming names of unity and peace.

✣ From the sermon "Apostolic Fears"

Are You Overcoming the World?

Ye are of God, little children, and have overcome them: because greater is he that is in you, than he that is in the world.
—1 JOHN 4:4

My first word shall be a question. Are you overcoming the world, or are you overcome by it? Do you know what it is to come out from the world and be separate, or are you yet entangled by it and conformed to it? If you have any desire to be saved, I entreat you to answer this question.

If you know nothing of separation, I warn you affectionately that your soul is in great danger. The world passes away; and those who cling to the world, and think only of the world, will pass away with it to everlasting ruin! Awake to know your peril before it be too late. Awake and flee from the wrath to come. The time is short. The end of all things is at hand. The shadows are lengthening. The sun is going down. The night comes when no man can work. The great white throne will soon be set. The judgment will begin. The books will be opened. Awake, and come out from the world while it is called today!

Yet a little while, and there will be no more worldly occupations and worldly amusements, no more getting money and spending money, no more eating and drinking and feasting and dressing and ball going and theaters and races and cards and gambling. What will you do when all these things have passed away forever? How can you possibly be happy in an eternal heaven, where holiness is all in all and worldliness has no place? Oh, consider these things and be wise! Awake, and break the chains that the world has thrown around you! Awake, and flee from the wrath to come!

❖ From the sermon "The World"

Experimental Knowledge of Jesus Christ

Nevertheless I have somewhat against thee, because thou hast left thy first love. Remember therefore from whence thou art fallen, and repent, and do the first works; or else I will come unto thee quickly, and will remove thy candlestick out of his place, except thou repent.
—REVELATION 2:4–5

If we want to grow in grace and have more hope, we must seek a more experimental knowledge of our Lord Jesus Christ. How little do we know of Him! Our cold affections toward Him are a witness against ourselves. If our eyes were more open to what He is and does for us, we would love Him more. There are some Christians whose minds seem ever running on the doctrine of sanctification to the exclusion of everything else. They can argue warmly about little points of practice; yet they are cold about Christ. They live by rule, they walk strictly, they do many things, they fancy in a short time they shall be very strong. But all this time they lose sight of this grand truth that nothing is so sanctifying as knowledge of the Lord Jesus and communion with Him. "Abide in me," He says Himself, "and I in you. As the branch cannot bear fruit of itself, except it abide in the vine; no more can ye, except ye abide in me" (John 15:4). Christ must be the spring of our holiness as well as the rock of our faith. Christ must be all in all.

I doubt not He is precious to you that believe. Precious He ought to be because of His offices, and precious because of His work. Precious He ought to be for what He has done already. He has called us, quickened us, washed us, justified us. Precious He ought to be for what He is doing even now: strengthening us, interceding for us, sympathizing with us.

Precious He ought to be for what He will do yet: He will keep us to the end, raise us, gather us at His coming, present us faultless before God's throne, give us rest with Him in His kingdom. But oh, reader, Christ ought to be far more precious to us than He ever has been yet! Nothing else will either save, satisfy, or sanctify a sinful soul. We all need a more experimental knowledge of Christ!

❖ From the sermon "Where Are You?"

Chief Privilege of a True Christian

Therefore being justified by faith, we have peace with God through our Lord Jesus Christ.
                                        —ROMANS 5:1

When the apostle Paul wrote his epistle to the Romans, he used five words which the wisest of the heathen could never have used. Socrates and Plato and Aristotle and Cicero and Seneca were wise people. On many subjects they saw more clearly than most people in the present day. They were people of mighty minds and of a vast range of intellect. But not one of them could have said as the apostle did, "[I] have peace with God" (Rom. 5:1).

When Paul used these words, he spoke not for himself only, but for all true Christians. Some of them no doubt have a greater sense of this privilege than others. All of them find an evil principle within, warring against their spiritual welfare day by day. All of them find their adversary, the devil, waging an endless battle with their souls. All of them find that they must endure the enmity of the world. But all, notwithstanding, to a greater or less extent "have peace with God." This peace with God is a calm, intelligent sense of friendship with the Lord of heaven and earth. He who has it feels as if there was no barrier and separation between himself and his holy maker. He can think of himself as under the eye of an all-seeing being and yet not feel afraid. He can believe that this all-seeing being beholds him and yet is not displeased.

If you don't have this peace with God, you are truly poor. You have nothing that will last, nothing that will wear, nothing that you can carry with you when your turn comes to die. Naked you came into this world, and naked in every sense you will go forth. Your body may be carried to the grave with pomp and ceremony. A solemn service may be read over your coffin. A marble monument may be put up in your honor. But after all, it will be but a pauper's funeral if you die without peace with God.

❖ From the sermon "Justification"

The High Calling

Brethren, I count not myself to have apprehended: but this one thing I do, forgetting those things which are behind, and reaching forth unto those things which are before, I press toward the mark for the prize of the high calling of God in Christ Jesus.

—PHILIPPIANS 3:13–14

I beseech you to cleave to the Lord with all your heart and to press toward the mark for the prize of your high calling. I can well conceive that you find your way very narrow. There are few with you and many against you. Your lot in life may seem hard, and your position may be difficult. But still cleave to the Lord, and He will never forsake you. Cleave to the Lord in the midst of persecution. Cleave to the Lord though men laugh at you and mock you and try to make you ashamed. Cleave to the Lord though the cross be heavy and the fight be hard. He was not ashamed of you upon the cross of Calvary; then do not be ashamed of Him upon earth, lest He should be ashamed of you before His Father who is in heaven. Cleave to the Lord, and He will never forsake you. In this world there are plenty of disappointments, in properties and families and houses and lands and situations. But no man ever yet was disappointed in Christ. No man ever failed to find Christ all that the Bible says He is, and a thousand times better than He had been told before!

Look forward—look onward and forward to the end! Your best things are yet to come.

Time is short. The end is drawing near. The latter days of the world are upon us. Fight the good fight. Labor on. Work on. Strive on. Pray on. Read on. Labor hard for your own soul's prosperity. Labor hard for the prosperity of the souls of others. Strive to bring a few more with you to heaven, and by all means to save some. Do something, by God's help, to make heaven more full and hell more empty.

❖ From the sermon "Our Souls"

Biblical Examples of Patience

Let us run with patience the race that is set before us. —HEBREWS 12:1

Look at Moses in Hebrews 11:24–26: "By faith Moses, when he was come to years, refused to be called the son of Pharaoh's daughter; choosing rather to suffer affliction with the people of God, than to enjoy the pleasures of sin for a season; esteeming the reproach of Christ greater riches than the treasures in Egypt: for he had respect unto the recompence of the reward."

Look at Job, when God permitted Satan to afflict him: "Naked," he says, "came I out of my mother's womb, and naked shall I return thither: the LORD gave, and the LORD hath taken away; blessed be the name of the LORD" (Job 1:21). "What? Shall we receive good at the hand of God, and shall we not receive evil?" (Job 2:10).

Look at David, the man after God's own heart. How many waves of trouble passed over that honored head; how many years he fled from the hand of Saul, how much tribulation did he suffer from his own family. Mark too, as you read his psalms, how often you come on that expression "waiting upon God." It seems as if he thought it the highest grace a Christian can attain to.

Look last at your blessed Lord Himself. Peter says, "For even hereunto were ye called: because Christ also suffered for us, leaving us an example, that ye should follow his steps: who did no sin, neither was guile found in his mouth: who, when he was reviled, reviled not again; when he suffered, he threatened not; but committed himself to him that judgeth righteously" (1 Peter 2:21–23). Paul says, "For consider him that endured such contradiction of sinners against himself, lest ye be wearied and faint in your minds. Ye have not yet resisted unto blood, striving against sin. And ye have forgotten the exhortation which speaketh unto you as unto children, My son, despise not thou the chastening of the Lord, nor faint when thou art rebuked of him: for whom the Lord loveth he chasteneth, and scourgeth every son whom he receiveth" (Heb. 12:3–6).

O yes, beloved, we must run with patience, or we shall never obtain. Today is the cross, but tomorrow is the crown. Today is the battle, but tomorrow is the rest. Be patient and hope unto the end!

✣ From the sermon "The Christian Race"

Sorrowful Warnings

Look to yourselves, that we lose not those things which we have wrought, but that we receive a full reward. — 2 JOHN 1:8

I have a word of sorrowful warning for some into whose hands these pages will fall. Some of you know in your own hearts and consciences— though I could say it weeping—you know well that you are not walking with God. You, to whom I now speak, know well that God's ways are not your ways, that although you profess and call yourselves Christians, your hearts are not right in His sight. You have no heartfelt hatred for sin. You have no heartfelt love for God's commandments. You have no delight in God's Word. You have no pleasure in the company of His people. His day is a weariness to you. His service is a burden. His ordinances are not precious to your soul. Your first and best thoughts are given to the life that now is; you spend but the wreck and remnant of them on the life to come. Your treasure is on earth and not in heaven. Your affections are set on things below and not on things above. Your friendship is with the world and not with God. Will the world give comfort in death? No! But Jesus will. Can the world help you in the day of judgment? No! No! None can help you then but Christ!

The world you think so much of now passes away. He only who does the will of God abides forever. But God, our Savior, still loves you. God is not willing that anyone should perish. He sends you by my mouth a message of peace this day. Turn from the broad way and come unto Christ while there is yet time. Turn before the fountain is sealed, now open for sin and uncleanness, before the Father's house is closed forever and not one more allowed to enter, before the Spirit and the Bride cease to invite. Be wise, repent, return, and come.

Reader, you cannot prevent my grieving over you, although you may be at ease yourself. God is my witness, this day I have given you a warning!

✣ From the sermon "The Lord Our Righteousness"

Surely It Is Night!

The night is far spent, the day is at hand: let us therefore cast off the works of darkness, and let us put on the armour of light.
—ROMANS 13:12

Let us consider the present condition of the world. The apostle Paul calls it "night." "The night," he says, "is far spent." I have no doubt that word seems strange to some people. They think it surprising that our present time should be called night. They are living in days of learning, science, civilization, commerce, freedom, and knowledge. They see around them things that their forefathers never dreamed of—railways, manufacturing plants, gas, electricity, steam engines, education for all, and inexpensive books. I know it all and am thankful for it.

Nevertheless, I say that in the things of God, the world is still in a state of night. I believe that God looks down on this globe of ours as it rolls round the sun, and as He looks upon it, He pronounces it very dark! I believe that the angels go to and fro and make report of all they see on our earth, and their constant report is, "Very dark!" And I am sure that believers in the Lord Jesus in every land are of one mind on this subject. They cry and sigh because of the abominations they see around them. To them the world appears very dark!

Is it not dark in many professedly Christian countries? There are two-thirds of all the professing Christians on earth who are unsound in the faith. Their religion simply is not scriptural. They have added to it many things which are not to be found in the Bible. They have left out of it many things which the Bible has plainly commanded. Is there not much darkness under the eyes of every true believer? Go to the most godly, quiet, and orderly parish in our land at this moment. Ask any well-informed child of God residing in it how many true Christians it contains, and what is the proportion of the converted to the unconverted. Mark well the answer he will give. I doubt if you will find a parish in Great Britain where one-third of the people are converted! And if such be the report of parishes that are like the green tree, what must be the state of things in the dry? Surely it is night!

✣ From the sermon "Coming Events and Present Duties"

Rest for Your Souls

Thus saith the LORD, Stand ye in the ways, and see, and ask for the old paths, where is the good way, and walk therein, and ye shall find rest for your souls. But they said, We will not walk therein.
—JEREMIAH 6:16

"Walk in the old paths," says the Lord, "and ye shall find rest for your souls." I cannot doubt that our Lord Jesus Christ had these words of the prophet in His mind when He proclaimed that glorious invitation that is so wisely quoted in our Communion service, "Come unto me, all ye that labour and are heavy laden, and I will give you rest" (Matt. 11:28). One thing, at any rate, is quite certain. Whether under the Old Testament or the New, nothing could be held out to man more suitable to his spiritual needs than rest. Walk in the "old paths," is the promise, and you shall have "rest."

Let it never, never be forgotten that rest of conscience is the secret need of a vast portion of mankind. Sin and the sense of guilt are the root of all the heart weariness in the world. Men are not at ease because they are not at peace with God. Men often feel their sinfulness, though they know not what the feeling really means. They only know there is something wrong within, but they do not understand the cause. "Who will show us any good?" is the universal cry. But there is universal ignorance of the disease from which the cry springs. The laboring and heavy laden are everywhere. They are a multitude that man can scarcely number; they are to be found in every climate and in every country under the sun.

Now, rest for the laboring and heavy laden is one of the chief promises that the Word of God offers to man, both in the Old Testament and the New. "Come to me," says the world, "and I will give you riches and pleasure." "Come with me," says the devil, "and I will give you greatness, power, and wisdom." "Come unto Me," says the Lord Jesus Christ, "and I will give you rest." "Walk in the old paths," says the prophet Jeremiah, "and you shall find rest for your souls."

✣ From the sermon "The Good Way"

God's Gift to the World

In this was manifested the love of God toward us, because that God sent his only begotten Son into the world, that we might live through him.
—1 JOHN 4:9

The way the truth before us is stated by our Lord Jesus Christ demands special attention. It would be well for many who talk big, swelling words about the love of God in the present day if they would mark the way in which the Lord Jesus sets it before us. The love of God toward the world is not a vague, abstract idea of mercy that we are obliged to take on trust without any proof that it is true. It is a love that has been manifested by a mighty gift. It is a love that has been put before us in a plain, unmistakable, tangible form.

God the Father was not content to sit in heaven, idly pitying His fallen creatures on earth. He has given the mightiest evidence of His love toward us by a gift of unspeakable value. He has "spared not his own Son, but delivered him up for us all, how shall he not with him also freely give us all things?" (Rom. 8:32). He has so loved us that He has given us Christ! A higher proof of the Father's love could not have been given.

Who can estimate the value of God's gift when He gave to the world His only begotten Son? It is something unspeakable and incomprehensible! It passes human understanding.

There are two that we have no arithmetic to compute and no line to measure. He gave us One who was nothing less than His own fellow, fully and truly God, His only begotten Son! He who thinks lightly of man's need and man's sin would do well to consider man's Savior! Sin must indeed be exceeding sinful when the Father must need give His only Son to be the sinner's friend and Savior!

❖ From the sermon "Do You Believe?"

Are You a Vile Sinner before God?

When Jesus heard it, he saith unto them, They that are whole have no need of the physician, but they that are sick: I came not to call the righteous, but sinners to repentance.
—MARK 2:17

You tell me you have been a vile sinner before God. I answer that the blood of Christ cleanses from all sin. You tell me you have broken God's laws a million times. I answer that Christ is the end of the law for righteousness to everyone who believes. You tell me you have no righteousness, you will never be fit for heaven; I offer you the perfect righteousness of the Lord Jesus Himself. All that He has done shall be accounted yours. I repeat, the complete righteousness of the Lord Jesus shall be placed upon you as a pure white garment that shall cover all your iniquities, and who shall dare to raise his voice against you? But you tell me you have such a cold, dead, wicked heart. I answer, if you come at once unto the Lord Jesus, He shall pour the Holy Spirit upon you and give you a new one, and you shall become a new creature.

This very day I set before the worst among you pardon and peace and immortality, without money and without price. I do not tell you to go and become saints, to go and live a new life before you can receive these blessings. I call upon you to return at once with all your sins upon you, and lay them at your Savior's feet and they shall be forgiven. I know nothing of conditions; I am not sent to one and not to another. Return unto Jesus all you that are far off, old or young, high or low, rich or poor, whether you be now sleeping in utter carelessness; whether you be godless blasphemers of the truth; whether you be talking, self-deceiving hypocrites; whether you be self-righteous, formal Pharisees; whether you be cold, heartless listeners to truth; whether you be wretched backsliders from the narrow way, return unto Jesus, I beseech you, for He has redeemed you.

✧ From the sermon "The Grace of God in Vain"

Exhortation

And whatsoever ye do in word or deed, do all in the name of the Lord Jesus, giving thanks to God and the Father by him.
—COLOSSIANS 3:17

Live a holy life, my brethren. Walk worthy of the church to which you belong. Live like citizens of heaven. Let your light shine before men, so that the world may profit by your conduct. Let them know whose you are and whom you serve. Be epistles of Christ, known and read by all men; written in such clear letters that none can say, "We do not know whether he is a member of Christ or not." Live a courageous life, my brethren. Confess Christ before men.

Whatever station you occupy, in that station confess Christ. Why should you be ashamed of Him? He was not ashamed of you on the cross. He is ready to confess you now before His Father in heaven. Be bold. Be very bold. The good soldier is not ashamed of his uniform. The true believer ought never to be ashamed of Christ.

Live a joyful life, my brethren. Live like men who look for that blessed hope, the second coming of Jesus Christ. This is the prospect to which we should all look forward. It is not so much the thought of going to heaven as of heaven coming to us that should fill our minds. There is a good time coming for all the people of God, a good time for all the church of Christ, a good time for all believers. But there is a bad time coming for the impenitent and unbelieving, a bad time for those who serve their own lusts and turn their backs on the Lord, but a good time for true Christians. For that good time, let us wait and watch and pray. The scaffolding will soon be taken down, the last stone will soon be brought out, the topstone will be placed upon the edifice. In a little while, the full beauty of the building shall be clearly seen. The great master builder will soon come Himself. A building shall be shown to assembled worlds in which there shall be no imperfection. The Savior and the saved shall rejoice together. The whole universe shall acknowledge that in the building of Christ's church, all was well done!

❖ From the sermon "The True Church"

Thoughts on the Holy Spirit

And because ye are sons, God hath sent forth the Spirit of his Son into your hearts, crying, Abba, Father. —GALATIANS 4:6

For one thing, be thankful for the Spirit. Who has made you to differ? Whence came all these feelings in your heart that thousands around you know not and you yourself knew not at one time? To what do you owe that sense of sin and that drawing toward Christ and that hunger and thirst after righteousness and that taste for the Bible and prayer that, with all your doubts and infirmities, you find within your soul? Did these things come of nature? Oh no! Did you learn these things in the schools of this world? Oh no, no! They are all of grace. Grace sowed them, grace watered them, grace began them, grace has kept them up. Learn to be more thankful. Praise God more every day you live, praise Him more in private, praise Him more in public, praise Him in your own family, praise Him above all in your own heart. This is the way to be in tune for heaven. The anthem there will be, "What has God wrought?"

For another thing, be filled with the Spirit. Seek to be more and more under His blessed influence. Strive to have every thought and word and action and habit brought under obedience to the leadings of the Holy Spirit. Grieve Him not by inconsistencies and conformity to the world. Quench Him not by trifling with little infirmities and small besetting sins. Seek rather to have Him ruling and reigning more completely over you every week that you live. Pray that you may yearly grow in grace and in the knowledge of Christ. This is the way to do good to the world. An eminent Christian is a lighthouse, seen far and wide by others and doing good to myriads whom he never knows. This is the way to enjoy much inward comfort in this world, to have bright assurance in death, to leave broad evidence behind us, and at last to receive a great crown!

✤ From the sermon "Having the Spirit"

One Blood

And hath made of one blood all nations of men for to dwell on all the face of the earth, and hath determined the times before appointed, and the bounds of their habitation. —ACTS 17:26

We are all "made of one blood." Then the Bible account of the origin of man is true. The book of Genesis is right. The whole family of mankind, with all its thousand millions, has descended from one pair, from Adam and Eve. This is a humbling fact, no doubt, but it is true. Kings and their subjects, rich and poor, learned and unlearned, prince and pauper, the educated Englishman and the untutored African, the fashionable lady of London and the North American squaw—all, all might trace their pedigree, if they could trace it through sixty centuries, to one man and one woman. No doubt in the vast period of six thousand years, immense varieties of ethnicity have gradually been developed. Hot climates and cold climates have affected the color and physical peculiarities of nations. Civilization and culture have produced their effect on the habits, demeanor, and mental attainments of the inhabitants of different parts of the globe. The story written by Moses is true. All the dwellers in Europe, Asia, Africa, and America originally sprang from Adam and Eve. We were all "made of one blood."

Of "one blood" we were all born. In "one blood" we all need to be washed. To all partakers of Adam's "one blood" we are bound, if we love life, to be charitable, sympathizing, loving, and kind. The time is short. We are going, going, and shall soon be gone to a world where there is no evil to remedy and no scope for works of mercy. Then for Christ's sake, let us all try to do some good before we die and to lessen the sorrows of this sin-burdened world.

✣ From the sermon "One Blood"

God Is Always Watching

Can any hide himself in secret places that I shall not see him? saith the LORD. Do not I fill heaven and earth? saith the LORD.
—JEREMIAH 23:24

However hard it is to comprehend this doctrine, it is one that is most useful and wholesome for our souls. To keep continually in mind that God is always present with us; to live always as in God's sight; to act and speak and think as always under His eye—all this is eminently calculated to have a good effect upon our souls. Here are three thoughts:

1. The thought of God's presence is a loud call to humility. How much that is evil and defective must the all-seeing eye see in every one of us! How small a part of our character is really known by man! "For man looketh on the outward appearance, but the LORD looketh on the heart" (1 Sam. 16:7). Man does not always see us, but the Lord is always looking at us, morning, noon, and night!

2. The thought of God's presence is a check and curb on the inclination to sin. The recollection that there is One who is always near us and observing us, who will one day have a reckoning with all mankind, may well keep us back from evil! Happy are those sons and daughters, who, when they leave the family home and launch forth into the world, carry with them the abiding remembrance of God's eye.

3. The thought of God's presence is a spur to the pursuit of true holiness. The highest standard of sanctification is to walk with God as Enoch did, and to walk before God as Abraham did. Where is the man who would not strive to live to please God if he realized that God was always standing at his elbow! To get away from God is the secret aim of the sinner. To get nearer to God is the longing desire of the saint. The real servants of the Lord are "a people near unto him" (Ps. 148:14)!

❖ From the sermon "The Real Presence"

Gather His Wheat

Whose fan is in his hand, and he will throughly purge his floor, and gather his wheat into the garner; but he will burn up the chaff with unquenchable fire.
                                                            —MATTHEW 3:12

When the Lord Jesus comes the second time, He shall collect His believing people into a place of safety. He will send His angels and gather them from every quarter. The sea shall give up the dead that are in it and the graves the dead that are in them, and the living shall be changed. Not one poor sinner of mankind who has ever laid hold on Christ by faith shall be overlooked in that company. Not one single grain of wheat shall be missing and left outside when judgments fall upon a wicked world. There shall be a barn for the wheat of the earth, and into that barn all the wheat shall be brought.

Ah, reader, it is a sweet and comfortable thought that "the Lord cares for the righteous." But how much the Lord cares for them, I fear, is little known and dimly seen. They have their trials, beyond question, and these both many and great. The flesh is weak. The world is full of snares. The cross is heavy. The way is narrow. The companions are few. But still they have strong consolations if their eyes were but open to see them. Like Hagar, they have a well of water near them, even in the wilderness, though they often do not find it out. Like Mary, they have Jesus standing by their side, though often they are not aware of it for very tears. Take comfort, I say once more, if you have really come to Christ. Take comfort and know your privileges. Cast every care on Jesus. Tell every need to Jesus. Roll every burden on Jesus, your sins, unbelief, doubts, fears, anxieties—lay them all on Christ! He loves to see you doing so. He loves to be employed as your high priest. He loves to be trusted. He loves to see His people ceasing from the vain effort to carry their burdens for themselves.

✤ From the sermon "The Great Separation"

No Home Like Christ!

For we know that if our earthly house of this tabernacle were dissolved, we have a building of God, an house not made with hands, eternal in the heavens. —2 CORINTHIANS 5:1

I will show you what Christ is, even in this life, to true Christians. Heaven, beyond doubt, is the final home in which a true Christian will dwell at last. Toward that he is daily traveling, nearer to that he is daily coming. Body and soul united once more, renewed, beautified, and perfected, will live forever in the Father's great house in heaven. To that home we have not yet come. We are not yet in heaven. But is there meanwhile no home for our souls? Is there no spiritual dwelling place to which we may continually repair in this desolate world and, repairing to it, find rest and peace? Thank God there is no difficulty in finding an answer to that question. There is a home provided for all laboring and heavy-laden souls, and that home is Christ.

In the midst of a dying, changing, disappointing world, a true Christian has always something which no power on earth can take away. Morning, noon, and night, he has near him a living refuge, a living home for his soul. You may rob him of life and liberty and money; you may take from him health and lands and house and friends. But, do what you will, you cannot rob him of his home. Like those humblest of God's creatures that carry their shells on their backs, wherever they are, so the Christian, wherever he goes, carries his home!

No home like Christ! In Him there is room for all and room for all sorts. None are unwelcome guests and visitors, and none are refused admission. The door is always open and never bolted. The best robe, the fatted calf, the ring, the shoes, are always ready for all comers! No home like Christ! In Him there is boundless and unwearied mercy for all, even after admission. None are rejected and cast forth again after probation because they are too weak and bad to stay! No home like Christ! Communion once begun with Him shall never be broken off. Once joined to the Lord by faith, you are joined to Him for an endless eternity!

✣ From the sermon "Our Home"

Neglect of Prayer Leads to Backsliding

*Watch and pray, that ye enter not into temptation: the spirit indeed
is willing, but the flesh is weak.* —MATTHEW 26:41

There is such a thing as going back in religion after making a good
profession. People may run well for a season, like the Galatians, and
then turn aside after false teachers. People may profess loudly while their
feelings are warm, as Peter did, and then in the hour of trial deny their
Lord. People may lose their first love as the Ephesians did. People may
cool down in their zeal to do good, like John Mark, the companion of
Paul. People may follow an apostle for a season, and like Demas go back
to the world. All these things people may do.

It is a miserable thing to be a backslider. Of all unhappy things
that can befall a person, I suppose it is the worst. A stranded ship, a
broken-winged eagle, a garden overrun with weeds, a harp without
strings, a church in ruins—all these are sad sights, but a backslider is
sadder still. A wounded conscience, a mind sick of itself, a memory full
of self-reproach, a heart pierced through with the Lord's arrows, a spirit
broken with the inward accusation, all this is a taste of hell. It is a hell
on earth. Truly that saying of the wise man is solemn and weighty, "The
backslider in heart shall be filled with his own ways" (Prov. 14:14). Now
what is the case of most backslidings? I believe, as a general rule, one of
the chief causes is neglected private prayer. Of course, the secret history
of falls will not be known until the last day. I can only give my opinion
as a minister of Christ and a student of the heart. I repeat distinctly that
backsliding generally first begins with neglect of private prayer!

❖ From the sermon "Call to Prayer"

Love Is the Greatest Grace!

And now abideth faith, hope, charity, these three;
but the greatest of these is charity.
—1 CORINTHIANS 13:13

The reasons why love is called the greatest of the three graces appear to me plain and simple. Let me show what they are. Love is called the greatest of graces because it is the one in which there is some likeness between the believer and his God. God has no need of faith. He is dependent on no one. There is none superior to Him in whom He must trust. God has no need of hope. To Him all things are certain, whether past, present, or to come. But God is love, and the more love His people have, the more similar they are to their Father in heaven.

Love, for another thing, is called the greatest of the graces because it is most useful to others. Faith and hope, beyond doubt, however precious, have special reference to a believer's own private individual benefit. Faith unites the soul to Christ, brings peace with God, and opens the way to heaven. Hope fills the soul with cheerful expectation of things to come and, amid the many discouragements of things seen, comforts with visions of the things unseen.

Love, in the last place, is the greatest of the graces because it is the one that endures the longest. In fact, it will never die. Faith will one day be swallowed up in sight and hope in certainty. Their office will be useless in the morning of the resurrection, and like old almanacs, they will be laid aside. But love will live on through the endless ages of eternity! Heaven will be the abode of love. The inhabitants of heaven will be full of love. One common feeling will be in all their hearts, and that will be love!

�֎ From the sermon "Christian Love"

The Place of No Sorrow

*And God shall wipe away all tears from their eyes; and there shall
be no more death, neither sorrow, nor crying, neither shall there be
any more pain: for the former things are passed away.*
—REVELATION 21:4

Brethren, think of an eternal habitation in which there is no sorrow.
Who is there here below that is not acquainted with sorrow? It came in
with thorns and thistles at Adam's fall, it is the bitter cup that all must
drink, it is before us and behind us, it is on the right hand and the left,
it is mingled with the very air we breathe. Our bodies are racked with
pain, and we have sorrow. Our worldly goods are taken from us, and we
have sorrow. We are encompassed with difficulties and troubles, and we
have sorrow. Our friends forsake us and look coldly on us, and we have
sorrow. We are separated from those we love, and we have sorrow. Those
on whom our hearts' affections are set go down to the grave and leave us
alone, and we have sorrow.

And then, too, we find our own hearts frail and full of corruption,
and that brings sorrow.

We are persecuted and opposed for the gospel's sake, and that brings
sorrow. We see those who are near and dear to us refusing to walk with
God, and that brings sorrow. Oh, what a sorrowing, grieving world we
live in! Blessed be God! There shall be no sorrow in heaven.

There shall not be one single tear shed within the courts above.
There shall be no more disease and weakness and decay. The coffin and
the funeral and the grave shall be things unknown. Our faces shall no
more be pale and sad. No more shall we go out from the company of
those we love and be parted asunder; that word "farewell" shall never be
heard again. There shall be no anxious thought about tomorrow to mar
and spoil our enjoyment. Our needs will have come to a perpetual end,
and all around us shall be harmony and love!

❖ From the sermon "Heaven"

What Shall Heaven Be Like?

We are confident, I say, and willing rather to be absent from the body, and to be present with the Lord. —2 CORINTHIANS 5:8

I pity that man who never thinks about heaven. I use that word in the broadest and most popular sense. I mean by "heaven" the future dwelling place of all true Christians, when the dead are raised and the world has passed away. Cold and unfeeling must that heart be which never gives a thought to that dwelling place! Dull and earthly must that mind be which never considers heaven! We may die any day. "In the midst of life, we are in death." We must all die sooner or later. The youngest, the fairest, the strongest, the cleverest, all must go down one day before the scythe of the king of terrors. This world shall not go on forever as it does now. Its affairs shall at last be wound up. The King of Kings will come and take His great power and reign over all. The judgment shall be set, the books shall be opened, the dead shall be raised, and the living shall be changed.

And where do we all hope to go then? Why, if we know anything of true faith in the Lord Jesus Christ, then we hope to go to heaven. Surely there is nothing unreasonable in asking men to consider the subject of heaven. Now, what will heaven be like? Before we go to our eternal home, we should try to become acquainted with it. Suffice it to say that heaven is the eternal presence of everything that can make a saint happy and the eternal absence of everything that can cause sorrow. Sickness and pain and disease and death and poverty and labor and money and care and ignorance and misunderstanding and slander and lying and strife and contention and quarrels and envies and jealousies and bad tempers and infidelity and skepticism and wickedness and superstition and heresy and schism and wars and fightings and bloodshed and murders and lawsuits—all, all these things shall have no place in heaven. On earth, in this present time, they may live and flourish. In heaven even their footprints shall not be known!

✤ From the sermon "Shall We Know One Another in Heaven?"

Outward Show of Religion

Having a form of godliness, but denying the power thereof: from such turn away. —2 TIMOTHY 3:5

Enormous luxury, extravagance, self-indulgence, mammon worship, and an idolatry of fashion and amusements are sorrowful marks of our times. With all our outward show of religion, is there any proportionate increase of internal reality? With all this immense growth of external Christianity, is there any corresponding growth of vital godliness? Is there more faith, repentance, and holiness among the worshipers in our churches? Is there more of that saving faith without which it is impossible to please God, more of that repentance unto salvation without which a man must perish, and more of that holiness without which no man shall see the Lord? Is our Lord Jesus Christ more known and trusted and loved and obeyed? Is the inward work of the Holy Spirit more realized and experienced among our people? Are the grand verities of justification, conversion, sanctification more thoroughly grasped and rightly esteemed by our congregations? Is there more private Bible reading, private prayer, private self-denial, private mortification of the flesh, private exhibition of meekness, gentleness, and unselfishness? In a word, is there more private religion at home in all the relations of life? These are very serious questions, and I wish they could receive very satisfactory answers.

There is nothing like testing systems by their results. Let us ask quietly whether there has been any increase of Christian liberality and spiritual-mindedness in the land in proportion to the enormous increase of attention to external worship. I am afraid the reply will be found very unsatisfactory. In many cases the money given by a congregation to help missions at home and abroad and to promote direct work for the salvation of souls in any way would be found absurdly out of proportion to the money expended on organist, choir, ferns, flowers, and general decoration. Can this be right? And is this a healthy state of things?

❖ From the sermon "Signs of the Times"

Special National Sins

But if ye will not do so, behold, ye have sinned against the LORD: and be sure your sin will find you out. —NUMBERS 32:23

Does anyone ask what the special national sins of England are? I will mention some which appear to my eyes to stand out prominently in this country at the present time. I may be quite wrong. I only give my judgment as one who looks on attentively and marks the signs of the times.

1. The first national sin I will name is covetousness. The excessive love of money and the desire to be rich in this world are what I mean. Never, surely, was there such a race for riches as at the present day. To make money and die rich seems to be thought the highest virtue and the greatest wisdom.

2. The second national sin I will name is luxury and love of pleasure. Never, surely, was there a time when people ran so greedily after excitement, amusement, and gratification of their senses.

3. The third national sin I will name is neglect of the Lord's Day. That blessed day is rapidly becoming in many quarters the day for visiting and pleasure, and not the day of God.

4. The fourth national sin I will name is drunkenness. The quantity of intoxicating drink consumed every year in England is something frightful. The number of alehouses, gin palaces, and beer shops in our large towns is a standing proof that we are an intemperate people. There are more people every Sunday night in gin shops than there are in churches and chapels.

5. The fifth national sin I will name is immorality: "Thou shalt not commit adultery" (Ex. 20:14). In town and in country among rich and among poor, the tone of feeling about purity among the young is at the lowest ebb.

6. The last national sin I will name is the growing disposition to skepticism and infidelity. Little by little, men in high places are ceasing to honor God. Year after year, the Bible is more openly impugned and its authority impaired. To believe the Bible was once a mark of a Christian.

I believe firmly that these things are crying to God against England. They are an offense against the King of Kings, for which He is punishing us at this very day.

✤ From the sermon "The Finger of God"

Church Work

Therefore I endure all things for the elect's sakes, that they may also obtain the salvation which is in Christ Jesus with eternal glory.
—2 TIMOTHY 2:10

We live in days when there is an immense increase of what is called "church work." The contrast between the ways of the present age and the ways of our grandfathers in trying to do good is very great indeed. To preach the gospel and expound the Scriptures both on Sundays and weekdays; to visit the sick frequently; to go from house to house as a pastor, endeavoring by kindly influence over all the members of families to get at hearts and consciences; to keep up efficient day schools, night schools, and Bible classes; to create and maintain an interest about the souls of others by foreign and home missions—this used to be the work of the clergyman, and this was the kind of work in which he was ever trying to enlist the practical sympathy of his parishioners. It was good, solid, healthy, soul-helping, Christlike work.

A great change has taken place in the last forty years. A quantity of work is continually being carried on by both clergymen and laymen that, however well meant, can hardly be called Christian and in reality has a painful tendency to throw true Christian work into the background, if not to throw it entirely out! No one, for instance, can fail to observe that a large number of professors are spending all their time and strength on church music, church decorations, church programs, and an incessant round of church attractions. Others are equally absorbed in such subjects as temperance, social work, feeding the poor, and improved dwellings for the working classes. Others are incessantly getting up popular concerts, secular lectures, and evening recreations. They proclaim everywhere that the way to do good is to amuse people!

It is quite certain that musical services and church decorations and concerts and bazaars and improved cookery and the like will not save souls. I certainly see on every side a vast increase of what people call church work. But I own to a strong suspicion that there is little or no increase of true religion. There is more show and glitter and display, undoubtedly.

But I doubt extremely whether there is more spiritual reality and more growth of practical godliness and zeal to save souls!

❖ From the sermon "The Parable of the Good Samaritan"

None So Dangerous as Self-Righteousness

And he spake this parable unto certain which trusted in themselves
that they were righteous, and despised others.   —LUKE 18:9

Are there none to whom this parable is applicable in the present day?
Truly, if it were so, the ministers of Jesus would have comparatively a
light employment and an idle post. We do not often meet with men
who deny the divinity of Christ or the personality of the Holy Spirit or
disbelieve the Bible or doubt the existence of a God, and so bring upon
themselves swift destruction. But alas! We have daily proof that the disease spoken of in our text is as deep-seated and hard to cure as ever. And
of all the mischievous delusions that keep men out of heaven, of all the
soul-destroying snares that Satan employs to oppose Christ's gospel, there
is none we find so dangerous, none so successful, as self-righteousness!

Perhaps you think this strange, and I dare say there are few who
would not say, if asked the ground of their hopes and how they expect
to be saved, "We trust in the merits of Christ." But I fear that too many
of you are making the Lord Jesus but half your Savior and could never
stand the sifting of an inquiry that would draw out into daylight the
secrets of your hearts.

How much would then come out by degrees about doing as well as
you could and being no worse than others and having been sober and
industrious and well-behaved and having attended church regularly and
having had a Bible and a Prayer Book of your own ever since you can
remember, and the like. Besides many other self-approving thoughts,
which often never appear until a deathbed. And all prove the root of all
evil, which is pride, to be still vigorous and flourishing within. Oh, this
pride of heart, beloved! It is fearful to see the harm that it does and the
carelessness with which it is regarded! You cannot search your heart too
diligently, for this self-righteousness is the subtlest enemy of all.

✤ From the sermon "Self-Righteousness"

Your Time Is Short

And as it is appointed unto men once to die,
but after this the judgment.
—HEBREWS 9:27

The day may come when after a long fight with disease, we shall feel that medicine can do no more and that nothing remains but to die. Friends will be standing by, unable to help us. Hearing, eyesight, even the power of praying, will be fast failing us. The world and its shadows will be melting beneath our feet. Eternity, with its realities, will be looming large before our minds. What shall support us in that trying hour? What shall enable us to feel "I will fear no evil"? (Ps. 23:4). Nothing, nothing can do it but close communion with Christ. Christ dwelling in our hearts by faith, Christ putting His right arm under our heads, Christ felt to be sitting by our side, Christ can alone give us the complete victory in the last struggle.

Let us cleave to Christ more closely, love Him more heartily, live to Him more thoroughly, copy Him more exactly, confess Him more boldly, follow Him more fully. Religion like this will always bring its own reward. Worldly people may laugh at it. Weak brethren may think it extreme. But it will wear well. At even time it will bring us light. In sickness it will bring us peace. In the world to come it will give us a crown of glory that fades not away.

The time is short. The fashion of this world passes away. A few more sicknesses, and all will be over. A few more funerals, and our own funeral will take place. A few more storms and tossings, and we shall be safe in harbor. We travel toward a world where there is no more sickness, where parting and pain and crying and mourning are done with for evermore.

Heaven is becoming every year fuller and earth emptier. The friends ahead are becoming more numerous than the friends astern. "For yet a little while, and he that shall come will come, and will not tarry" (Heb. 10:37).

❖ From the sermon "Sickness"

SEPTEMBER 19

Abuse Not God's Mercies

How shall we escape, if we neglect so great salvation; which at the first began to be spoken by the Lord, and was confirmed unto us by them that heard him.
—HEBREWS 2:3

There is an awful readiness in all men to abuse God's mercies. Even the children of God are not as free from the sad infection. There is a busy devil near the best of saints who would gladly persuade them to make their privileges a plea for the careless living, and to turn their soul's food into poison. I cannot look around the church and the end to which many high professors come without feeling that there is need for caution. "Wherefore let him that thinketh he standeth take heed lest he fall" (1 Cor. 10:12). Would we know what it is to abuse the doctrine of perseverance? It is abused when believers make their safety an excuse for inconsistencies in practice. It is abused when they make their security from final ruin an apology for a low standard of sanctification and a distant walk with God.

Would we know what it is to use the doctrine of perseverance aright? Let us watch jealously over the daily workings of our own hearts. Let us mortify and nip in the bud the least inclination to spiritual indolence. Let us settle down in our minds as a ruling principle of our lives that the mercies of God are only turned to a good account when they have a sanctifying effect on our hearts. Let us root it finally in our inward man, that the love of Christ is never so really valued as when it constrains us to increased spiritual-mindedness. Let us set before our minds that the safer we feel, the more holy we ought to be. The more we realize that God has done much for us, the more we ought to do for God. The greater our debt, the greater should be our gratitude. The more we see the riches of grace, the richer should we be in good works.

❖ From the sermon "Never Perish"

The Nature of Repentance

The time is fulfilled, and the kingdom of God is at hand: repent ye, and believe the gospel.
—MARK 1:15

Let us see that we set down our feet firmly on this point. The importance of the inquiry cannot be overrated. Repentance is one of the foundation stones of Christianity. Sixty times at least we find repentance spoken of in the New Testament. What was the first doctrine our Lord Jesus Christ preached? We are told that He said, "Repent ye, and believe the gospel" (Mark 1:15). What did the apostles proclaim when the Lord sent them forth the first time? They "preached that men should repent" (Mark 6:12). What was the charge that Jesus gave His disciples when He left the world? That "repentance and remission of sins should be preached in his name among all nations" (Luke 24:47). What was the concluding appeal of the first sermons that Peter preached? "Repent, and be baptized" (Acts 2:38). "Repent ye therefore, and be converted" (Acts 3:19).

Repentance is a thorough change of man's natural heart upon the subject of sin. We are all born in sin. We naturally love sin. We take to sin as soon as we can act and think, just as the bird takes to flying and the fish takes to swimming. There never was a child who required schooling or education in order to learn deceitfulness, selfishness, passion, self-will, gluttony, pride, and foolishness. These things are not picked up from bad companions or gradually learned by a long course of tedious instruction. They spring up of themselves, even when boys and girls are brought up alone. The seeds of them are evidently the natural product of the heart. The aptitude of all children to these evil things is an unanswerable proof of the corruption and fall of man. Now when this heart of ours is changed by the Holy Spirit, when this natural love of sin is cast out, then takes place that change which the Word of God calls "repentance." The man in whom the change is wrought is said to "repent." He may be called, in one word, a "penitent" man.

❖ From the sermon "Repentance"

Fountain from Which True Peace Is Drawn

There is no peace, saith my God, to the wicked.
—ISAIAH 57:21

The peace of the true Christian is not a vague, dreamy feeling without reason and without foundation. He can show cause for it. He builds upon solid ground. He has peace with God because he is justified. Without justification it is impossible to have real peace with God. Conscience forbids it. Sin is a mountain between a man and God and must be taken away.

The sense of guilt lies heavy on the heart and must be removed. Unpardoned sin will murder peace. The true Christian knows all this well. His peace arises from a consciousness of his sins being forgiven and his guilt being put away. His house is not built on sandy ground. His well is not a broken cistern that can hold no water. He has peace with God because he is justified.

He is justified, and his sins are forgiven. However many and however great, they are cleansed away, pardoned, and wiped out. They are blotted out of the book of God's remembrance. They are sunk into the depths of the sea. They are cast behind God's back. They are searched for and not found. They are remembered no more. Though they may have been like scarlet, they are become white as snow. Though they may have been red like crimson, they are as wool. And so he has peace.

Settle it in your mind that there can be no peace with God unless we feel that we are justified. We must know what has become of our sins. We must have a reasonable hope that they are forgiven and put away. We must have the witness of our conscience that we are reckoned not guilty before God. Without this it is vain to talk of peace with God. We have nothing but the deception and imitation of it. "There is no peace, saith my God, to the wicked" (Isa. 57:21).

❖ From the sermon "Justification"

Hold Fast to What Is Good

Prove all things; hold fast that which is good.
—1 THESSALONIANS 5:21

The words of the apostle on this subject are pithy and forcible. "Hold fast," he says, "that which is good." It is as if he said to us, "When you have found the truth for yourself, and when you are satisfied that it is Christ's truth—that truth which the Scriptures set forth—then get a firm hold upon it, grasp it, keep it in your heart, never let it go!" He speaks as one who knew what the hearts of all Christians are. He knew that our grasp of the gospel, at our best, is very cold; that our love soon waxes feeble; that our faith soon wavers; that our zeal soon flags; that familiarity with Christ's truth often brings with it a species of contempt; that, like Israel, we are apt to be discouraged by the length of our journey; and, like Peter, ready to sleep one moment and fight the next but, like Peter, not ready to watch and pray.

All this Paul remembered, and like a faithful watchman he cries, by the Holy Spirit, "Hold fast that which is good." He speaks as if he foresaw by the Spirit that the good tidings of the gospel would soon be corrupted, spoiled, and plucked away from the church at Thessalonica. He speaks as one who foresaw that Satan and all his agents would labor hard to cast down Christ's truth. He writes as though he would forewarn men of this danger and he cries, "Hold fast that which is good." Reader, the advice is always needed as long as the world stands. If we love the open Bible, if we love the preaching of the gospel, if we love the freedom of reading that Bible and the opportunity of hearing that gospel with no man forbidding us, if we love civil liberty, if we love religious liberty, if these are precious to our souls, we must all make up our minds to hold fast, lest by and by we lose all!

❖ From the sermon "Prove All Things"

I Give My Sheep Eternal Life

And I give unto them eternal life; and they shall never perish, neither shall any man pluck them out of my hand.   —JOHN 10:28

The Lord Jesus says of His sheep, "I give unto them eternal life." What is the portion that Jesus gives His people? "Eternal life," a perfect, never-ending happiness for that which is the most important part of a man, his immortal soul. They shall not be hurt by the second death, which alone is to be really feared. What greater things could our Lord bestow upon His people? Health and riches and honor and pleasures, houses and lands, and wives and children—what are they? How long do they last? It is but threescore years and ten, and we must leave them all, and six feet of vile earth is room enough for us. Naked came we into the world, and naked must we return unto the dust and carry nothing with us. What is the difference between the rich and the poor in death? They both go unto one and the same place. The worm feeds sweetly on them both. It is but a short time and you would not be able to distinguish between their bones.

But if the poor man sleeps in Jesus while the rich man dies in his sins, oh, what a mighty gulf then is between them! The rich will take up his abode in that fire which is never quenched; the poor will awake to find he has an everlasting treasure in heaven, even eternal life. Eternal life! Compared to which this world's concerns, weighty and important as they seem, are like a drop of water. Consider with yourselves how glorious that doctrine is, how thoroughly it takes away all excuse from the impenitent. Pardon and forgiveness are here unconditionally bestowed. We are not told that we must pay off so much every day and then shall be saved; that would drive us to doubt and despair. But if a man will only hear Christ's voice and follow Him, "Behold," says Jesus, "I give unto him eternal life; there remains no condemnation for him!"

❖ From the sermon "The Privileges of the True Christian"

The Bible Is What the Bible Is

For whatsoever things were written aforetime were written for our learning, that we through patience and comfort of the scriptures might have hope.
— ROMANS 15:4

Let me say, the Bible is what the Bible is. All through the Bible, from Genesis down to Revelation, there is only one simple account of the way in which a man or woman must be saved. It is always the same: only by our Lord Jesus Christ, through faith; never by our own works and righteousness. You see it dimly revealed at first; it looms through the mist of a few promises, but there it is. You see it more clearly later; it is taught by the pictures and symbols of the law of Moses. You have it still more clearly as time goes by. The prophets saw in visions many particulars about the Redeemer that was to come.

You have the complete revelation in the sunshine of New Testament history: Christ incarnate, Christ crucified, Christ rising again, Christ preached to the world. But one golden thread runs through the whole Bible—no salvation except by faith in Jesus Christ. The bruising of the serpent's head predicted in the day of the fall; the clothing of our first parents with animal skins; the sacrifices of Noah, Abraham, Isaac, and Jacob; the Passover; and all the particulars of the Jewish law, the high priest, the altar, the daily offering of the lamb, the holy of holies entered only by blood, the scapegoat, the cities of refuge—all are many witnesses to the truth set forth in the text. All preach with one voice: salvation only by Jesus Christ.

I do not know what use you make of your Bible, whether you read it or whether you do not, whether you read it all, or whether you read only the parts that you like. But this I tell you plainly: if you read and believe the whole Bible, you will find it hard to escape the doctrine that there is no salvation except through the person and blood of Jesus Christ. I do not see how you can consistently reject what I have been endeavoring to prove. Christ is the way, and the only way. Christ is the truth, and the only truth. Christ is the life, and the only life.

❖ From the sermon "Only One Way—Christ!"

Bearing Sorrows

He healeth the broken in heart, and bindeth up their wounds.
—PSALM 147:3

Let us consider the universal liability of man to sorrows. The testimony of Scripture that man is born to trouble (Job 5:7) is continually echoed by thousands who know nothing of the Scriptures but simply speak the language of their own experience. The world, nearly all men agree, is full of trouble. It is a true saying that we come into life crying, pass through it complaining, and leave it disappointed. Of all God's creatures, none is so vulnerable to sorrow as man. Body and mind and affections and family and property are all liable in their turn to become sources and avenues of sorrow. And from this no rank or class possesses any immunity. There are sorrows for the rich as well as for the poor, for the learned as well as for the unlearned, for the young as well as for the old, for the castle as well as for the cottage.

And neither wealth nor science nor high position can prevent their forcing their way into our homes and breaking in upon us sometimes like an armed man! These are ancient things, I know. The poets and philosophers of old Greece and Rome knew them as well as we do. But it is well to be put in remembrance. For what shall best help man to meet and bear sorrow? That is the question! If our condition is such since the fall that we cannot escape sorrow, then what is the surest remedy for making it tolerable?

I maintain that the apostle Paul's doctrine of a risen Christ comes in with a marvelous power and exactly meets our necessities. We have one sitting at the right hand of God as our sympathizing friend who has all power to help us and can be touched with the feeling of our infirmities, even Jesus, the Son of God. He knows the heart of a man and all his condition, for He Himself was born of a woman and took part of flesh and blood. He knows what sorrow is, for He Himself in the days of His flesh wept and groaned and grieved. He has proved His love toward us by bearing our manners for thirty-three years in this world, by a thousand acts of kindness, and ten thousand words of consolation, and by finally dying for us on the cross!

❖ From the sermon "Foundational Truths"

I Am a Friend of God

Henceforth I call you not servants; for the servant knoweth not what his lord doeth: but I have called you friends; for all things that I have heard of my Father I have made known unto you.

—JOHN 15:15

Seek every day to have closer communion with Him who is your friend and to know more of His grace and power. True Christianity is not merely the believing a certain set of dry theological propositions; it is to live in daily personal communication with an actual living person, Jesus the Son of God. "To me," said Paul, "to live is Christ" (Phil. 1:21)! Seek every day to glorify your Lord and Savior in all your ways. "A man that hath friends must shew himself friendly" (Prov. 18:24), and no man surely is under such mighty obligations as the friend of Christ. Avoid everything that would grieve your Lord. Fight hard against besetting sins, against inconsistency, against backwardness to confess Him before men. Say to your soul, whenever you are tempted to do what is wrong, "Soul, soul, is this your kindness to your friend?"

Think above all of the mercy which has been shown you and learn to rejoice daily in your friend! What though your body is bowed down with disease? What though your poverty and trials are very great? What though your earthly friends forsake you and you are alone in the world? All this may be true. But if you are in Christ, then you have a friend, a mighty friend, a loving friend, a wise friend, a friend who never fails! Oh, think, think much upon your friend! Yet in a little while your friend shall come to take you home to heaven, and you shall dwell with Him forever! Yet in a little while you shall see as you have been seen and know as you have been known. And then you shall hear assembled worlds confess that he is the rich and happy person, who has had Christ for his friend!

❖ From the sermon "The Best Friend"

The Means of Grace

His divine power hath given unto us all things that pertain unto life and godliness, through the knowledge of him that hath called us to glory and virtue.
— 2 PETER 1:3

When I speak of the means of grace, I have in my mind's eye five principal things: the reading of the Bible, private prayer, public worship, the sacrament of the Lord's Supper, and the rest of the Lord's Day. They are means that God has graciously appointed in order to convey grace to man's heart by the Holy Spirit or to keep up the spiritual life after it has begun. As long as the world stands, the state of a man's soul will always depend greatly on the manner and spirit in which he uses means of grace. The manner and spirit I say deliberately and of purpose. Our feeling about them is just one of the many tests of the state of our souls.

How can that man be thought to love God who reads about Him and His Christ as a mere matter of duty, content and satisfied if he has just moved his mark onward over so many chapters? How can that man suppose he is ready to meet Christ who never takes any trouble to pour out his heart to Him in private as a friend and is satisfied with saying over a string of words every morning and evening under the name of prayer, scarcely thinking what he is about? How could that man be happy in heaven forever who finds Sunday a dull, gloomy, tiresome day, who knows nothing of hearty prayer and praise and cares nothing whether he hears truth or error from the pulpit or scarcely listens to the sermon? What can be the spiritual condition of that man whose heart never burns within him when he receives that bread and wine which specially remind us of Christ's death on the cross and the atonement for sin?

❖ From the sermon "Self-Inquiry"

Arm Yourself against False Teaching

In meekness instructing those that oppose themselves; if God perad-venture will give them repentance to the acknowledging of the truth.
—2 TIMOTHY 2:25

False doctrines of every kind are continually set before us in the most subtle and specious forms. It cannot be thought unseasonable if I offer some practical safeguards against idolatry. What it is, whence it comes, where it is, what will end it, all this we have seen. Let me point out how we may be safe from it, and I will say no more. Let us arm ourselves, then, for one thing, with a thorough knowledge of the Word of God. Let us read our Bibles more diligently than ever and become familiar with every part of them. Let the word dwell in us richly. Let us beware of anything that would make us give less time and less heart to the perusal of its sacred pages. The Bible is the sword of the Spirit; let it never be laid aside. The Bible is the true lantern for a dark and cloudy time; let us beware of traveling without its light.

Above all, let us keep up continual communion with the Lord Jesus! Let us abide in Him daily, feed on Him daily, look to Him daily, lean on Him daily, live upon Him daily, draw from His fullness daily. Let us realize this, and the idea of other mediators, other comforters, other intercessors will seem utterly absurd. "What need is there?" We shall reply, "I have Christ, and in Him I have all. What have I to do with idols? I have Jesus in my heart, Jesus in the Bible, and Jesus in heaven, and I want nothing more!" Let us settle it firmly in our minds, that Christ Jesus has done everything needful in order to present us without spot before the throne of God, and that simple childlike faith on our part, is the only thing required to give us a saving interest in the work of Christ.

❖ From the sermon "Coming Events and Present Duties"

Doubts about the Truth of Christianity

But let him ask in faith, nothing wavering. For he that wavereth is like a wave of the sea driven with the wind and tossed. —JAMES 1:6

I will try to explain the reason why so many professing Christians are continually frightened and shaken in their minds by doubts about the truth of Christianity. That this is the case of many, I have a very strong impression. I suspect there are thousands of churchgoing Christians who would repudiate with indignation the charge of skepticism and yet are constantly troubled about the truth of Christianity. Some new book or lecture or sermon appears from the pen of men like Darwin or Colenso, and at once these worthy people are scared and panic-stricken and run from clergyman to clergyman to pour out their anxieties and fears, as if the very ark of God was in danger. "Can these new ideas be really true?" they cry. "Must we really give up the Old Testament and the flood and the miracles and the resurrection of Christ? Alas! alas! what shall we do?" In short, like Ahaz, they are "as the trees of the wood are moved with the wind" (Isa. 7:2).

Now what is the cause of this readiness to give way to doubts? Why are so many alarmed about the faith of eighteen centuries and frightened out of their wits by attacks that no more shake the evidence of Christianity than the scratch of a pin shakes the Great Pyramid of Egypt? The reason is soon told. The answer lies in a nutshell. The greater part of modern Christians is utterly ignorant of the truths and evidences of Christianity and the enormous difficulties of infidelity. The education of the vast majority of people on these subjects is wretchedly meager and superficial, or it is no education at all. Not one in a hundred churchgoers, probably, has ever read a page of the books on the evidences of the Christian faith! What wonder if the minds of such people are like a city without walls and utterly unable to resist the attacks of the most commonplace infidelity, much less of the refined and polished skepticism of these latter days!

❖ From the sermon "What Can You Know?"

Ready to Be Offered

For I am now ready to be offered, and the time of my departure is at hand. I have fought a good fight, I have finished my course, I have kept the faith: Henceforth there is laid up for me a crown of righteousness, which the Lord, the righteous judge, shall give me at that day: and not to me only, but unto all them also that love his appearing. —2 TIMOTHY 4:6–8

In these words you see the apostle Paul looking three ways: downward, backward, forward. Downward to the grave, backward to his own ministry, forward to that great day, the day of judgment. Happy is that soul among us who can look where Paul looked and then speak as Paul spoke. He looks downward to the grave, and he does it without fear. Hear what he says: "I am ready to be offered." I am like an animal brought to the place of sacrifice and bound with cords to the horns of the altar. The wine and oil have been poured on my head. The last ceremonies have been gone through. Every preparation has been made. It only remains to receive the death blow, and then all is over.

He looks backward to his ministerial life, and he does it without shame. Hear what he says. "I have fought a good fight." There he speaks as a soldier. I have fought that good battle with the world, the flesh, and the devil from which so many shrink and draw back. He looks forward to the great day of reckoning, and he does it without doubt. Mark his words: "Henceforth there is laid up for me a crown of righteousness." A glorious reward, he seems to say, is ready and laid up in store for me, even that crown which is only given to the righteous. In the great day of judgment, the Lord shall give this crown to me and to all besides me who have loved Him as an unseen Savior and longed to see Him face-to-face. My work is over. This one thing now remains for me to look forward to, and nothing more.

❖ From the sermon "Ready to Be Offered"

Unbelief of the Present Day

And for this cause God shall send them strong delusion, that they should believe a lie: That they all might be damned who believed not the truth, but had pleasure in unrighteousness.
—2 THESSALONIANS 2:11–12

That there is a good deal of unbelief in this age, it is vain to deny. The number of people who attend no place of worship and seem to have no religion is very considerable. A vague kind of skepticism or agnosticism is one of the common spiritual diseases in this generation. It meets us at every turn and crops up in every company. Among high and low and rich and poor, in town and country, in universities and manufacturing towns, in castles and in cottages, you will continually find some form of unbelief. It is no longer a pestilence that walks in darkness but a destruction which wastes at noon day. It is even considered clever and intellectual and a mark of a thoughtful mind. Society seems leavened with it. He who avows his belief of everything contained in the Bible must make up his mind in many companies, to be smiled at contemptuously and thought an ignorant and weak man!

Now there is no doubt that, as I have already said, the seat of unbelief in some people is the head. They refuse to accept anything that they cannot understand or that seems above their reason. Inspiration, miracles, the Trinity, the incarnation, the atonement, the Holy Spirit, the resurrection, the future state—all these mighty verities are viewed with cold indifference as disputable points, if not absolutely rejected. "Can we entirely explain them? Can we satisfy their reasoning faculties concerning them?" If not, they must be excused if they stand in doubt. What they cannot fully understand they tell us they cannot fully believe, and so they never exhibit any religion while they live, though, strangely enough, they like to be buried with religious forms when they die.

❖ From the sermon "What Can You Know?"

An Epistle of Christ

Forasmuch as ye are manifestly declared to be the epistle of Christ ministered by us, written not with ink, but with the Spirit of the living God; not in tables of stone, but in fleshy tables of the heart.
—2 CORINTHIANS 3:3

Believing reader, I trust I may say of you that you love the Lord Jesus Christ in sincerity. Know then that I want you to be a bright and shining light to those around you. I want you to be such a plain epistle of Christ that all may read something of God on the face of your conversation. I want you so to live that all may see that you are one of the people of Jesus, and thus to glorify your Father who is in heaven. Alas! I say it with shame—we many of us bring little glory to the Lord who bought us. We are far from walking worthy of our vocation. How weak is our faith! How fleeting our sorrow for sin! How faint our self-denial! How soon spent our patience! How thin and threadbare our humility! How formal our prayers! How cold our love!

We are called God's witnesses, but truly our witness is often little better than silence, it is but an uncertain sound. We are called the light of the world, but we are, many of us, poor, glimmering sparks that can only just be seen. We are called the salt of the earth, but we scarcely do anything to make our savor felt and known. We are called pilgrims and strangers, but those who observe us might sometimes think this world was our only home. Oh, believing reader, these things ought not so to be.

Brother or sister, what are you doing in the world? Where is the proof of your growth in grace? Are you awake or are you asleep? Is there no sort of besetting sin you are shamefully sparing? Is there no time you might employ more usefully? Are there no daily habits you might alter for the better? Are there no spots upon your spiritual garments that you never seek to have washed out? Are there no friends and relations you are letting alone in their sins? Oh, that you may deal more honestly with yourself than you have done hitherto! The Lord is at hand.

❖ From the sermon "The Lord Our Righteousness"

Happiness in Serving Christ

Now the God of hope fill you with all joy and peace in believing,
that ye may abound in hope, through the power of the Holy Ghost.
—ROMANS 15:13

Believers, if you would have an increase of happiness in Christ's service, labor every year to be more thankful. Pray that you may know more and more what it is to "rejoice in the Lord" (Phil. 3:1). Learn to have a deeper sense of your own wretched sinfulness and corruption and to be more deeply grateful that by the grace of God you are what you are. Alas, there is too much complaining and too little thanksgiving among the people of God! There is too much murmuring and coveting things that we have not. There is too little praising and blessing for the many undeserved mercies that we have. Oh, that God would pour out upon us a great spirit of thankfulness and praise!

Believers, if you would have an increase of happiness in Christ's service, labor every year to do more good. Look around the circle in which your lot is cast and lay yourself out to be useful. Strive to be of the same character with God; He is not only good but "doest good" (Ps. 119:68). Alas, there is far too much selfishness among believers in the present day! There is far too much lazy sitting by the fire nursing our own spiritual diseases and croaking over the state of our own hearts! Up, and be useful in your day and generation! Is there no one that you can speak to? Is there no one that you can write to? Is there literally nothing that you can do for the glory of God and the benefit of your fellow men? Oh, I cannot think it! I cannot think it. There is much that you might do if you had only the desire. For your own happiness' sake, rise and do it, without delay. The bold, outspoken, working Christians are always the happiest!

❖ From the sermon "Happiness"

Train Your Children or
They Will Train Themselves

The rod and reproof give wisdom: but a child left to himself bringeth his mother to shame. —PROVERBS 29:15

If you want to train your children correctly, train them in the way they should go and not in the way that they want to go. Remember, children are born with a definite bias toward evil, and therefore if you let them choose for themselves, they are certain to choose wrong. The mother cannot tell what her tender little infant may grow up to be—tall or short, weak or strong, wise or foolish. He may be any of these things or not, it is all uncertain. But one thing the mother can say with certainty: he will have a corrupt and sinful heart. It is natural for us to do wrong. "Foolishness," says Solomon, "is bound in the heart of a child" (Prov. 22:15); and "A child left to himself bringeth his mother to shame" (Prov. 29:15). Our hearts are like the earth on which we walk. Leave it alone, and it is sure to bear weeds.

If, then, you want to be wise in dealing with your child, then you must not leave him to the guidance of his own will. Think for him, judge for him, act for him, just as you would for one who is weak and blind. But for pity's sake, do not allow him to pursue his own unruly tastes and inclinations. It must not be his tendencies and wishes that are favored. He does not yet know what is good for his mind and soul any more than what is good for his body. You do not let him decide what he will eat and what he will drink and how he will be clothed. Be consistent, and deal with his mind in the same manner. Train him in the way that is scriptural and right, and not in the way that he thinks is right.

❖ From the book *The Duties of Parents*

How the Holy Spirit Works in Believers, Part 1

Whereby are given unto us exceeding great and precious promises: that by these ye might be partakers of the divine nature, having escaped the corruption that is in the world through lust.

—2 PETER 1:4

In speaking of the manner of the Holy Spirit's working, I shall simply state certain great leading facts. They are facts attested alike by Scripture and experience. They are facts patent to the eyes of every candid and well-instructed observer. They are facts that I believe it is impossible to gainsay.

I say then that the Holy Spirit works on the heart of a man in a mysterious manner. Our Lord Jesus Christ Himself tell us that in well-known words: "The wind bloweth where it listeth, and thou hearest the sound thereof, but canst not tell whence it cometh, and whither it goeth: so is every one that is born of the Spirit" (John 3:8). We cannot explain how and in what way the almighty Spirit comes into man and operates upon him. But neither also can we explain a thousand things that are continually taking place in the natural world. We cannot explain how our wills work daily on our bodily members and make them walk or move or rest at our discretion; yet no one ever thinks of disputing the fact. So it ought to be with the work of the Spirit. We ought to believe the fact, though we cannot explain the manner.

I say furthermore that the Holy Spirit works on the heart of a man in a sovereign manner. He comes to one and does not come to another. He often converts one in a family, while others are left alone. There were two thieves crucified with our Lord Jesus Christ on Calvary. They saw the same Savior dying and heard the same words come from His lips. Yet only one repented and went to paradise, while the other died in his sins. There were many Pharisees besides Saul who had a hand in Stephen's murder. But Saul alone became an apostle. There were many slave captains in John Newton's time, yet none but he became a preacher of the gospel. We cannot account for this. But neither can we account for China being a heathen country and England a Christian land. We only know that so it is!

✣ From the sermon "The Holy Spirit"

How the Holy Spirit Works in Believers, Part 2

Whereby are given unto us exceeding great and precious promises: that by these ye might be partakers of the divine nature, having escaped the corruption that is in the world through lust.
—2 PETER 1:4

I say furthermore that the Holy Spirit always works on the heart of a man in such a manner as to be felt. I do not for a moment say that the feelings He produces are always understood by the person in whom they are produced. On the contrary, they are often a cause of anxiety and conflict and inward strife. All I maintain is that we have no warrant of Scripture for supposing that there is an indwelling of the Spirit that is not felt at all. Where He is, there will always be corresponding feelings.

I say furthermore that the Holy Spirit always works on the heart of a man in such a manner as to be seen in the man's life. I do not say that as soon as He comes into a man, that man becomes immediately an established Christian in whose life and ways nothing but spirituality can be observed. But this I say, that the almighty Spirit is never present in a person's soul without producing some perceptible results in that person's conduct! He never sleeps; He is never idle. We have no warrant of Scripture for talking of dormant grace. "Whosoever is born of God doth not commit sin; for his seed remaineth in him" (1 John 3:9). Where the Holy Spirit is, there will be something seen.

I say, finally, under this head, that the Holy Spirit generally works on the heart of man through the use of means. The Word of God, preached or read, is generally employed by Him as an instrument in the conversion of a soul. He applies that Word to the conscience; He brings that Word home to the mind. This is His general course of procedure. There are instances, undoubtedly, in which people are converted "without the word" (1 Peter 3:1). But, as a general rule, God's truth is the sword of the Spirit. By it He teaches, and teaches nothing else but what is written in the Word!

❖ From the sermon "The Holy Spirit"

The Heart Is Deceitfully Wicked

The heart is deceitful above all things, and desperately wicked: who can know it? I the LORD search the heart, I try the reins, even to give every man according to his ways, and according to the fruit of his doings.
—JEREMIAH 17:9–10

The first of these two verses contains a very strong saying, and one that the world in general is not at all disposed to believe. "The heart is deceitful above all things," says our text. "I deny it," says the unconverted man. "To be sure, my heart is very careless and very thoughtless, but it is an honest heart after all." "The heart is desperately wicked," says the text. "Nothing of the sort," replies the sinner. "I know that I neglect the means of grace very much, and perhaps I do not live as I ought to do, but I am sure I have a good heart at the bottom." "Who can know it?" asks the text. "Know it!" we are told. "Why, we do not pretend to be such saints as you want men to be, but at any rate we do know our own hearts; we do know what our faults are."

And so, beloved, it appears there are two statements, and one of them must be false. The everlasting Bible is on one side, and human reasoning on the other; God says one thing, and man says another. In short, unless you really know the character of your own heart, you will never value the gospel as you ought, you will never love the Lord Jesus Christ in sincerity, you will never see how absolutely necessary it was that He should suffer death upon the cross in order to deliver our souls from hell and bring us unto God. It is my earnest desire and prayer that you may all come unto Christ and be delivered from the wrath to come. But this will never be until you are convinced of sin, and you will never be thoroughly convinced until you know that the root and source and fountain of sin all is within you, even in your own hearts!

✣ From the sermon "A Bad Heart"

What Does It Mean to Be Saved?

That if thou shalt confess with thy mouth the Lord Jesus, and shalt believe in thine heart that God hath raised him from the dead, thou shalt be saved. —ROMANS 10:9

What is it to be saved? This is a matter that must be cleared up. Until we know this, we shall make no progress. By being saved I may mean one thing, and you may mean another. Let me show you what the Bible says it is to be saved, and then there will be no misunderstanding. To be saved is not merely to profess and call ourselves Christians. We may have all the outward parts of Christianity and yet be lost after all. We may be baptized into Christ's church, go to Christ's Table, have Christian knowledge, be reckoned Christian men and women, and yet be dead souls all our lives and at last, in the judgment day, be found on Christ's left hand, among the goats! No, this is not salvation! Salvation is something far higher and deeper than this. Now, what is it?

To be saved is to be delivered in this present life from the guilt of sin by faith in Jesus Christ, the Savior. It is to be pardoned, justified, and freed from every charge of sin by faith in Christ's blood and mediation. Whoever with his heart believes on the Lord Jesus Christ is a saved soul. He shall not perish. He shall have eternal life. This is the first part of salvation and the root of all the rest. But this is not all.

To be saved is to be delivered in this present life from the power of sin by being born again and sanctified by the Holy Spirit. It is to be freed from the hateful dominion of sin, the world, and the devil by having a new nature put in us by the Holy Spirit. Whoever is thus renewed in the spirit of his mind and converted is a saved soul. He shall not perish. He shall enter into the glorious kingdom of God. After all, the grand object of having a religion is to be saved. This is the great question that we have to settle with our consciences.

❖ From the sermon "Few Saved"

Doing Good in This World

Let your light so shine before men, that they may see your good works, and glorify your Father which is in heaven.
—MATTHEW 5:16

Let us be more active in endeavors to do good to the world. Surely we may all do far more for unconverted souls than we have ever done yet. Many of us, alas, take things so quietly that a man might suppose everyone about us was converted and the kingdom of Christ fully set up. I pray you, let us lay aside these lazy habits. Are all our friends and relations in Christ? Are all our neighbors and acquaintances inside the ark? Have all within our reach received the truth in the love of it? Have we asked them all to come in? Have we told them all the way of salvation and our own experience that the way is good? Have we done all that we can? Have we tried every means? Is there no one left to whom we can show Christian kindness and offer the gospel? Can we lift up our hands to God as one by one souls around us are taken away and say, "Our eyes, O Lord, have not seen this blood, and its loss cannot in any wise be laid at our door!"

Surely, my brethren, grace ought to be as active a principle in trying to spread godliness as sin is in trying to spread evil. Surely, if we had a tenth part of the zeal that Satan shows to enlarge his kingdom we would be far fuller of care for other men's souls. Where is our mercy and compassion if we can see disease of soul about us and not desire to make it less? Let us awake to a right understanding of our responsibility in this matter. We complain of the world being full of wickedness. It is so. But do we each do our own part in trying to make it better?

❖ From the sermon "Consider Your Ways"

Cling to Justification by Faith Alone

But to him that worketh not, but believeth on him that justifieth the ungodly, his faith is counted for righteousness. —ROMANS 4:5

If you love life, cling with a fast hold to the doctrine of justification by faith. If you love inward peace, let your views of faith be very simple. Honor every part of the Christian religion. Contend to the death for the necessity of holiness. Use diligently and reverently every appointed means of grace, but do not give to these things the office of justifying your soul in the slightest degree. If you would have peace and keep peace, remember that faith alone justifies, and that not as a meritorious work but as the act that joins the soul to Christ. Believe me, the crown and glory of the gospel is justification by faith without the deeds of the law.

No doctrine can be imagined so glorifying to God. It honors all His attributes, His justice, mercy, and holiness. It gives the whole credit of the sinner's salvation to the Savior He has appointed. It honors the Son and so honors the Father who sent Him (John 5:23). It gives people no partnership in their redemption but makes salvation to be wholly of the Lord. It must be of God. No doctrine can be imagined so calculated to put man in his right place. It shows him his own sinfulness, weakness, and inability to save his soul by his own works. It leaves him without excuse if he is not saved at last. It offers to him peace and pardon "without money and without price" (Isa. 55:1). It must be of God.

No doctrine can be imagined so satisfying to a true Christian. It supplies him with a solid ground of comfort, the finished work of Christ. If anything was left for the Christian to do, where would his comfort be? He would never know that he had done enough and was really safe. But the doctrine that Christ undertakes all and that we have only to believe and receive peace meets every fear. It must be of God.

✤ From the sermon "Justification"

The Unchanging Christ

Jesus Christ the same yesterday, and to day, and for ever.
—HEBREWS 13:8

Always the same! Unchanging! That is a glorious character; a character that belongs to nothing that is of the earth; a character that He alone deserves, who is the Lord from heaven.

Before the mountains were brought forth or the earth and world were formed, from everlasting Jesus Christ was, like the Father, very God. From the beginning He was foreordained to be the Savior of sinners. He was always the Lamb slain from the foundation of the world, without whose blood there could be no remission. The same Jesus to whom alone we may look for salvation, that same Jesus was the only hope of Abel and Enoch and Noah and Abraham and all the patriarchs. What we are privileged to see distinctly they doubtless saw indistinctly, but the Savior both we and they rest upon is one. It was Christ Jesus who was foretold in all the prophets and foreshadowed and represented in all the law, the daily sacrifice of the lamb, the cities of refuge, the brazen serpent. All these were so many emblems to Israel of that Redeemer who was yet to come and without whom no man could be saved. There never was but one road to heaven; Jesus Christ was the way, the truth, and the life yesterday as well as today.

He is always the same in love toward human souls. It was love toward a fallen world that made Him lay aside for a season His glorious majesty and honor and take upon Him the form of a servant upon earth. It was love that constrained Him to endure the cross and despise the shame and lay down His life for us, the ungrateful and the ungodly. It was love that moved Him to shed tears over bloody-minded, unbelieving Jerusalem because she would not know the things belonging to her peace. And it is just the same love that He feels toward sinners now. He never changes.

✤ From the sermon "The Unchanging Christ"

Self-Consecration

Know ye not, that to whom ye yield yourselves servants to obey, his servants ye are to whom ye obey; whether of sin unto death, or of obedience unto righteousness? —ROMANS 6:16

That a life of daily self-consecration and daily communion with God should be aimed at by everyone who professes to be a believer; that we should strive to attain the habit of going to the Lord Jesus Christ with everything we find a burden, whether great or small, and casting it upon Him. All this, I repeat, no well-taught child of God will dream of disputing. But surely the New Testament teaches us that we want something more than generalities about holy living, which often prick no conscience and give no offense. The details and particular ingredients of which holiness is composed in daily life ought to be fully set forth and pressed on believers by all who profess to handle the subject.

True holiness does not consist merely of believing and feeling but of doing and bearing and a practical exhibition of active and passive grace. Our tongues, our tempers, our natural passions and inclinations, our conduct as parents and children, masters and servants, husbands and wives, rulers and subjects, our dress, our employment of time, our behavior in business, our demeanor in sickness and health, in riches and in poverty—all, all these are matters that are fully treated by inspired writers. They are not content with a general statement of what we should believe and feel and how we are to have the roots of holiness planted in our hearts. They dig down lower. They go into particulars. They specify minutely what a holy man ought to do and be in his own family and by his own fireside if he abides in Christ. True holiness, we surely ought to remember, does not consist merely of inward sensations and impressions. It is much more than tears and sighs and bodily excitement and a quickened pulse and a passionate feeling of attachment to our own favorite preachers and our own religious party and a readiness to quarrel with everyone who does not agree with us. It is something of the image of Christ (Rom. 8:29), which can be seen and observed by others in our private life and habits and character and doings.

❖ From the book *Holiness*

Our Great Hope

*Now we beseech you, brethren, by the coming of our Lord Jesus
Christ, and by our gathering together unto him.*
— 2 THESSALONIANS 2:1

Paul evidently thought that the gathering at the last day was a cheering
object that Christians ought to keep before their eyes. He classes it with
that second coming of our Lord, which he says elsewhere believers love
and long for. He exalts it in the distant horizon as one of those good
things to come, which should animate the faith of every pilgrim in the
narrow way. Not only, he seems to say, will each servant of God have rest
and a kingdom and a crown, he will also have besides a happy "gathering
together." Now, where is the peculiar blessedness of this gathering? Why
is it a thing that we ought to look forward to with joy and expect with
pleasure? Let us see.

For one thing, the "gathering together" of all true Christians will be
a state of things totally unlike their present condition. To be scattered,
and not gathered, seems the rule of man's existence now. Of all the millions who are annually born into the world, how few continue together
until they die! Children who draw their first breath under the same roof
and play by the same fireside are sure to be separated as they grow up
and to draw their last breath far distant from one another. The same law
applies to the people of God. They are spread abroad like salt, one in
one place and one in another, and never allowed to continue long side
by side. It is doubtless good for the world that it is so. A town would be
a very dark place at night if all the lighted candles were crowded together
into one room. But as good as it is for the world, it is no small trial to
believers. Many a day they feel desolate and alone; many a day they long
for a little more communion with their brethren and a little more companionship with those who love the Lord! Well, they may look forward
with hope and comfort. The hour is coming when they shall have no
lack of companions. Let them lift up their heads and rejoice. There will
be a "gathering together" by and by!

❖ From the sermon "The Great Gathering"

The Doctrine of Particular Redemption

Even as the Son of man came not to be ministered unto, but to minister, and to give his life a ransom for many.
—MATTHEW 20:28

I confess, boldly, that I hold the doctrine of particular redemption in a certain sense as strongly as anyone. I believe that none are effectually redeemed but God's elect. They, and they alone, are set free from the guilt and power and consequences of sin. But I hold no less strongly that Christ's work of atonement is sufficient for all mankind. There is a sense in which He has tasted death for every man and has taken upon Him the sin of the world (Heb. 2:9; John 1:29, respectively). I dare not pare down and file away what appear to me the plain statements of Scripture. I dare not shut a door which God seems, to my eyes, to have left open. I dare not tell any man on earth that Christ has done nothing for him and that he has no warrant to apply boldly to Christ for salvation. I must abide by the statements of the Bible. Christ is God's gift to the whole world.

Let us observe what a giving religion true Christianity is. Gift, love, and free grace are the grand characteristics of the pure gospel. The Father loves the world and gives His only begotten Son. The Son loves us and gives Himself for us. The Father and the Son together give the Holy Spirit to all who ask. All three persons in the blessed Trinity give grace upon grace to those who believe. Never let us be ashamed of being giving Christians if we profess to have any hope in Christ. Let us give freely, liberally, and self-denyingly, according as we have power and opportunity. Let not our love consist in nothing more than vague expressions of kindness and compassion. Let us make proof of it by actions. Let us help forward the cause of Christ on earth by money, influence, pains, and prayer. If God so loved us as to give His Son for our souls, we should count it a privilege and not a burden to give what we can to do good to people.

✣ From the sermon "Faith"

Have You Got a Home for Your Soul?

For here have we no continuing city, but we seek one to come.
—HEBREWS 13:14

Have you got a home for your soul? Is it safe? Is it pardoned? Is it prepared to meet God? With all my heart, I wish you a happy home. But remember my question. Amid the greetings and salutations of home, amid the meetings and partings, amid the laughter and merriment, amid the joys and sympathies and affections—think, think of my question. Have you got a home for your soul? Our earthly homes will soon be closed forever. Time hastens on with giant strides. Old age and death will be upon us before many years have passed away. Oh, seek an abiding home for the better part of you, the part that never dies! Before it be too late, seek a home for your soul.

Seek Christ that you may be safe. Woe to the man who is found outside the ark when the flood of God's wrath bursts at length on a sinful world! Seek Christ that you may be happy. None have a real right to be cheerful, merry, lighthearted, and at ease except those who have got a home for their souls. Once more I say, seek Christ without delay.

If Christ is the home of your soul, accept a friendly caution. Beware of being ashamed of your home in any place or company. The man who is ashamed of the home where he was born, the parents who brought him up when a baby, the brothers and sisters who played with him— that man, as a general rule, may be set down as a mean and despicable being. But what shall we say of the man who is ashamed of Him who died for him on the cross? What shall we say of the man who is ashamed of his Master and ashamed of his home? Take care that you are not that man. Whatever others around you please to think, never be ashamed of being a Christian. Let them laugh and mock and jest and scoff, if they will. They will not scoff in the hour of death and in the day of judgment. Hoist your flag, show your colors, nail them to the mast. Take care that you are never ashamed of your Master. Never be ashamed of your home!

✤ From the sermon "Our Home"

Heirs of God!

For as many as are led by the Spirit of God, they are the sons of God. For ye have not received the spirit of bondage again to fear; but ye have received the Spirit of adoption, whereby we cry, Abba, Father. The Spirit itself beareth witness with our spirit, that we are the children of God: And if children, then heirs; heirs of God, and joint-heirs with Christ; if so be that we suffer with him, that we may be also glorified together. —ROMANS 8:14–17

The people of whom Paul speaks in the verses before our eyes are the richest people upon earth. It must needs be so. They are called "heirs of God, and joint-heirs with Christ." The inheritance of these people is the only inheritance really worth having. All others are unsatisfying and disappointing. They bring with them many cares. They cannot cure an aching heart or lighten a heavy conscience. They cannot keep off family troubles. They cannot prevent sicknesses, bereavements, separations, and deaths. But there is no disappointment among the "heirs of God."

The inheritance I speak of is the only inheritance that can be kept forever. All others must be left in the hour of death if they have not been taken away before. The owners of millions can carry nothing with them beyond the grave. But it is not so with the "heirs of God." Their inheritance is eternal. The inheritance I speak of is the only inheritance which is within everybody's reach. Most men can never obtain riches and greatness, though they labor hard for them all their lives. But glory, honor, and eternal life are offered to every man freely who is willing to accept them on God's terms. Whoever will may be an heir of God, and joint-heir with Christ!

❖ From the sermon "Heirs of God"

Jesus Says, "Come"

Come unto me, all ye that labour and are heavy laden, and I will give you rest.
— MATTHEW 11:28

I love that word "come." To me it seems full of grace, mercy, and encouragement. "Come now," says the Lord in Isaiah, "and let us reason together…: though your sins be as scarlet, they shall be as white as snow" (Isa. 1:18). "Come" is the word put in the mouth of the king's messenger in the parable of the guest supper: "All things are ready: come unto the marriage" (Matt. 22:4). "Come" is the last word in the Bible to sinners: "The Spirit and the bride say, Come" (Rev. 22:17).

Jesus does not say, "Go and get ready." This is the word of the Pharisee and self-righteous. "Go and work out a righteousness. Do this and that and be saved." Jesus says, "Come." Come is a word of merciful invitation. It seems to say, "I want you to escape the wrath to come. I am not willing that any should perish. I have no pleasure in death. I would gladly have all men saved, and I offer all the water of life freely. So come to Me."

"Come" is a word of gracious expectation. It seems to say, "I am here waiting for you. I sit on my mercy seat expecting you to come. I wait to be gracious. I wait for more sinners to come in before I close the door. I want more names written down in the Book of Life before it is closed forever. So come to Me." "Come" is a word of kind encouragement. It seems to say, "I have got treasures to bestow if you will only receive them. I have that to give which makes it worthwhile to come: a free pardon, a robe of righteousness, a new heart, a star of peace. So come to Me." Brethren, I ask you to hear these words and lay them to heart. I plead for my Master. I stand here an ambassador. I ask you to come and be reconciled to God. Tell Him you have heard that He receives sinners; that you are such a one, and you want to be saved. Tell Him you have nothing to plead but His own word, that He said, "Come," and therefore you come to Him!

❖ From the sermon "Come unto Me"

Private Judgment

Prove all things; hold fast that which is good.
—1 THESSALONIANS 5:21

When I say the right of private judgment, I mean that every individual Christian has a right to judge for himself or herself by the Word of God whether that which is put before him or her as religious truth is God's truth or is not. When I say the duty of private judgment, I mean that God requires every Christian man to use the right of which I have just spoken to compare human words and human writings with God's revelation and to make sure that he is not deluded and taken in by false teaching.

And when I say the necessity of private judgment, I mean this: that it is absolutely needful for every Christian who loves his soul and would not be deceived to exercise the right and discharge the duty to which I have referred, seeing that experience shows the neglect of private judgment has always been the cause of immense evils in the church of Christ. Here, we must remember, the apostle Paul is writing to the Thessalonians, to a church that he himself had founded. Mark what he says: "Prove all things." He does not say, "Whatever apostles, whatever evangelists, pastors, and teachers, whatever your bishops, whatever your ministers tell you is truth—that you are to believe." No! He says, "Prove all things." He does not say, "Whatever the universal church pronounces true, that you are to hold." No! He says, "Prove all things." The principle laid down is this: prove all things by the Word of God—all ministers, all teaching, all preaching, all doctrines, all sermons, all writings, all opinions, all practices—prove all by the Word of God.

Measure all by the measure of the Bible. Compare all with the standard of the Bible.

Weigh all in the balances of the Bible. Examine all by the light of the Bible. Test all in the crucible of the Bible. That which can abide the fire of the Bible receive, hold, believe, and obey. That which cannot abide the fire of the Bible reject, refuse, repudiate, and cast away.

✤ From the sermon "Private Judgment"

The Bible Alone

Heaven and earth shall pass away,
but my words shall not pass away.
—MATTHEW 24:35

The Bible alone gives us true views of God. By nature man knows nothing clearly or fully about Him. All his conceptions of Him are low, groveling, and debased. What could be more degraded than the gods of the Canaanites and Egyptians, of Babylon, of Greece, and of Rome? What can be viler than the gods of the Hindus and other heathen in our own time? By the Bible we know that God hates sin. The destruction of the old world by the flood; the burning of Sodom and Gomorrah; the drowning of Pharaoh and the Egyptians in the Red Sea; the cutting off the nations of Canaan; the overthrow of Jerusalem and the temple; the scattering of the Jews—all these are unmistakable witnesses.

By the Bible we know that God loves sinners. His gracious promise in the day of Adam's fall, His long-suffering in the time of Noah, His deliverance of Israel out of the land of Egypt, His gift of the law at Mount Sinai, His bringing the tribes into the promised land, His forbearance in the days of the judges and kings, His repeated warnings by the mouth of His prophets, His restoration of Israel after the Babylonian captivity, His sending His Son into the world in due time to be crucified, His commanding the gospel to be preached to the Gentiles—all these are speaking facts. The Bible alone explains the state of things that we see in the world around us. There are many things on earth that a natural person cannot explain. The amazing inequality of conditions, the poverty and distress, the oppression and persecution, the shakings and tumults, the failures of statesmen and legislators, the constant existence of uncured evils and abuses—all these things are often puzzling to him or her. One sees but does not understand. But the Bible makes it all clear that there is a good time certainly coming, and coming perhaps sooner than people expect it—a time of perfect knowledge, perfect justice, perfect happiness, and perfect peace!

❖ From the sermon "Inspiration"

How the Word of God Is Corrupted

For we are not as many, which corrupt the word of God: but as
of sincerity, but as of God, in the sight of God speak we in Christ.
—2 CORINTHIANS 2:17

We corrupt the Word of God most dangerously when we throw any
doubt on the absolute inspiration of any part of Holy Scripture. This
is not merely corrupting the cup but the whole fountain! This is not
merely corrupting the bucket of living water, which we profess to present to our people, but poisoning the whole well. Once wrong on this
point, the whole substance of our religion is in danger. It is a flaw in the
foundation. It is a worm at the root of our theology. Once we allow this
worm to gnaw the root, then we will not be surprised if the branches,
the leaves, and the fruit decay little by little.

Second, we corrupt the Word of God when we make defective statements of doctrine. We do so when we add to the Bible the opinions of
the church or of the church fathers, as if they were of equal authority.
We do so when we take away from the Bible for the sake of pleasing
men. We do so when, from a feeling of false liberality, we keep back any
statement that seems narrow and harsh or hard. We do so when we try
to soften down anything that is taught about eternal punishment or the
reality of hell.

In the third place, we corrupt the Word of God when we make a
defective practical application of it. We do so when we do not discrimi-
nate between classes in our congregations, when we address everyone as
being possessed of grace because of their baptism or church membership, and do not draw the line between those who have the Spirit and
those who have not. Are we not in danger of defective handling of the
Word in our practical exhortations by not bringing home the statements
of the Bible to the various classes in our congregations? We speak plainly
to the poor, but do we also speak plainly to the rich? Do we speak plainly
in our dealings with the upper classes? This is a point on which, I fear,
we need to search our consciences.

❖ From the sermon "Not Corrupting the Word"

To Those Who Have the Holy Spirit

That he would grant you, according to the riches of his glory, to be strengthened with might by his Spirit in the inner man; that Christ may dwell in your hearts by faith; that ye, being rooted and grounded in love.
—EPHESIANS 3:16–17

Let me give a word of exhortation to all readers of this who have received the Spirit of Christ, to the penitent, the believing, the holy, the praying, the lovers of the Word of God. Be filled with the Spirit. Seek to be more and more under His blessed influence. Strive to have every thought and word and action and habit brought under obedience to the leading of the Holy Spirit. Grieve Him not by inconsistencies and conformity to the world. Quench Him not by trifling with little infirmities and small besetting sins. Seek rather to have Him ruling and reigning more completely over you every week that you live. Pray that you may yearly grow in grace and in the knowledge of Christ. This is the way to do good to the world. An eminent Christian is a lighthouse, seen far and wide by others, and doing good to myriads whom he never knows. This is the way to enjoy much inward comfort in this world, to have bright assurance in death, to leave broad evidence behind us, and at last to receive a great crown.

Finally, pray daily for a great outpouring of the Spirit on the church and on the world. This is the grand need of the day; it is the thing that we need far more than money, machinery, and men. The company of preachers in Christendom is far greater than it was in the days of Paul; but the actual spiritual work done on the earth, in proportion to the means used, is undoubtedly far less. We need more of the presence of the Holy Spirit, more in the pulpit, and more in the congregation, more in the pastoral visit, and more in the school. Where He is there will be life, health, growth, and fruitfulness. Where He is not, all will be dead, tame, formal, sleepy, and cold. Then let everyone who desires to see an increase of pure and undefiled religion pray daily for more of the presence of the Holy Spirit in every branch of the visible church of Christ!

✣ From the sermon "The Holy Spirit"

Three Points on Contentment

Not that I speak in respect of want: for I have learned, in what-soever state I am, therewith to be content. I know both how to be abased, and I know how to abound: every where and in all things I am instructed both to be full and to be hungry, both to abound and to suffer need. I can do all things through Christ which strength-eneth me. —PHILIPPIANS 4:11–13

Let me tell you why there is so little contentment in the world. The sim-ple answer is because there is so little grace and true religion. Few know their own sin; few feel their desert; and so few are content with such things as they have. Humility, self-knowledge, a clear sight of our own utter vileness and corruption—these are the true roots of contentment.

Let me tell you, second, what you should do if you want to be content. You must know your own heart, seek God for your portion, take Christ for your Savior, and use God's Word for your daily food. Contentment is not to be learned at the feet of Gamaliel but at the feet of Jesus Christ. He who has God for his friend and heaven for his home can wait for his good things and be content with little here below.

Let me tell you, last, that there is one thing with which we ought never to be content. That thing is a little religion, a little faith, a little hope, and a little grace. Let us never sit down satisfied with a little of these things. On the contrary, let us seek them more and more.

One thing there is which should never satisfy and content us, and that is anything that stands between our souls and Christ!

✣ From the sermon "Be Content"

Four Points of Self-Examination

Examine yourselves, whether ye be in the faith; prove your own selves. Know ye not your own selves, how that Jesus Christ is in you, except ye be reprobates?
—2 CORINTHIANS 13:5

I offer a word of friendly exhortation. I offer to everyone within these old cathedral walls tonight some food for thought and matter for self-examination.

1. First of all, how are you using your time? Life is short and very uncertain. You never know what a day may bring forth. Business and pleasure, money getting and money spending, eating and drinking, marrying and giving in marriage—all, all will soon be over and done with forever. Are you wasting time or turning it to good account?

2. Second, where shall you be in eternity? It is coming, coming, coming very fast upon us. You are going, going, going very fast into it. But where will you be? On the right hand or on the left in the day of judgment? Among the lost or among the saved? Oh, rest not, rest not until your soul is insured! Make sure work; leave nothing uncertain. It is a fearful thing to die unprepared and fall into the hands of the living God.

3. Third, would you be safe for time and eternity? Then seek Christ and believe in Him. Come to Him just as you are. Seek Him while He may be found, call upon Him while He is near. There is still a throne of grace. It is not too late. Christ waits to be gracious; He invites you to come to Him. Before the door is shut and the judgment begins, repent, believe, and be saved.

4. Last, would you be happy? Cling to Christ and live the life of faith in Him. Abide in Him and live near to Him. Follow Him with heart and soul and mind and strength, and seek to know Him better every day. So doing you shall have great peace while you pass through temporary things and in the midst of a dying world shall "never die" (John 11:26).

❖ From the sermon "Thoughts on Immortality"

Jesus at the Right Hand of the Father

If ye then be risen with Christ, seek those things which are above, where Christ sitteth on the right hand of God. —COLOSSIANS 3:1

Let your faith's eye see Jesus as your priest in heaven and rejoice in the sight. What will you see there? You will see the same Savior who died for you exalted to the place of highest honor and doing the work of an intercessor and advocate for your soul. All was not done when He suffered for your sins on Calvary. He rose again and ascended up to heaven to carry on there the work that He began on earth. There, as our priest and representative, He ever lives to make intercession for us. He presents our names before the Father. He continually pleads our cause. He obtains for us a never-ending supply of mercy and grace. He watches over our interests with an eye that never sleeps. He is ready morning, noon, and night to hear our confessions, to grant us absolution, to strengthen us for duty, to comfort us in trial, to guide us in perplexity, to hold us up in temptation, and to preserve us safe on our journey heavenward until we reach home.

What will you get by looking upward to Jesus? Comfort and strength in all the daily battles of life. What thought more cheering than the thought that Jesus is ever looking at you and watching over you! What idea more strengthening than the idea that you are never alone, never forgotten, never neglected, never without a friend who is "able also to save them to the uttermost that come unto God by him, seeing he ever liveth to make intercession for them" (Heb. 7:25)! Look up to Him daily if you would be a happy Christian. Pour out your heart before Him if you would enjoy the consolations of the gospel. This daily look to a living interceding Jesus is one great secret of strength and comfort in religion!

❖ From the sermon "Are You Looking?"

The Cross of Christ

Who his own self bare our sins in his own body on the tree, that we,
being dead to sins, should live unto righteousness: by whose stripes
ye were healed.
                                                          —1 PETER 2:24

The "cross" sometimes means that wooden cross on which the Lord Jesus Christ was nailed and put to death on Calvary. This is what Paul had in his mind's eye when he told the Philippians that Christ "became obedient unto death, even the death of the cross" (Phil. 2:8). This is not the cross in which Paul boasted. He would have shrunk with horror from the idea of boasting in a mere piece of wood. I have no doubt he would have denounced the Roman Catholic adoration of the crucifix as profane, blasphemous, and idolatrous.

The "cross" sometimes means the afflictions and trials that believers in Christ have to go through if they follow Christ faithfully for their religion's sake. This is the sense in which our Lord uses the word when He says, "And he that taketh not his cross, and followeth after me, is not worthy of me" (Matt. 10:38). This also is not the sense in which Paul uses the word when he writes to the Galatians. He knew that cross well; he carried it patiently. But he is not speaking of it here.

Jesus Christ crucified was the joy and delight, the comfort and the peace, the hope and the confidence, the foundation and the resting place, the ark and the refuge, the food and the medicine of Paul's soul. He did not think of what he had done and suffered himself. He did not meditate on his own goodness and his own righteousness. He loved to think of what Christ had done and suffered—of the death of Christ, the righteousness of Christ, the atonement of Christ, the blood of Christ, the finished work of Christ. In this he did boast.

This was the sun of his soul.

❖ From the sermon "The Cross of Christ"

Lay Aside Every Weight

Wherefore seeing we also are compassed about with so great a cloud of witnesses, let us lay aside every weight, and the sin which doth so easily beset us, and let us run with patience the race that is set before us.
—HEBREWS 12:1

By this he means that we must give up everything that is really hurtful to our souls. We must cast away everything that hinders us upon our road toward heaven: the lust of the flesh, the lust of the eye, and the pride of life. The love of riches, pleasures, and honors; the spirit of lukewarmness and carelessness and indifference about the things of God—all must be rooted out and forsaken if we are anxious for the prize. We must mortify the deeds of the body; we must crucify our affections for this world. We must look well to our habits and inclinations and employments, and if we find anything coming in as a stumbling block between ourselves and salvation, we must be ready to lay it aside as if it were a millstone about our necks, although it cost us as much pain as cutting off a hand or plucking out a right eye. Away with everything that keeps us back. Our feet are slow at the very best. We have a long course to run. We cannot afford to carry weight if we are really contending for everlasting life.

But above all we must take heed that we lay aside the sin that does most easily beset us, the sin which from our age or habit or taste or disposition or feelings possesses the greatest power over us. I know of two that are always at our elbows, two sins that try the most advanced Christians even to the end, and these are pride and unbelief. Pride in our own difference from others, pride in our reputation as Christians, pride in our spiritual attainments. Unbelief about our own sinfulness, unbelief about God's wisdom, unbelief about God's mercy. Oh, they are heavy burdens, and sorely do they keep us back, and few really know they are carrying them. Few indeed are those who will not discover them at the very bottom of the chamber of their hearts, waiting an opportunity to come out!

❖ From the sermon "The Christian Race"

The Gift of His Son

For God so loved the world, that he gave his only begotten Son,
that whosoever believeth in him should not perish, but have ever-
lasting life. —JOHN 3:16

The gift of His Son: let us next inquire in what way it pleased God to manifest this love. We had all sinned. Who then could put away this sin and present us clean and spotless before His throne? We had all failed utterly of keeping His holy laws. How then could we be clothed for the wedding feast of our Master? Beloved, here is wisdom! This is the very point that the learned of this world could never understand. How, they have asked, can perfect justice and perfect mercy be reconciled? How can God justify His sinful creature and yet be that Holy One whose law must needs be fulfilled? But all is explained in this simple verse, if you can receive it; and thus it was, "he gave his only begotten Son."

Observe the magnitude of this gift, "his only begotten Son." Can anything give you a more tender idea of God's love? Observe again the expression "he gave," not because we had merited anything, for it was a free gift; not for our deserving, for it was all of grace. "By grace are ye saved," says Paul to the Ephesians (Eph. 2:8). "The gift of God is eternal life," says the same apostle to the Romans (Rom. 6:23). And for what purpose was His Son given? Beloved, He was given to atone for our guilt by the sacrifice and death of Himself as a lamb without spot and blemish. By so doing He made a full, perfect, and sufficient oblation and satisfaction for the sins of the whole world. He was given to bear our iniquities and carry our transgressions upon the accursed tree, the cross; for being innocent Himself He was for our sakes accounted guilty, that we for His sake might be accounted pure. He was given to fulfill the demands of that law which we have broken; and He did fulfill them. He "was in all points tempted," says Paul, "like as we are, and yet without sin" (Heb. 4:15).

The prince of this world had nothing in Him, and thus He brought in an everlasting righteousness, which like a pure white raiment is unto all and upon all those who believe.

✤ From the sermon "Saving Faith"

The Foundation upon Which This Church Is Built

And I say also unto thee, That thou art Peter, and upon this rock I will build my church; and the gates of hell shall not prevail against it.
—MATTHEW 16:18

The Lord Jesus Christ tells us, "Upon this rock I will build my church." What did the Lord Jesus Christ mean when He spoke of this foundation? Did He mean the apostle Peter, to whom He was speaking? I think assuredly not. I can see no reason, if he meant Peter, why He did not say, "on you" will I build my church. If He had meant Peter, He would have said, "I will build my church on you," as plainly as He said, "I will give you the keys." No! It was not the person of the apostle Peter, but the good confession that the apostle had just made. It was not Peter, the erring, unstable man, but the mighty truth that the Father had revealed to Peter. It was the truth concerning Jesus Christ Himself, which was the rock. It was Christ's mediatorship and Christ's messiahship. It was the blessed truth that Jesus was the promised Savior, the real intercessor between God and man. This was the rock and this was the foundation on which the church of Christ was to be built.

My brethren, this foundation was laid at a mighty cost. It was necessary that the Son of God should take our nature upon Him and in that nature live, suffer, and die not for His own sins, but for ours. It was necessary that in that nature Christ should go to the grave and rise again. It was necessary that in that nature Christ should go up to heaven to sit at the right hand of God, having obtained eternal redemption for all His people. No other foundation but this could have borne the weight of that church of which our text speaks. No other foundation could have met the necessities of a world of sinners.

Here is the point that demands our personal attention. Are we on the rock? Are we really joined to the one foundation? Look to your foundation, my beloved, if you would know whether or not you are members of the one true church.

✤ From the sermon "The True Church"

Perilous Times!

This know also, that in the last days perilous times shall come. For men shall be lovers of their own selves, covetous, boasters, proud, blasphemers, disobedient to parents, unthankful, unholy, without natural affection, trucebreakers, false accusers, incontinent, fierce, despisers of those that are good, traitors, heady, highminded, lovers of pleasures more than lovers of God; having a form of godliness, but denying the power thereof: from such turn away. —2 TIMOTHY 3:1–5

I am going to write things that will not please everybody. I am prepared for that. "If I yet pleased men, I should not be the servant of Christ" (Gal. 1:10). Some will think me to be a foolish alarmist and deny that there is any danger. Be it so. The faithful prophets are never popular. Some will think me to be a gloomy, melancholy man and charge me with ignoring the immense amount of good that is going on in the country. Be it so. Infidelity abounds. Look at the drunkenness of the times. In spite of Christianity, temperance, teetotalism, and education, we are a very intemperate people. The testimony of judges and magistrates about the effects of drinking as a main cause of crime is enough to make one's blood run cold. Is not this perilous?

Look at the immorality in our times. I do not only allude to the coarser forms of sin in this respect when I say this, though I might say much. I have in view the widespread decay of morals among young women of all classes. I challenge anyone to deny that novels and romances are read nowadays in many a household, which contain scenes and descriptions that would not have been tolerated thirty years ago. There is a hideous familiarity with that which is racy and indelicate. Is not this perilous?

Look at the covetousness of our times. I do not speak so much of miserly habits as of the intense love of money that overspreads all classes. To pile up a fortune in a few years, to speculate successfully, to obtain the power of every kind of self-indulgence at a bound—how thoroughly this is the life of many people! The history of joint-stock companies and banks and railways in the last few years is a disgraceful tale and shows how men will do anything to get money. Is not this perilous?

✣ From the sermon "Perilous Times"

What Can We Learn from Sickness?

So teach us to number our days,
that we may apply our hearts unto wisdom.
—PSALM 90:12

Sickness, disease, decay, and death are the common lot of all mankind without exception. This is the old story. It is the history of every child of Adam for the last six thousand years except for Enoch and Elijah. No medical skill can prevent death. Our physicians and surgeons are unwearied in their efforts to find new remedies and modes of treatment. They compass sea and land in order to prevent disease, discover remedies, diminish pain, and lengthen life. But in spite of all that medicine and surgery can do, there is something that the ablest doctors find beyond their reach. When the time appointed by God comes, they cannot keep men and women alive. After all, there is nothing amazing in this. The tent in which our soul lives, the human body, is a most frail and complicated machine. From the sole of the foot to the crown of the head, there is not a part of us which is not liable to disease. When I think of the variety of ailments that may assail our frame, I do not so much wonder that we die at last as we live so long!

Brethren, when your time comes to be ill, I beseech you not to forget what the illness means. Beware of fretting and murmuring and complaining and giving way to an impatient spirit. Regard your sickness as a blessing in disguise, a good and not an evil, a friend and not an enemy. No doubt we would all prefer to learn spiritual lessons in the school of ease and not under the rod. But rest assured that God knows better than we do how to teach us. The light of the last day will show you that there was a meaning and a need-be in all your bodily ailments. The lessons that we learn on a sickbed, when we are shut out from the world, are often lessons that we would never learn elsewhere. Settle it down in your minds that, however much you may dislike it, sickness is not an unmixed evil!

✣ From the sermon "Christ in the Sick Room"

The Importance of the Local Body of Believers

Not forsaking the assembling of ourselves together, as the manner of
some is; but exhorting one another: and so much the more, as ye see
the day approaching. —HEBREWS 10:25

No careful reader of the Bible can fail to observe that many separate visible churches are mentioned in the New Testament. At Corinth, at Ephesus, at Thessalonica, at Antioch, at Smyrna, at Sardis, at Laodicea, and several other places. At each we find a distinct body of professing Christians, a body of people baptized in Christ's name and professing the faith of Christ's gospel. And these bodies of people we find spoken of as the churches of the places that are named. We read of the churches of Judea, the churches of Syria, the churches of Galatia, the churches of Asia, the churches of Macedonia. In each case, the expression means the bodies of baptized Christians in the countries mentioned.

We know, for one thing, that these churches were all mixed bodies. They consisted not only of converted people but of many unconverted people also. They contained not only believers but members who fell into gross errors and mistakes, both of faith and practice. This is clear from the account we have of the churches at Corinth, at Ephesus, and at Sardis. Of Sardis, the Lord Jesus Himself says that there were "a few," a few only, in it who had not "defiled their garments" (Rev. 3:4). We know, moreover, that even in the apostles' times, churches received plain warnings that they might perish and pass away altogether. To the church at Rome the threat was held out that it would be "cut off"; to the church at Ephesus, that its candlestick would be taken away; to the church at Laodicea, that it would be utterly rejected (Rom. 11:22; Rev. 2:5; 3:16).

We know, moreover, that in all these churches there was public worship, preaching, reading of the Scriptures, prayer, praise, discipline, order, government, the ministry, and the sacraments. Mixed and imperfect as these churches plainly were, within their pale were to be found nearly all the existing believers and members of the body of Christ. Everything in the New Testament leads us to suppose that there could have been few believers, if any, who were not members of one or another of the professing churches scattered up and down the world.

❖ From the sermon "The Church"

Come Out from among Them

Wherefore come out from among them, and be ye separate, saith the Lord, and touch not the unclean thing; and I will receive you. And will be a Father unto you, and ye shall be my sons and daughters, saith the Lord Almighty. —2 CORINTHIANS 6:17–18

The text that heads this page touches a subject of vast importance in religion. That subject is the great duty of separation from the world. This is the point that Paul had in view when he wrote to the Corinthians, "Come out, be separate." The subject is one that demands the best attention of all who profess and call themselves Christians. In every age of the church, separation from the world has always been one of the grand evidences of a work of grace in the heart. He who has been really born of the Spirit, and made a new creature in Christ Jesus, has always endeavored to "come out from" the world and live a separate life. They who have only had the name of Christian, without the reality, have always refused to come out and be separate from the world.

The subject perhaps was never more important than it is at the present day. There is a widely spread desire to make things pleasant in religion, to saw off the corners and edges of the cross, and to avoid, as far as possible, self-denial. On every side we hear professing Christians declaring loudly that we must not be narrow and exclusive and that there is no harm in many things which the holiest saints of old thought bad for their souls. That we may go anywhere and do anything and spend our time in anything and read anything and keep any company and plunge into anything, and all the while may be very good Christians! This, this is the maxim of thousands. In a day like this, I think it good to raise a warning voice and invite attention to the teaching of God's Word. It is written in that Word, "Come out…and be ye separate"!

✣ From the sermon "The World"

Five Fruits of True Repentance

Bring forth therefore fruits worthy of repentance.
—LUKE 3:8

1. True repentance begins with knowledge of sin. The eyes of the penitent man are opened. He sees with dismay and confusion the length and breadth of God's holy law and the extent, the enormous extent, of his own transgressions. He discovers, to his surprise, that in thinking himself a good sort of man and a man with a good heart, he has been under a huge delusion.

2. True repentance goes on to work sorrow for sin. The heart of a penitent man is touched with deep remorse because of his past transgressions. He is cut to the heart to think that he should have lived so madly and so wickedly. He mourns over time wasted, over talents misspent, over God dishonored, over his own soul injured. The remembrance of these things is grievous to him.

3. True repentance proceeds further to produce confession of sin. The tongue of a penitent man is loosed. He feels he must speak to that God against whom he has sinned. Something within him tells him he must cry to God and pray to God and talk with God about the state of his own soul. He must pour out his heart and acknowledge his iniquities at the throne of grace.

4. True repentance, furthermore, shows itself in a thorough breaking off from sin. The life of a penitent man is altered. The course of his daily conduct is entirely changed. A new King reigns within his heart. He puts off the old man. What God commands he now desires to practice, and what God forbids he now desires to avoid.

5. True repentance, in the last place, shows itself by producing in the heart a settled habit of deep hatred of all sin. The mind of a penitent man becomes a mind habitually holy. He abhors that which is evil and cleaves to that which is good. He delights in the law of God. He comes short of his own desires not infrequently. He finds in himself an evil principle warring against the Spirit of God.

✣ From the sermon "Repentance"

The Mighty Truth of the Gospel

Wherefore he is able also to save them to the uttermost that come unto God by him, seeing he ever liveth to make intercession for them.
—HEBREWS 7:25

Let us never lose sight of this mighty truth of the gospel, the intercession and priestly office of our Lord and Savior Jesus Christ. I believe that losing sight of this great truth is one principal reason why so many have fallen away from the faith in some quarters, have forsaken the creed of their Protestant forefathers, and have gone back to the darkness of Rome. Once firmly established upon this mighty truth—that we have one Priest and altar; that we have an unfailing, never-dying, ever-living intercessor who has transferred His office to none—and we shall see that we need turn aside nowhere else. We need not hew for ourselves broken cisterns which can hold no water when we have in the Lord Jesus Christ a fountain of living waters, ever flowing and free to all. We need not seek any human priest upon earth when we have a divine Priest living for us in heaven.

Let us beware of regarding the Lord Jesus Christ only as one that is dead. Here, I believe, many greatly err. They think much of His atoning death, and it is right that they should do so. But we ought not to stop short there. We ought to remember that He not only died and went to the grave but that He rose again and ascended up on high, leading captivity captive. We ought to remember that He is now sitting on the right hand of God to do a work as real, as true, as important to our souls as the work which He did when He shed His blood. Christ lives and is not dead. He lives as truly as any one of us. Christ sees us, hears us, knows us, and is acting as a priest in heaven on behalf of His believing people. The thought of His life ought to have as great and important a place in our souls as the thought of His death upon the cross.

✣ From the sermon "Christ's Power to Save"

What Is Regeneration?

Jesus answered, Verily, verily, I say unto thee, Except a man be born
of water and of the Spirit, he cannot enter into the kingdom of God.
—JOHN 3:5

Regeneration means that change of heart and nature which a man goes through when he becomes a true Christian. As Ezekiel describes it: "And I will give them one heart, and I will put a new spirit within you; and I will take the stony heart out of their flesh, and will give them an heart of flesh" (11:19); "A new heart also will I give you, and a new spirit will I put within you: and I will take away the stony heart out of your flesh, and I will give you an heart of flesh" (36:26). The apostle John sometimes calls it being "born of God," sometimes being "born again," sometimes being "born of the Spirit" (John 1:13; 3:3, 6).

The epistle to the Romans speaks of it "as those that are alive from the dead" (Rom. 6:13). In the second epistle to the Corinthians Paul says, "Therefore if any man be in Christ, he is a new creature: old things are passed away; behold, all things are become new" (2 Cor. 5:17). The epistle to the Ephesians speaks of it as a resurrection together with Christ: "And you hath he quickened, who were dead in trespasses and sins" (Eph. 2:1). Furthermore, he says "that ye put off concerning the former conversation the old man, which is corrupt according to the deceitful lusts…and that ye put on the new man, which after God is created in righteousness and true holiness" (Eph. 4:22, 24). The epistle to Titus calls it "washing of regeneration, and renewing of the Holy Ghost" (Titus 3:5).

All these expressions come to the same thing in the end. They are all the same truth, only viewed from different sides. And all have one and the same meaning. They describe a great radical change of heart and nature, a thorough alteration and transformation of the whole inner man, a participation in the resurrection life of Christ.

❖ From the sermon "Regeneration"

Pharisees and Sadducees

*Then Jesus said unto them, Take heed and beware of the leaven of
the Pharisees and of the Sadducees.* —MATTHEW 16:6

"Take heed," He says, "be on your guard against the yeast of the Pharisees and of the Sadducees." The danger of which He warns them is false
doctrine. He says nothing about the sword of persecution or the love of
money or the love of pleasure. All these things no doubt were perils and
snares to which the souls of the apostles were exposed, but against these
things our Lord raises no warning voice here. The doctrine of the Pharisees may be summed up in three words: they were formalists, tradition
worshipers, and self-righteous. They attached such weight to the traditions of men that they practically regarded them of more importance
than the inspired writings of the Old Testament. They valued themselves
on excessive strictness in their attention to all the ceremonial requirements of the Mosaic law. They made a great deal about the external parts
of religion, and such things that could be seen by men.

The doctrine of the Sadducees, on the other hand, may be summed
up in three words: freethinking, skepticism, and rationalism. The practical effect of their teaching was to shake men's faith in any revelation and
to throw a cloud of doubt over men's minds that was only one degree
better than infidelity. I believe our Lord delivered this solemn warning for the perpetual benefit of that church which He came to earth to
establish. He knew that there always would be Pharisees in spirit and
Sadducees in spirit among professing Christians. He knew that their succession would never fail, and their generation never become extinct, and
that though the names of Pharisees and Sadducees were no more, yet
their principles would always exist. He knew that during the time that
the church existed until His return, there would always be some who
would add to the Word and some who would subtract from it, some
who would tone it down by adding to it other things, and some who
would bleed it to death by subtracting from its principal truths. And this
is the reason why we find Him delivering this solemn warning: "Take
heed and beware of the leaven of the Pharisees and of the Sadducees"!

✣ From the sermon "Take Heed"

Happiness from Another World

Happy is that people, that is in such a case: yea, happy is that people, whose God is the LORD.
—PSALM 144:15

To be truly happy, a man must have sources of gladness which are not dependent on anything in this world. There is nothing upon earth which is not stamped with the mark of instability and uncertainty. All the good things which money can buy are but momentary: they either leave us, or we are obliged to leave them! All the sweetest relationships in life are liable to come to an end; death may come any day and cut them off. The person whose happiness depends entirely on things here below is like one who builds his house on sand or leans his or her weight on a reed!

Tell me not of your happiness if it daily hangs on the uncertainties of earth. Your home may be rich in comforts; your wife and children may be all you could desire; your means may be amply sufficient to meet all your needs. But oh, remember, if you have nothing more than this to look to, that you stand on the brink of a precipice! Your rivers of pleasure may any day be dried up. Your joy may be deep and earnest, but it is fearfully short-lived! It has no root. It is not true happiness. To be really happy, a man must be able to look on every side without uncomfortable feelings. He must be able to look back to the past without guilty fears. He must be able to look around him without discontent. He must be able to look forward without anxious dread. He must be able to sit down and think calmly about things past, present, and to come, and feel prepared. The man who has a weak side in his condition, a side that he does not like looking at or considering, that man is not really happy!

✢ From the sermon "Happiness"

Lessons from Athens

*Now while Paul waited for them at Athens, his spirit was stirred
in him, when he saw the city wholly given to idolatry. Therefore
disputed he in the synagogue with the Jews, and with the devout
persons, and in the market daily with them that met with him.*
—ACTS 17:16–17

What did Paul see at Athens? The answer of the text is clear and unmistakable. He saw a "city wholly given to idolatry." Idols met his eyes in
every street. The temples of idol gods and goddesses occupied every
prominent position. The magnificent statue of Minerva, at least forty
feet high according to Pliny, towered above the Acropolis and caught
the eye from every point. A vast system of idol worship overspread the
whole place and thrust itself everywhere on his notice. The ancient
writer Pausanias expressly says that "the Athenians surpassed all states in
the attention which they paid to the worship of the gods." In short, the
city, as the marginal reading says, was "full of idols."

And yet this city, I would have you remember, was probably the
most favorable specimen of a heathen city which Paul could have seen. In
proportion to its size, it very likely contained the most learned, civilized,
philosophical, highly educated, artistic, intellectual population on the face
of the globe. But what was it in a religious point of view? If the true God
was unknown at Athens, what must He have been in the darker places of
the earth? Leave man without a Bible, and he will have a religion of some
kind; for human nature, corrupt as it is, must have a God. But it will be
a religion without light or peace or hope. "In the wisdom of God the
world by wisdom knew not God" (1 Cor. 1:21). Old Athens is a standing
lesson which we shall do well to observe. It is vain to suppose that nature,
unaided by revelation, will ever lead fallen man to nature's God. Without
a Bible the Athenian bowed down to sticks and stones and worshiped the
work of his own hands. Place a heathen philosopher, a Stoic, or an Epi-
curean by the side of an open grave and ask him about a world to come,
and he could have told you nothing certain, satisfactory, or peace-giving.

❖ From the sermon "Athens"

How Paul Felt at Athens

Now while Paul waited for them at Athens, his spirit was stirred in him, when he saw the city wholly given to idolatry. Therefore disputed he in the synagogue with the Jews, and with the devout persons, and in the market daily with them that met with him.

—ACTS 17:16–17

Paul saw a "city wholly given to idolatry." How did the sight affect him? What did he feel? It is instructive to observe how the same sight affects different people. Place two men on the same spot; let them stand side by side; let the same objects be presented to their eyes. The emotions called forth in the one man will often be wholly different from those called forth in the other. The thoughts which will be wakened up and brought to birth will often be as far as the poles asunder.

He was stirred with holy compassion. It troubled his heart to see so many myriads perishing for lack of knowledge, without God, without Christ, having no hope, traveling in the broad road which leads to destruction! He was stirred with holy sorrow. It troubled his heart to see so much talent misapplied. Here were hands capable of excellent works, minds capable of noble conceptions. And yet the God who gave life and breath and power was not glorified. He was stirred with holy indignation against sin and the devil. He saw the god of this world blinding the eyes of multitudes of his fellow human beings and leading them captive at his will. He saw his divine Master unknown and unrecognized by His own creatures and idols receiving the homage due to the King of Kings.

Reader, these feelings which stirred the apostle are a leading characteristic of a man born of the Spirit. Do you know anything of them? Where there is true grace, there will always be tender concern for the souls of others. Where there is true sonship to God, there will always be zeal for the Father's glory. It is written of the ungodly that they not only commit things worthy of death but "have pleasure in them that do them" (Rom. 1:32). It may be said with equal truth of the godly that they not only mourn over sin in their own hearts but mourn over sin in others.

✤ From the sermon "Athens"

What Did Paul Do at Athens?

Now while Paul waited for them at Athens, his spirit was stirred in him, when he saw the city wholly given to idolatry. Therefore disputed he in the synagogue with the Jews, and with the devout persons, and in the market daily with them that met with him.
—ACTS 17:16–17

He did something. He was not the man to stand still and confer with flesh and blood in the face of a city full of idols. He might have reasoned with himself that he stood alone, that he was a Jew by birth, that he was a stranger in a strange land, that he had to oppose the rooted prejudices and old associations of learned men, that to attack the old religion of a whole city was to beard a lion in his den, that the doctrines of the gospel were little likely to be effective on minds steeped in Greek philosophy. But none of these thoughts seem to have crossed the mind of Paul. He saw souls perishing. He felt that life was short and time passing away. He had confidence in the power of his Master's message to meet every man's soul; he had received mercy himself and knew not how to hold his peace. He acted at once, and what his hand found to do, he did with his might. Oh, that we had more men of action in these days!

And he did what he did with holy wisdom as well as holy boldness. He commenced aggressive measures alone and waited not for companions and helpers. But he commenced them with consummate skill and in a manner most likely to obtain a footing for the gospel.

First, we are told, he disputed "with the Jews" in the synagogue and the "devout persons," or proselytes, who attended the Jewish worship. Afterward he went on to dispute, or hold discussions, "in the market daily with them that met with him." He advanced step-by-step like an experienced general. Here, as elsewhere, Paul is a model to us; he combined fiery zeal and boldness with judicious tact and sanctified common sense. Oh, that we had more men of wisdom in these days!

✣ From the sermon "Athens"

The Hope of Heaven

In my Father's house are many mansions: if it were not so, I would have told you. I go to prepare a place for you. And if I go and prepare a place for you, I will come again, and receive you unto myself; that where I am, there ye may be also. And whither I go ye know, and the way ye know.
—JOHN 14:2–4

Brethren, you all hope to go to heaven yourselves. There is not one of you but wishes to be in eternal happiness after death. But on what are your hopes founded? Heaven is a prepared place. Those who shall dwell there are all of one character. The entrance into it is only by one door. Brethren, remember that. And then, too, I read of two sorts of hope: a good hope and a bad hope; a true hope and a false hope; a living hope and a dead hope; the hope of the righteous and the hope of the wicked; the hope of the believer and of the hypocrite. I read of some who have hope through grace, a hope that does not make ashamed, and of others who have no true hope and are without God in the world.

Yes, brethren, these are the men and women that enter heaven; nothing can keep them out. Tell me not of deathbed evidence and visions and dreams of dying people. There is no evidence like that of Christ's followers. Repentance, faith, and holiness—this is a character against which the gates shall never be closed. Repent and believe in Christ and be converted, and then, whatever happens to others, you, at least, shall enter heaven; you shall never be cast out. Christian, look up and take comfort. Jesus has prepared a place for you, and those who follow Him shall never perish, neither shall any man pluck them out of His hands. Look forward to that glorious abode He has provided. Look forward in faith, for it is yours. Oh, Christian brothers and sisters, think what a glorious meeting that shall be!

✣ From the sermon "Heaven"

Put On the Armor of Light

The night is far spent, the day is at hand: let us therefore cast off the works of darkness, and let us put on the armour of light.
—ROMANS 13:12

How are you to put on the armor of light? Listen to me once more and I will tell you. You ought to aim at every grace and habit which befits a believer in Christ and a child of God and a citizen of a heavenly kingdom. You ought not to leave eminent holiness and spirituality to a few, as if none but a few favored ones could be eminent saints. You ought to labor to wear the armor of light yourself, the belt of truth, the breastplate of righteousness, the helmet of hope, and the sword of the Spirit (Eph. 6:14–17). Wherever you may live and whatever may be your trials, however great your difficulties and however small your helps, nothing should prevent your aiming at the highest standard—to behave like one who believes that Christ is coming again! You should resolve, by God's help, so to live that the day of Christ shall find you needing as little change as possible! You should seek to have your tastes so heavenly, your affections so spiritual, your will so subdued, your mind so unworldly, that when the Lord appears, you may be thoroughly in tune for His kingdom!

Oh, that everyone into whose hands this address may fall may so walk with God that, like Enoch, he may be only translated from a lower degree of communion with God to a higher one, from walking by faith to walking by sight. This would be putting on the armor of light. Live as if you thought that Christ might come at any time. Do everything as if you did it for the last time. Say everything as if you said it for the last time. Read every chapter in the Bible as if you did not know whether you would be allowed to read it again. Pray every prayer as if you felt it might be your last opportunity. Hear every sermon as if you were hearing once and forever.

This is the way to be found ready. This is the way to turn Christ's second appearing to good account. This is the way to put on the armor of light!

❖ From the sermon "Coming Events and Present Duties"

Your Tears Will Be Wiped Away

And God shall wipe away all tears from their eyes; and there shall be no more death, neither sorrow, nor crying, neither shall there be any more pain: for the former things are passed away.
—REVELATION 21:4

Beloved children, a Bible text stands at the top of this page. I would like you to read it twice over. I am going to tell you something which, I hope, will make you remember that text as long as you live. I am going to tell you about three places of which the Bible says a great deal. It matters little what we know about some places, but it matters much to know something about the three places of which I am now going to speak. First of all, there is a place where there is a great deal of crying. What is that place? It is the world in which you and I live. This world is a place where there is much crying and where things do not always go on pleasantly. Crying came into the world by reason of sin. Sin is the cause of all the weeping and tears and sorrow and pain which are upon earth.

There is a place where there is nothing else but crying. What is this place? It is the place to which all bad people go when they are dead. It is the place which the Bible calls hell. In hell there is no laughter and smiling. There is nothing but weeping and wailing and gnashing of teeth! In hell there is no happiness. Those who go there cry all day and all night without stopping. They have no rest. They never go to sleep and wake up happy. They never stop crying in hell.

There is a place where there is no crying at all! What is this place? It is heaven. It is the place to which all godly people go when they are dead. In heaven, there all is joy and happiness. There, no tears are shed. There, sorrow and pain and sickness and death can never enter in. There can be no crying in heaven because there is nothing that can cause grief. Best of all, the Lord Jesus Christ Himself will be in the midst of heaven! His people shall at last see Him face-to-face and never leave His presence!

✣ From the sermon "No More Crying"

How to Be Made Holy

We are sanctified through the offering of the body of Jesus Christ once for all. —HEBREWS 10:10

Would you be holy? Would you become a new creature? Then begin with Christ! You will do just nothing until you feel your sin and weakness and flee to Him! He is the beginning of all holiness. He is not only wisdom and righteousness to His people, but sanctification also. Men sometimes try to make themselves holy first, and sad work they make of it! They toil and labor and turn over many new leaves and make many changes, and yet, like the woman with the issue of blood, they feel nothing bettered but rather worse. They run in vain and labor in vain! Little wonder, for they are beginning at the wrong end! They are building up a wall of sand. Their work runs down as fast as they throw it up. They are bailing water out of a leaky vessel. The leak gains on them, not they on the leak. Another foundation of holiness can no man lay than that which Paul laid, even Christ Jesus. Without Christ, we can do nothing. Sanctification outside of Christ is filth and sin! Redemption outside of Christ is bondage and slavery! "But of him are ye in Christ Jesus, who of God is made unto us wisdom, and righteousness, and sanctification, and redemption" (1 Cor. 1:30).

Would you be holy? Would you be partakers of the divine nature? Then go to Christ!

Wait for nothing! Wait for nobody! Do not linger! Think not to make you yourself ready. Go and say to Him, in the words of that beautiful hymn:

> Nothing in my hand I bring,
> Simply to Your cross I cling!
> Naked, flee to You for dress;
> Helpless, look to You for grace!

❖ From the sermon "We Must Be Holy"

Riches and Poverty

*There was a certain rich man, which was clothed in purple and fine
linen, and fared sumptuously every day: and there was a certain
beggar named Lazarus, which was laid at his gate, full of sores.*

—LUKE 16:19–20

The Lord Jesus begins the parable by telling us of a rich man and a
beggar. He says not a word in praise either of poverty or of riches. He
describes the circumstances of a wealthy man and the circumstances of
a poor man but neither condemns the temporal position of one nor
praises that of the other. The contrast between the two men is painfully
striking. Look on this picture and on that. Here is one who possessed
abundance of this world's good things. He "was clothed in purple and
fine linen, and fared sumptuously every day." Here is another who has
literally nothing. He is a friendless, diseased, half-starved pauper. He lies
at the rich man's gate "full of sores" and begs for crumbs.

Both are children of Adam. Both came from the same dust and
belong to one family.

Both are living in the same land and subjects of the same government.
And yet how different is their condition! We must take heed that we do
not draw lessons from the parable which it was never meant to teach. The
rich are not always evil men and do not always go to hell. The poor are not
always holy men and do not always go to heaven. We must not rush into
the extreme of supposing that it is sinful to be rich. We must not run away
with the idea that there is anything wicked in the difference of condition
here described and that God intended all men to be equal.

Labor to do good to all men; pity your poorer brethren and help
every reasonable endeavor to raise them from their low estate. Do not
slacken your hand from any endeavor to increase knowledge, to promote
morality, to improve the temporal condition of the poor. But never,
never forget that you live in a fallen world, that sin is all around you, and
that the devil is abroad. And be very sure that the rich man and Lazarus
are emblems of two classes of people which will always be in the world
until the Lord comes!

❖ From the sermon "Riches and Poverty"

Lazarus Though Poor, Yet Rich

There was a certain rich man, which was clothed in purple and fine linen, and fared sumptuously every day: and there was a certain beggar named Lazarus, which was laid at his gate, full of sores, and desiring to be fed with the crumbs which fell from the rich man's table: moreover the dogs came and licked his sores.

—LUKE 16:19–21

But who that reads the parable to the end can fail to see that in the highest sense Lazarus was not poor but rich? He was a child of God. He was an heir of glory. He possessed durable riches and righteousness. His name was in the Book of Life. His place was prepared for him in heaven. He had the best of clothing, the righteousness of a Savior. He had the best of friends; God Himself was his portion. He had the best of food; he had food to eat which the world knew nothing of. And, best of all, he had these things forever! They supported him in life; they did not leave him in the hour of death. They went with him beyond the grave; they were his to eternity. Surely, in this point of view, we may well say not "poor Lazarus," but "rich Lazarus!"

Reader, you would do well to measure all men by God's standard, to measure them not by the amount of their income but by the condition of their souls. When the Lord God looks down from heaven upon men, He takes no account of many things which are highly esteemed by the world. He looks not at men's money or lands or titles. He looks only at the state of their souls and reckons them accordingly. Oh, that you would strive to do likewise! Oh, that you would value grace above titles or intellect or gold! Often, far too often, the only question asked about a man is, "How much is he worth?" It would be well for us all to remember that every man is pitiably poor until he is rich in faith and rich toward God.

✤ From the sermon "Riches and Poverty"

Lessons from the Dead

And it came to pass, that the beggar died, and was carried by the angels into Abraham's bosom: the rich man also died, and was buried; and in hell he lift up his eyes, being in torments, and seeth Abraham afar off, and Lazarus in his bosom.   —LUKE 16:22–23

Lazarus died, and the rich man also died. As different and divided as they were in their lives, they had both to drink of the same cup at the last. Both went to the house appointed for all living. Both went to that place where rich and poor meet together. Dust they were, and unto dust they returned. This is the lot of all men. It will be our own unless the Lord shall first return in glory. After all our scheming and contriving and planning and studying—after all our inventions and discoveries and scientific attainments—there remains one enemy we cannot conquer and disarm, and that is death! Death is a mighty leveler! He spares none; he waits for none! He will not tarry until you are ready. He will not be kept out by doors and bars and bolts.

Reader, I know that these are ancient things. I do not deny it for a moment. I am writing stale, old things that all men know, but I am also writing things that all men do not feel. Oh, no! If they did feel them, they would not speak and live as they do. Oh, that men would learn to live as those who must one day die! Truly it is poor work to set our affections on a dying world and its short-lived comforts, and for the sake of an inch of time to lose a glorious immortality! Here we are toiling and laboring and wearying ourselves about trifles and running to and fro like ants upon a heap, and yet after a few years we shall all be gone, and another generation will fill our place. Live for eternity, reader! Seek a portion which can never be taken from you, and never forget John Bunyan's golden rule: "He who would live well, let him make his dying day his company-keeper."

✣ From the sermon "Riches and Poverty"

How Precious a Believer's Soul Is in the Sight of God

And it came to pass, that the beggar died, and was carried by the angels into Abraham's bosom: the rich man also died, and was buried; and in hell he lift up his eyes, being in torments, and seeth Abraham afar off, and Lazarus in his bosom. —LUKE 16:22–23

The rich man in the parable dies and is buried. Perhaps he had a splendid funeral, proportioned to his expenditure while he was yet alive. But we hear nothing further of the moment when soul and body were divided. The next thing we hear of is that he is in hell. The poor man in the parable dies also. What kind of burial he had, we know not. A pauper's funeral is a melancholy business! But this we do know, that the moment Lazarus dies, he is carried by the angels into Abraham's bosom, carried to a place of rest where all the faithful are waiting for the "resurrection of the just" (Luke 14:14).

Ah, reader, the men of the world little think whom they are despising when they mock Christ's people! They are mocking those whom angels are not ashamed to attend upon. They are mocking the brothers and sisters of Christ Himself! Little do they consider that these are those for whose sakes the days of tribulation are shortened. These are those by whose intercession kings reign peacefully. Little do they reckon that the prayers of men like Lazarus have more weight in the affairs of nations than hosts of armed men.

Believers in Christ who read these pages, you little know the full extent of your privileges and possessions. Like children at school, you know not half of what your Father is doing for your welfare. Learn to live by faith more than you have done. Acquaint yourself with the fullness of the treasure laid up for you in Christ even now!

❖ From the sermon "Riches and Poverty"

Assured Hope Is Exceedingly to Be Desired

My flesh and my heart faileth: but God is the strength of my heart, and my portion for ever.
—PSALM 73:26

Know then, for one thing, that assurance is a thing to be desired because of the present joy and peace it affords. Doubts and fears have great power to mar the comfort of a true believer. Uncertainty and suspense are bad enough in any condition—in the matter of our health, our property, our families, our affections, our earthly callings—but never so bad as in the affairs of our souls. Now so long as a believer cannot get beyond "I hope and I wish," he manifestly feels a certain degree of uncertainty about his spiritual state. The very words imply as much; he says "I hope" because he dare not say "I know."

Assurance, my brethren, goes far to set a child of God free from this painful kind of bondage and mightily ministers to comfort. It gives him joy and peace in believing. It makes him patient in tribulation, contented in trial, calm in affliction, unmoved in sorrow, not afraid of evil tidings. It sweetens his bitter cups, it lessens the burden of his crosses, it smooths the rough places on which he travels, it lightens the valley of the shadow of death. It makes him feel as if he had something solid beneath his feet and something firm under his hand, a sure friend by the way and a sure home in the end. He feels that the great business of life is a settled business; debt, disaster, work, and all other business is by comparison small. Assurance will help a man to bear poverty and loss; it will teach him to say, "I know that I have in heaven a better and more enduring substance. Silver and gold have I none, but grace and glory are mine and can never be taken away." Assurance will support a man in sickness, make all his bed, smooth his pillow. It will enable him to say, "If my earthly house of this tabernacle fail, I have a building of God, a house not made with hands, eternal in the heavens. I desire to depart and be with Christ. My flesh and my heart faileth: but God is the strength of my heart, and my portion for ever" (see 2 Cor. 5:2; Phil. 1:23; Ps. 73:26, respectively).

✤ From the sermon "Ready to Be Offered"

How to Live in the Last Days

See then that ye walk circumspectly, not as fools, but as wise, redeeming the time, because the days are evil.
—EPHESIANS 5:15–16

Here are six points of advice while you live awaiting the return of the Lord Jesus Christ:

Our first duty is to make sure work of the salvation of our own souls. Let us never rest until we know and feel that we ourselves have got hold of thoroughgoing, solid Bible religion and that we are justified, converted, and saved. Our second duty is to pray night and day that God may intervene and drive back the flood of evil which seems bursting on our country. Our third duty is to work hard to maintain true religion and to oppose error. With the Bible in our hands and Bible arguments on our lips, let us proclaim fearlessly, both in public and in private, our entire belief in the divine authority of God's Word. No man on earth has such a right to be bold as the believer in the Bible.

Our fourth duty is to impress on all around us the immense importance of the fifth and seventh commandments. It is clear as daylight to my mind, that myriads of my fellow countrymen are forgetting these two mighty laws of God. Ignorance of the spirit of the fifth commandment is the true secret of the abounding social disorder that we see around us.

Ignorance of the spirit of the seventh commandment accounts for much of that fearful immorality which is creeping into all classes of society. One remedy for perilous times is more full preaching of God's law. Our fifth duty is to cultivate and press on all around us a spirit of cheerfulness and contentment. Our last but not our least important duty is to be continually looking for the coming and kingdom of our Lord Jesus Christ. This is the great event which will wind up the affairs of all nations. Then, and then only, will sin, disorder, and superstition be put down completely and come to an end. When shall that event take place? I cannot tell. "Of that day and hour, no man knows!"

✤ From the sermon "Perilous Times"

My Sheep Will Never Perish

And I give unto them eternal life; and they shall never perish, neither shall any man pluck them out of my hand. —JOHN 10:28

Jesus says of His sheep, "They shall never perish! They shall never be finally cast away if they have once been sealed and numbered in My flock." They may have many a slip and many a fall. They may experience many a shortcoming and many a backsliding. But they shall never be lost eternally; they shall be kept by the power of God through faith unto salvation. Where are those fearful Christians who think they may be Christ's sheep and yet come short at last? Behold the assurance of Him who cannot lie: "They shall never perish!"

True Christians shall never perish. Are they not Christ's special property, the servants of His house, the members of His family, the children of His adoption? Then surely He will never let them be overthrown. He will watch them as tenderly as we watch over our own flesh and blood. He will cherish them as we cherish that which is most dear to our hearts. He never would have laid down His life for their sakes if He had intended to give them up.

"Never perish!" Kings of the earth and mighty men shall depart and be no more seen. Thrones and dominions and principalities, rich men and honorable men, shall be swept into the tomb. But the humblest Christian cottager shall never see death everlasting, and when the heavens shall pass away as a scroll and earth shall be burned up, that man shall be found to have a house not made with hands, eternal in the heavens. That man may be poor in this world and lightly esteemed, but I see in him one who shall be a glorious saint when those who perchance had more of this life's good things shall be in torment. I am confident that nothing shall ever separate him from the love of Christ. He may have his doubts, but I know he is provided for. He shall never be lost!

✣ From the sermon "The Privileges of the True Christian"

Consider Your Ways

Thus saith the LORD of hosts; Consider your ways.
—HAGGAI 1:7

I wish to write a few words to you about your souls. I want those souls to be saved. And I invite you all to take the advice I give you today, and that is to "consider your ways." I write to you because the time is short. The day of grace is slipping away, the day of judgment is drawing near, the thread of life is winding up; a few more short years, and every soul of us will have gone to his own place. We shall each of us be in heaven or hell!

There are some true Christians among you whom I long to see more holy and brighter. You are they who have found out your own sinfulness and lost estate and really believe on Jesus for the saving of your souls. The eyes of your understanding have been opened by the Spirit; He has led you to Christ, and you are new men. You have peace with God. Sin is no longer pleasant to you; the world has no longer the first place in your heart; all things are become new. You have ceased from trusting in your own works. You are willing to stand before the bar of God and rest your soul on the finished work of Him who died for the ungodly. This is all your confidence, that you have washed your robes and made them white in the blood of the Lamb. I thank God heartily for what He has wrought in your souls, but I ask you also to consider your ways.

Consider well what I have said. Death may be busy among us very soon. Let us all be found in Christ and prepared. Satan will be busy among us no doubt; let us all watch and pray. Let us beware of a spirit of slumber and formality, and especially in private reading and praying. Let our path to the fountain be worn with daily journeys; let our key to the treasury of grace be bright with constant use.

✤ From the sermon "Consider Your Ways"

Abiding in Christ

Whosoever transgresseth, and abideth not in the doctrine of Christ, hath not God. He that abideth in the doctrine of Christ, he hath both the Father and the Son.
—2 JOHN 1:9

Let us all seek to abide in Christ more thoroughly than we have hitherto. Christ is the true spring of life in every believer's soul, the head on which every member depends, the cornerstone of all real sanctification. Whenever I see a child of God becoming less holy than he was, I know the secret of it: he is clinging less firmly to Christ than he did. Our root must be right if our fruit is to abound. Brothers and sisters, let us strive after close union and communion with Christ. Let us go to Him oftener, speak with Him more frequently, trust Him more wholly, look to Him more constantly, lean upon Him more entirely. This is the way to go through the wilderness without fainting and to run the race set before us with patience. Let us live the life of faith in the Son of God. He is the vine, and we are the branches. Let all our strength be drawn from Him; separate from Him we can do nothing. He is the Sun of righteousness; let us seek our comfort in Him and not in our own frames and feelings.

He is the Bread of Life; let us feed on Him day by day, as Israel on the manna, and not on our own experiences. Let Christ become more and more all things to us! His blood our peace, His intercession our comfort, His word our warrant, His grace our strength, His sympathy our support, His speedy coming our hope. Brothers and sisters, let us cleave to Christ more closely. Let us draw near to the cross. Let us sit at the feet of Jesus. Let us drink into the spirit of the apostle when he said, "To me to live is Christ" (Phil. 1:21). Let us do this, and we shall grow.

❖ From the sermon "Consider Your Ways"

Why Is the New Birth Necessary?

Jesus answered and said unto him, Verily, verily, I say unto thee, Except a man be born again, he cannot see the kingdom of God.
—JOHN 3:3

The answer is short and simple: because of the natural sinfulness of every man's disposition. We are not born into the world with spotless, innocent minds, but corrupt and wicked and with a will to do that which is evil as soon as we have the power. The scriptural account is true to the letter; we are all conceived in sin and shaped in iniquity. I need not stop now to tell you how all this came to pass; I need only remind you that in the beginning it was not so. Our first parents, Adam and Eve, were created holy, harmless, undefiled, without spot or stain or blemish about them. And when God rested from His labor on the seventh day, He pronounced them, like all His other works, to be very good. But alas for us! Adam, by transgression, fell into sin and lost his first estate. He forfeited the likeness of God in which he had been made. And hence all we, who are his children, come into being with a defiled and sinful nature. We are fallen and we must needs be raised. We have about us the marks of the old Adam—the first, earthly and carnal—and we must needs be marked with the marks of the second Adam, the Lord Jesus, which are heavenly and spiritual. Do any of you feel a doubt of this? Consider only what we are by nature.

By nature we do not see Christ's spiritual kingdom upon earth. It is all hidden from our eyes. People may be sharp and knowing in worldly matters; they may be wise in the things of time. But when they come to spiritual religion, their understandings seem blind, there is a thick veil over their hearts, and they see nothing as they ought to see. Jesus tells us solemnly not one shall enter into the heavenly rest without being born again!

✣ From the sermon "Regeneration"

What Do You Think about Christ?

What think ye of Christ?
—MATTHEW 22:42

Beloved, I have told you more than once, and I tell you now again, that since I have had the charge of this district it has been my heart's desire and prayer to promote your salvation.

Morning and night I make my petition to my Father who is in heaven, that it will please Him to pour out the Holy Spirit upon you all and bring you unto Christ. Has not He said, "Ask, and you shall receive," and shall I not bring your case before Him?

What, I say to myself, will most awaken this people? What will most startle them? What will arouse them and make them think? What will most likely lead them to see the sinfulness of sin, the danger of trifling with their Maker and their Judge, the real value of their own souls, the exceeding mercy of God in Christ Jesus? Such were some of the reflections that passed through my mind when I chose the text you have heard: What do you think about Christ?

Beloved, the present state of your souls depends on the nature of the answer your conscience gives: What do you think about Christ? You cannot answer this satisfactorily unless you are true members of His body, really united to Him by a living faith, really renewed by the Holy Spirit. There is no middle path here. You cannot make it a matter of indifference whether you think rightly of Christ or not. The question is very short, very simple, but the answer to it involves life or death. I ask you a little, plain question, but if you cannot give the answer God requires, I warn you, in love and tenderness, you are traveling on the broad way that leads to destruction!

✣ From the sermon "What Do You Think about Christ?"

A Spiritual Disease, Which We Ought to Fear

But I fear, lest by any means, as the serpent beguiled Eve through his subtilty, so your minds should be corrupted from the simplicity that is in Christ.
—2 CORINTHIANS 11:3

There is a spiritual disease which we ought to fear: that "minds should be corrupted." I take "minds should be corrupted" to mean injury of our minds by the reception of false and unscriptural doctrines in religion. And I believe the sense of the apostle to be, "I am afraid that your minds would partake of erroneous and unsound views about Christianity. I am afraid that you should receive as truths, principles which are not the truth. I am afraid that you would depart from the faith once delivered to the saints and embrace views which are intrinsically destructive of the gospel of Christ."

The fear expressed by the apostle is painfully instructive and at first sight may create surprise. Who would have thought that under the very eyes of Christ's own chosen disciples, while the blood of Calvary was hardly yet dry, while the age of miracles had not yet passed away—who would have thought that in a day like this there was any danger of Christians departing from the faith? Yet nothing is more certain than that "the mystery of iniquity doth already work," began already to work before the apostles were dead (2 Thess. 2:7). "Even now," says John, "many antichrists have come" (see 1 John 2:18). And no fact in church history is more clearly proved than this, that false doctrine has never ceased to be the plague of Christendom for the last eighteen centuries.

Looking forward with the eye of a prophet, Paul might well say "I am afraid"—not only of the corruption of your morals but of your minds. The plain truth is that false doctrine has been the chosen device which Satan has employed in every age to stop the progress of the gospel of Christ. Finding himself unable to prevent the fountain of life from being opened, he has labored incessantly to poison the streams which flow from it. If he could not destroy it, he has too often neutralized its usefulness by addition, subtraction, or substitution. In a word he has led astray men's minds. Beware.

✣ From the sermon "Apostolic Fears"

No Other Book Like the Bible

The grass withereth, the flower fadeth:
but the word of our God shall stand for ever.
—ISAIAH 40:8

The Bible is given by inspiration of God. In saying this, I mean to assert that the Bible is utterly unlike all other books that were ever written because its writers were specially inspired or enabled by God for the work which they did. I say that this book comes to us with a claim which no other book possesses. It is stamped with divine authority. In this respect it stands entirely alone. Sermons and tracts and theological writings of all kinds may be sound and edifying, but they are only the handiwork of uninspired man.

The Bible alone is the book of God. It is a fact that there is an extraordinary fullness and richness in the contents of the Bible. It throws more light on a vast number of most important subjects than all the other books in the world put together. It boldly handles matters that are beyond the reach of man when left to himself. It treats of things that are mysterious and invisible: the soul, the world to come, and eternity, depths which man has no line to fathom. All who have tried to write of these things without Bible light have done little but show their own ignorance. They grope like the blind, they speculate, they guess, they generally make the darkness more visible, and land us in a region of uncertainty and doubt.

How dim were the views of Socrates, Plato, Cicero, and Seneca! A well-taught Sunday scholar, in this day, knows more spiritual truth than all these sages put together!

The Bible alone gives a reasonable account of the beginning and end of the globe on which we live. It starts from the birthday of sun, moon, stars, and earth in their present order and shows us creation in its cradle. It foretells the dissolution of all things, when the earth and all its works shall be burned up, and shows us creation in its grave. It tells us the story of the world's youth, and it tells us the story of its old age. It gives us a picture of its first days and a picture of its last. How vast and important is this knowledge!

❖ From the sermon "Inspiration"

Assurance in Death

For I am now ready to be offered, and the time of my departure is at hand. I have fought a good fight, I have finished my course, I have kept the faith: henceforth there is laid up for me a crown of righteousness, which the Lord, the righteous judge, shall give me at that day: and not to me only, but unto all them also that love his appearing. —2 TIMOTHY 4:6–8

Assurance such as Paul here expresses is not merely imagined or felt. It is not the result of high animal spirits or a lively temperament of body. It is a positive gift of the Holy Spirit, bestowed without reference to men's bodily frames or constitutions, and a gift which every believer in Christ should aim at and seek after. The Word of God appears to me to teach that a believer may arrive at an assured confidence with regard to his own salvation. I lay it down deliberately that a true Christian or converted man may reach a comfortable degree of faith such that in general he shall feel confident as to the safety and forgiveness of his own soul and shall seldom be troubled with doubts, distracted with hesitations, distressed with anxious questionings, be alarmed about his own state. He may have many an inward conflict with sin, but he shall look forward to death, like Paul, without trembling, and to judgment without dismay.

Such is my account of assurance. Mark it well. I say neither less nor more. The great majority of the worldly among ourselves oppose the doctrine of assurance. It offends and annoys them. They do not like others to feel comfortable and sure because they never feel so themselves. That they cannot receive it is certainly no marvel. But there are also some true believers who reject assurance. They shrink from it as a notion fraught with danger. They consider it borders on presumption. They seem to think it a proper humility to live in a certain degree of doubt. This is to be regretted and does much harm.

❖ From the sermon "Ready to Be Offered"

Ryle's Thoughts on Preaching

For we are not as many, which corrupt the word of God: but as of sincerity, but as of God, in the sight of God speak we in Christ.
—2 CORINTHIANS 2:17

A few words on each point must suffice. Three points:

1. We should aim to speak with "sincerity." Sincerity of aim, heart, and motive; to speak as those who are thoroughly convinced of the truth of what they speak; as those who have a deep feeling and tender love for those whom we address.

2. We should aim to speak "in Christ." We ought to strive to feel like men commissioned to speak for God and on His behalf. We forget how great the responsibility of the New Testament minister is and how awful the sin of those who, when a real messenger of Christ addresses them, refuse to receive his message and harden their hearts against it.

3. We should aim to speak "in the sight of God." We are to ask ourselves not, What did the people think of me? but, What was I in the sight of God? I have spoken as standing before God's sight.

In conclusion, we should all ask, do we ever handle the Word of God deceitfully? Do we realize what it is to speak as of God, as in the sight of God, and in Christ? I have often thought that one great secret of the marvelous honor which God has put on a man not in our denomination (I allude to Mr. Charles Spurgeon) is the extraordinary boldness and confidence with which he stands up in the pulpit to speak to people about their sins and their souls. It cannot be said he does it from fear of any or to please any. He seems to give every class of hearers its portion, to the rich and the poor, the high and the low, the king and the peasant, the learned and the illiterate. He gives to everyone the plain message according to God's Word. I believe that very boldness has much to do with the success which God is pleased to give to his ministry. Let us not be ashamed to learn a lesson from him in this respect. Let us go and do likewise.

❖ From the sermon "Not Corrupting the Word"

Prayer Leads to Contentment and Happiness

Continue in prayer, and watch in the same with thanksgiving.
—COLOSSIANS 4:2

We live in a world where sorrow abounds. This has always been the state since sin came in. There cannot be sin without sorrow. And until sin is driven out from the world, it is vain for anyone to suppose they can escape sorrow. Some without doubt have a larger cup of sorrow to drink than others. But few are to be found who live long without sorrows or cares of one sort or another. Our bodies, our property, our families, our children, our relations, our servants, our friends, our neighbors, our worldly callings—each and all of these are fountains of care. Sickness, deaths, losses, disappointments, partings, separations, ingratitude, slander—all these are common things. We cannot get through life without them. Some day or other they find us out. The greater are our affections the deeper are our afflictions, and the more we love the more we have to weep.

And what is the best means of cheerfulness in such a world as this? How shall we get through this valley of tears with the least pain? I know no better means than the habit of taking everything to God in prayer. The only way to really be happy in such a world as this is to be ever casting all our cares on God. It is trying to carry their own burdens, which so often makes believers sad. Jesus can make those happy who trust Him and call Him, whatever be their outward condition. He can give them peace of heart in a prison, contentment in the midst of poverty, comfort in the midst of bereavements, joy on the brink of the grave. There is a mighty fullness in Him for all His believing members, a fullness that is ready to be poured out on everyone that will ask in prayer. Oh, that people would understand that happiness does not depend on outward circumstances, but on the state of the heart!

❖ From the sermon "Call to Prayer"

Never Will I Leave Thee, nor Forsake Thee

Let your conversation be without covetousness; and be content with such things as ye have: for he hath said, I will never leave thee, nor forsake thee.
— HEBREWS 13:5

Let every believer grasp these words and store them up in his heart. Keep them ready and have them fresh in your memory; you will need them one day. The Philistines will be upon you, the hand of sickness will lay you low, the king of terror will draw near, the valley of the shadow of death will open up before your eyes. Then comes the hour when you will find nothing so comforting as a text like this—nothing so cheering, as a realizing sense of God's companionship.

Stick to that word "never." It is worth its weight in gold. Cling to it as a drowning man clings to a rope. Grasp it firmly, as a soldier attacked on all sides grasps his sword. God has said, and will stand to it, "I will never leave you!"

"Never!" Though your heart often faints, and you are sick of self and your many failures and infirmities, even then the promise will not fail.

"Never!" Though the devil whispers, "I shall have you at last! In a little while, your faith will fail, and you will be mine!" Even then, God will keep His word.

"Never!" Though waves of trouble go over your head and all hope seems taken away.

Even then the Word of God will stand.

"Never!" When the cold chill of death is creeping over you and friends can do no more and you are starting on that journey from which there is no return. Even then, Christ will not forsake you.

"Never!" When the day of judgment comes and the books are opened and the dead are rising from their graves and eternity is beginning. Even then the promise will bear all your weight. Christ will not leave His hold on your soul!

❖ From the sermon "Be Content"

Hold Fast to Your Christian Zeal

And let us not be weary in well doing:
for in due season we shall reap, if we faint not.
—GALATIANS 6:9

I have but one request to make, and that is that you will persevere. I beseech you to hold fast your zeal and never let it go. I beseech you never to go back from your first works, never to leave your first love, never to let it be said of you that your first things were better than your last. Beware of cooling down. You have only to be lazy and to sit still, and you will soon lose all your warmth! You will soon become another man from what you are now. Oh, do not think this a needless exhortation! It may be very true that wise, young believers are very rare. But it is no less true that zealous old believers are very rare also. Never allow yourself to think that you can do too much, that you can spend and be spent too much for Christ's cause. For one man that does too much, I will show you a thousand who do not do enough! Rather, think that "the night cometh, when no man can work" (John 9:4), and give, collect, teach, visit, work, pray, as if you were doing it for the last time. Lay to heart the words of that noble-minded man who said, when told that he ought to rest a little, "What should we rest for? Have we not all eternity to rest in?"

Fear not the reproach of men. Faint not because you are sometimes abused. Heed it not if you are sometimes called bigot, enthusiast, fanatic, madman, and fool. There is nothing disgraceful in these titles. They have often been given to the best and wisest of men. If you are only to be zealous when you are praised for it, if the wheels of your zeal must be oiled by the world's commendation, then your zeal will be but short-lived. Care nothing for the praise or frown of man!

✤ From the sermon "Christian Zeal"

It's Their Father's Hand
That Chastens Them!

For whom the Lord loveth he chasteneth,
and scourgeth every son whom he receiveth.
—HEBREWS 12:6

We live in such a beauteous and pleasant world, we are surrounded with so much that is smiling and mirthful, that if we were not often obliged to taste of sickness or trial or disappointments, we would soon forget our heavenly home and pitch our tents permanently in this Sodom. Therefore it is that God's people pass through great tribulations. Therefore it is they are often called upon to suffer the sting of affliction and anxiety or weep over the grave of those whom they have loved as their own soul.

It is their Father's hand that chastens them! It is thus He weans their affection from things below and fixes them on Himself. It is thus He trains them for eternity and cuts the threads that bind their truant hearts to earth one by one. No doubt such chastening is grievous for the time, but still it brings many a hidden grace to light and cuts down many a secret seed of evil. We shall see those who have suffered most shining among the brightest stars in the assembly of heaven. "For our light affliction, which is but for a moment, worketh for us a far more exceeding and eternal weight of glory" (2 Cor. 4:17)!

The purest gold is that which has been longest in the refiner's furnace. The brightest diamond is often that which has required the most grinding and polishing. The saints are men who have come out of great tribulation—they are never left to perish in it. The last night of weeping will soon be spent, the last wave of trouble will have rolled over us, and then we shall have a peace that passes all understanding! We shall be at home forever with the Lord! "Wherefore comfort one another with these words" (1 Thess. 4:18)!

❖ From the sermon "It's Their Father's Hand That Chastens Them"

Wipe Away All Our Tears

And God shall wipe away all tears from their eyes; and there shall be no more death, neither sorrow, nor crying, neither shall there be any more pain: for the former things are passed away.
—REVELATION 21:4

The Lord Jesus Christ Himself shall minister to their comforts. The same kind hand which raised them from the death of sin to the life of righteousness—which healed their spiritual diseases and brought them health and peace and made them new creatures upon earth—the same hand shall welcome them in heaven and conduct them as highly favored guests to a banquet of happiness such as no eye has ever seen nor heart ever conceived!

And then there shall be no more weeping, for God shall wipe away all tears from their eyes. A dwelling place in which there shall be no weeping! I know no part of heaven more difficult to imagine. We live in a world of sorrow, a very valley of tears—tears for ourselves and tears for others, tears over our own shortcomings, tears over the unbelief of those we love, tears over disappointed hopes, tears over the graves of those on whom our affections are set—and all because of sin! There would have been no sorrow if Adam had never fallen, but our very weeping is a proof of sin!

Yet it shall not always be so. A day is still to come when sadness shall flee away and God Himself shall say, "Refrain from weeping, for the former things are passed away." There shall be no sadness in heaven for there shall be no sin! The days of our tribulation shall be forgotten! We shall be able at last to love our God without coldness, to reverence His holiness without torment, to trust Him without despair, to serve Him without weariness, interruption, or distraction. The days of weakness and corruption will be past, and we shall be like our Lord in holiness as well as happiness, in purity as well as immortality!

❖ From the sermon "The Blood of the Lamb"

The Grace of God in Vain

We then, as workers together with him, beseech you also that ye receive not the grace of God in vain. —2 CORINTHIANS 6:1

Although the church of Corinth, to which these words were written, was certainly not a body without spot and blemish—although we learn by Paul's first epistle that in many things its members were to be blamed—still, with all its faults, it is plain this church was very different from the churches of our own day. There was less profession without practice, more fruit in proportion to the branches, a stronger growth of faith and holiness and love, a more abundant crop of wheat in proportion to the tares. And yet you see by the text how solemnly the apostle warns them of danger, how earnestly he entreats them not to hear the gospel only to their condemnation. He would not have them rest upon their outward privileges and opportunities. He would not have them soothe their consciences with the idea that all was safe because they were baptized in the name of Jesus, but as a faithful laborer in God's vineyard, he calls on them to examine themselves and beware lest they receive the grace of God in vain.

And are we better than they? Can we produce a greater list of evidence that God is truly in us? I speak as unto wise men; judge what I say. Verily, beloved, we are guilty in this matter. Let us rather confess that we have nothing whereof to glory, and as a shortcoming generation let us humbly consider what this text contains for our particular instruction.

Consider, O you men and women who are so difficult to please; consider, O you who are too backward to search the Scriptures for yourselves—you have a great work to do, the time is short, the fashion of this world passes away. Tremble lest you go on doubting and trifling and faultfinding until the end, and so be found among that wretched company who have received the grace of God in vain!

❖ From the sermon "The Grace of God in Vain"

Is Your Heart Right?

But ye are a chosen generation, a royal priesthood, an holy nation,
a peculiar people; that ye should shew forth the praises of him who
hath called you out of darkness into his marvellous light.
—1 PETER 2:9

Is your heart right? Then be thankful. Praise the Lord for His distinguishing mercy, which "called you out of darkness into his marvellous light" (1 Peter 2:9). Think what you were by nature. Think what has been done for you by free undeserved grace. Your heart may not be all that it ought to be, nor yet all that you hope it will be. But at any rate your heart is not the old hard heart with which you were born. Surely the man whose heart is changed ought to be full of praise.

Is your heart right? Then be humble and watchful. You are not yet in heaven but in the world. You are in the body. The devil is near you and never sleeps. Oh, keep your heart with all diligence! Watch and pray lest you fall into temptation. Ask Christ Himself to keep your heart for you. Ask Him to dwell in it and reign in it and garrison it and to put down every enemy under His feet. Give the keys of the citadel into the King's own hands and leave them there. It is a weighty saying of Solomon: "He that trusteth in his own heart is a fool" (Prov. 28:26).

Is your heart right? Then be hopeful about the hearts of other people. Who has made you to differ? Why should not anyone in the world be changed, when such a one as you has been made a new creature? Work on. Pray on. Speak on. Write on. Labor to do all the good you can to souls. Never despair of anyone being saved so long as he is alive. Surely the man who has been changed by grace ought to feel that there are no desperate cases. There are no hearts which it is impossible for Christ to cure!

❖ From the sermon "The Heart"

Jesus and the Little Children

And they brought unto him also infants, that he would touch them: but when his disciples saw it, they rebuked them. But Jesus called them unto him, and said, Suffer little children to come unto me, and forbid them not: for of such is the kingdom of God. Verily I say unto you, Whosoever shall not receive the kingdom of God as a little child shall in no wise enter therein. —LUKE 18:15–17

Let us observe for one thing in this passage how ignorantly people are apt to treat children in the matter of their souls. We read that there were some who "brought unto him also infants, that he would touch them: but when his disciples saw it, they rebuked them." They thought most probably that it was mere waste of their Master's time, and that little children could derive no benefit from being brought to Christ. They drew from our Lord a solemn rebuke. But Jesus called them unto Him and said, "Suffer little children to come unto me, and forbid them not: for of such is the kingdom of God."

The souls of young children are evidently precious in God's sight. Both here and elsewhere, there is plain proof that Christ cares for them no less than for grown-up people. The souls of young children are capable of receiving grace. They are born in sin and without grace cannot be saved. There is nothing, either in the Bible or experience, to make us think that they cannot receive the Holy Spirit and be justified, even from their earliest infancy.

Let us leave the whole passage with a deep sense of the value of children's souls and with a settled resolution to put on the mind of Christ in all our dealings with them. Let us regard children as a most important part of Christ's professing church, and a part which the great Head of the church does not like to see neglected. Let us train them from their earliest infancy in godly ways and sow the seed of Scripture truth in their minds, with strong confidence that it will one day bear fruit.

❖ From the book *Expository Thoughts on the Gospels: Luke*

Spiritual Sonship

For ye have not received the spirit of bondage again to fear; but ye have received the Spirit of adoption, whereby we cry, Abba, Father.
—ROMANS 8:15

Furthermore, all the sons of God have the feelings of adopted children toward their Father in heaven. What says the Scripture? "For ye have not received the spirit of bondage again to fear; but ye have received the Spirit of adoption, whereby we cry, Abba, Father" (Rom. 8:15)! The sons of God are delivered from that slavish fear of God which sin begets in the natural heart. They are redeemed from that feeling of guilt which made Adam hide himself in the trees of the garden and Cain go out from the presence of the Lord. They are no longer afraid of God's holiness and justice and majesty. They no longer feel as if there was a great gulf and barrier between themselves and God—and as if God was angry with them, and must be angry with them, because of their sins. From these chains and fetters of soul the sons of God are delivered.

Their feelings toward God are now those of peace and confidence. They see Him as a Father reconciled in Christ Jesus. They look on Him as a God whose attributes are all satisfied by their great Mediator and peacemaker, the Lord Jesus, as a God who is just and yet the justifier of everyone who believes on Jesus. As a Father, they draw near to Him with boldness. As a Father, they can speak to Him with freedom. They have exchanged the spirit of bondage for that of liberty, and the spirit of fear for that of love. They know that God is holy, but they are not afraid. They know that they are sinners, but they are not afraid. Though holy, they believe that God is completely reconciled. Though sinners, they believe they are clothed all over with Jesus Christ. Such is the feeling of the sons of God.

❖ From the sermon "Are You an Heir?"

Concerning Your Sanctification

For this is the will of God, even your sanctification.
—1 THESSALONIANS 4:3

Brethren, I write to you about your sanctification. There are those who think that you are a class in our congregations that require little writing to, you are within the pale of salvation, you may be almost let alone. I cannot see it. I believe you need your minister's care and exhortation as much as any, if not more. I believe that on your growth in grace and holiness not merely your own comfort but the salvation of many souls, under God, depends. I believe that the converted members of a church should be preached to, spoken to, warned, counseled, far more than they are. You need many words of direction. You are still in the wilderness. You have not crossed Jordan. You are not yet at home. I see Paul beseeching the Thessalonians that as they have received of Him, how they ought to walk and please God so they would abound more and more. I see him warning them not to sleep as others do, but to watch and be sober. I see Peter telling believers to give diligence to make their calling and election sure, to go on adding one grace to another, to grow in grace and in the knowledge of Christ.

I wish to follow in their steps. I would remind you "that this is the will of God, even your sanctification," and I ask you to make it plain that it is your will too. You were not chosen out of the world to go to sleep, but that you might be holy. You were not called of God that you might sit still, but that you might walk worthy of your calling. Why do I say these things? Is it because I think that you do not know them? No! But I want to stir you up by putting you in remembrance. Is it because I wish to discourage the poor in spirit and make the heart of the righteous sad? No, indeed! I would not willingly do this. Is it because I think true Christians can ever fall away? God forbid you should suppose I mean such a thing. But I say what I say because I am jealous for my Lord's honor.

✣ From the sermon "Consider Your Ways"

Troubled by Doubts and Fears?

Peace I leave with you, my peace I give unto you: not as the world giveth, give I unto you. Let not your heart be troubled, neither let it be afraid.   —JOHN 14:27

You have doubts and fears! But what do you expect? What would you have? Your soul is married to a body full of weakness, passions, and infirmities. You live in a world that lies in wickedness, a world in which the great majority do not love Christ. You are constantly liable to the temptations of the devil. That busy enemy, if he cannot shut you out of heaven, will try hard to make your journey uncomfortable. Surely all these things ought to be considered.

I say to every believer that so far from being surprised that you have doubts and fears, I would suspect the reality of your peace if you had none. I think little of that grace which is accompanied by no inward conflict. There is seldom life in the heart when all is still, quiet, and in one way of thinking. Believe me, a true Christian may be known by his warfare as well as by his peace. These very doubts and fears which now distress you are tokens of good. They satisfy me that you have really got something which you are afraid to lose.

Beware that you do not help Satan by becoming an unjust accuser of yourself and an unbeliever in the reality of God's work of grace. I advise you to pray for more knowledge of your own heart, of the fullness of Jesus, and of the devices of the devil. Let doubts and fears drive you to the throne of grace, stir you up to more prayer, send you more frequently to Christ. But do not let doubts and fears rob you of your peace. Believe me, you must be content to go to heaven as a sinner saved by grace. And you must not be surprised to find daily proof that you really are a sinner so long as you live.

✢ From the sermon "Justification"

Christ's Continual Priesthood

But this man, because he continueth ever,
hath an unchangeable priesthood.
—HEBREWS 7:24

Christ's continual priesthood is the grand secret of daily comfort in Christianity. It is hard to do our duty in that place of life which God has appointed us and not to get absorbed in it. We are such poor weak creatures that we cannot do two things at once. The cares and business and occupations of life, however noble, often seem to drink up all our thoughts and swallow up all our attention. But, oh, what an unspeakable comfort it is to remember that we have a Great High Priest in heaven who never forgets us night or day and is continually interceding for us and providing for our safety! Happy is that man who knows how to begin and end each day with his Priest! This is indeed to live the life of faith.

Christ's continual priesthood is the grand secret of a saint's perseverance to the end.

Left to ourselves, there would be little likelihood of our getting safely home to heaven. We might begin well and end ill. So weak are our hearts, so busy is the devil, so many are the temptations of the world that nothing could prevent our making shipwreck!

But thanks be to God, the priesthood of Christ secures our safety. He who never slumbers and never sleeps is continually watching over our interests and providing for our need. While Satan pours water on the fire of grace and strives to quench it, Christ pours on oil and makes it burn more brightly. Start us in the narrow way of life with pardon, grace, and a new heart and then leave us to ourselves, and we should soon fall away. But grant us the continual intercession of an almighty Priest in heaven—God as well as man and man as well as God—and we shall never be lost. "Because I live," says our Lord, "ye shall live also" (John 14:19).

❖ From the sermon "Do You Have a Priest?"

The Great Battle

Thou therefore endure hardness, as a good soldier of Jesus Christ.
—2 TIMOTHY 2:3

All men ought to love peace. War is an immense evil, though it is a necessary evil sometimes. Battles are bloody and distressing events, though sometimes nations cannot maintain their rights without them. But all men ought to love peace. All ought to pray for a quiet life. All this is very true, and yet there is one war which it is a positive duty to carry on; there is one battle which we ought to be always fighting. The battle I speak of is the battle against the world, the flesh, and the devil. With these enemies we never ought to be at peace. From this warfare no man ought ever to seek to be discharged while he is alive.

Every professing Christian is the soldier of Christ. He is bound by his baptism to fight Christ's battle against sin, the world, and the devil. The man that does not do this breaks his vow. He is a spiritual defaulter. He does not fulfill the engagement made for him. The man that does not do this is practically renouncing his Christianity. The very fact that he belongs to a church, attends a Christian place of worship, and calls himself a Christian is a public declaration that he desires to be reckoned a soldier of Jesus Christ.

Armor is provided for the professing Christian if he will only use it. "Put on," says Paul to the Ephesians, "the whole armour of God.... Stand therefore, having your loins girt about with truth, and having on the breastplate of righteousness.... And take the helmet of salvation, and the sword of the Spirit, which is the word of God.... Above all, taking the shield of faith" (Eph. 6:13–17). And not least, the professing Christian has the best of leaders, Jesus the Captain of salvation, through whom we may be more than conquerors. We have the best of provisions, the Bread and Water of Life, and the best of pay promised, an eternal weight of glory.

✢ From the sermon "The Great Battle"

The Trials of Christ's Church

And I say also unto thee, That thou art Peter, and upon this rock I will build my church; and the gates of hell shall not prevail against it.
—MATTHEW 16:18

There is mention made of "the gates of hell." By that expression we are to understand the power of the devil! The history of Christ's true church has always been one of conflict and war. It has been constantly assailed by a deadly enemy, Satan, the prince of this world. The devil hates the true church of Christ with an undying hatred. He is ever stirring up opposition against all its members. He is ever urging the children of this world to do his will and injure and harass the people of God. If he cannot bruise the head, he will bruise the heel. If he cannot rob believers of heaven, he will aggravate them as they travel the road to heaven.

For six thousand years this hostility has gone on. Millions of the ungodly have been the devil's agents and done the devil's work, though they did not know it. The Pharaohs, the Herods, the Neros, the Julians, the Diocletians, the Bloody Marys were Satan's tools when they persecuted the disciples of Jesus Christ. Warfare with the powers of hell has been the experience of the whole body of Christ. It has always been a bush burning though not consumed—a woman fleeing into the wilderness but not swallowed up. The visible churches have their times of prosperity and seasons of peace, but never has there been a time of peace for the true church. Its conflict is perpetual. Its battle never ends.

Warfare with the powers of hell is the experience of every individual member of the true church. Each has to fight. What are the lives of all the saints but records of battles? The gates of hell have been continually assaulting the people of Christ. Do not be cast down by the hatred of hell. The warfare of the true child of God is as much a mark of grace as the inward peace which he enjoys. No cross, no crown! No conflict, no saving Christianity! "Blessed are ye," said our Lord Jesus Christ, "when men shall revile you, and persecute you, and shall say all manner of evil against you falsely, for my sake" (Matt. 5:11).

✢ From the sermon "The True Church"

Remember Lot's Wife

Remember Lot's wife. —LUKE 17:32

There are few warnings in Scripture more solemn than that which heads this page. The Lord Jesus Christ says to us, "Remember Lot's wife." Lot's wife professed religion. Her husband was a "righteous man" (2 Peter 2:8). She left Sodom with him on the day when Sodom was destroyed. She looked back toward the city from behind her husband, against God's express command. She was struck dead at once and turned into a pillar of salt. And the Lord Jesus Christ holds her up as a beacon to His church. He says, "Remember Lot's wife."

It is a solemn warning when we think of the people Jesus names. He does not bid us remember Abraham or Isaac or Jacob or Sarah or Hannah or Ruth. No, He singles out one whose soul was lost forever. He cries to us, "Remember Lot's wife." It is a solemn warning when we consider the subject Jesus is upon. He is speaking of His own second coming to judge the world. He is describing the dreadful state of unreadiness in which many will be found. The last days are on His mind when He says, "Remember Lot's wife."

It is a solemn warning when we think of the person who gives it. The Lord Jesus is full of love, mercy, and compassion. He is one who will not break the bruised reed nor quench the smoking flax. He could weep over unbelieving Jerusalem and pray for the men that crucified Him. Yet even He thinks it good to remind us of lost souls. Even He says, "Remember Lot's wife." It is a solemn warning when we think of the people to whom it was first given. The Lord Jesus was speaking to His disciples. He was not addressing the scribes and Pharisees, who hated Him, but Peter, James, and John and many others who loved Him. Yet even to them He thinks it good to address a caution. Even to them He says, "Remember Lot's wife."

✣ From the sermon "A Woman to Be Remembered"

The Sin Which Lot's Wife Committed

But his wife looked back from behind him,
and she became a pillar of salt.
—GENESIS 19:26

The history of the sin which Lot's wife committed is given by the Holy Spirit in few and simple words: She looked back from behind her husband, and she became a pillar of salt. We are told no more than this. There is a naked solemnity about the history. The sum and substance of her transgression lies in these three words: "She looked back." Does that sin seem small in the eyes of any reader of this message? Does the fault of Lot's wife appear a trifling one to be visited with such a punishment? This is the feeling, I dare say, that rises in some hearts. Give me your attention while I reason with you on the subject. There was far more in that look than strikes you at first sight; it implied far more than it expressed. Listen, and you shall hear.

That look was a little thing, but it revealed the true character of Lot's wife. Little things will often show the state of a man's mind even better than great ones. And little symptoms are often the signs of deadly and incurable diseases. The apple that Eve ate was a little thing, but it proved that she had fallen from innocence and become a sinner. A little cough in a morning seems an unimportant ailment, but it is often evidence of failing in the constitution and leads on to decline, consumption, and death. A straw may show which way the wind blows, and one look may show the rotten condition of a sinner's heart.

That look was a little thing, but it told of disobedience in Lot's wife. She seemed to doubt whether God was really going to destroy Sodom. She appeared not to believe there was any danger or any need for such a hasty flight. "But without faith it is impossible to please him" (Heb. 11:6). The moment a man begins to think he knows better than God and that God does not mean anything when He threatens, his soul is in great danger. When we cannot see the reason of God's dealings—our duty is to hold our peace and believe.

✤ From the sermon "A Woman to Be Remembered"

Hope Drawn from the Scriptures!

My soul fainteth for thy salvation: but I hope in thy word.
—PSALM 119:81

What says David? "I hope in thy word." "Remember the word unto thy servant, upon which thou hast caused me to hope" (Ps. 119:49). What says Paul? "For whatsoever things were written aforetime were written for our learning, that we through patience and comfort of the scriptures might have hope" (Rom. 15:4). If our hope is sound, we ought to be able to turn to some text or fact or doctrine of God's Word as the source of it. Our confidence must arise from something which God has caused to be written in the Bible for our learning and which our heart has received and believed.

It is not enough to have the good opinion of others about the state of our souls. We may be told by others on our deathbeds to keep up our spirits and not to be afraid. We may be reminded that we have lived good lives, or had a good heart, or done nobody any harm, or not been so bad as many. And all this time our friends may not bring forward a word of Scripture and may be feeding us poison! Such friends are miserable comforters. However well-meaning, they are downright enemies to our souls. The good opinion of others without the warrant of God's Word will never make up a good hope.

I warn everyone to beware of a hope not drawn from Scripture. It is a false hope, and many will find out this to their cost. That glorious and perfect book, the Bible, however people despise it, is the only fountain out of which man's soul can derive peace. Many sneer at the old book while living who find their need of it when dying. Honor your Bible, read your Bible, stick to your Bible. There is not on earth a scrap of solid hope for the other side of the grave which is not drawn out of the Word.

✣ From the sermon "Our Hope"

Beware the Love of Money

For the love of money is the root of all evil: which while some cov-
eted after, they have erred from the faith, and pierced themselves
through with many sorrows. —1 TIMOTHY 6:10

Money, in truth, is one of the most unsatisfying of possessions. It takes away some cares, no doubt, but it brings with it quite as many cares as it takes away! There is trouble in the getting of it; there is anxiety in the keeping of it; there are temptations in the use of it; there is guilt in the abuse of it; there is sorrow in the losing of it; there is perplexity in the disposing of it. Two-thirds of all the striving, quarrels, and lawsuits in the world arise from one simple cause: money! Money most certainly is one of the most heart-ensnaring possessions. It seems desirable at a distance yet often proves a poison when in our hand! No man can possibly tell the effect of money on his soul if it suddenly falls to his lot to possess it. Many a one did run well as a poor man who forgets God when he becomes rich.

Readers, I know that this is a painful and delicate subject. But it must not on that account be avoided by the minister of Christ. It is a subject for the times, and it needs pressing home. I desire to speak to myself and to all who make any profession of religion. Of course, I cannot expect worldly and utterly ungodly people to view this subject in Bible light. To them the Bible is no rule of faith and practice, so to quote texts to them would be of little use. But I do ask all professing Christians to consider well what Scripture says against covetousness and selfishness and on behalf of liberality in giving money! Has anyone who reads these pages money? Then take heed and beware of covetousness! Remember you carry weight in the race toward heaven!

✤ From the sermon "Riches and Poverty"

Pondering Christ's Death Daily

All we like sheep have gone astray; we have turned every one to his own way; and the LORD hath laid on him the iniquity of us all.
—ISAIAH 53:6

If we would look rightly to Jesus, we must look daily at His death as the only source of inward peace. We need inward peace. So long as our conscience is asleep, deadened by indulged sin, or dulled and stupefied by incessant pursuit of the things of this world, so long can that man get on tolerably well without peace with God. But once let conscience open its eyes and shake itself and rise and move, and it will make the stoutest child of Adam feel ill at ease. The irrepressible thought that this life is not all, that there is a God and a judgment, and a something after death—an undiscovered destiny from which no traveler returns—that thought will come up at times in every man's mind and make him long for inward peace.

We need peace. Now, there is only one source of peace revealed in Scripture, and that is the sacrifice of the death of Christ and the atonement which He has made for sin by that vicarious death on the cross. To obtain a portion in that great peace, we have only to look by faith to Jesus, as our substitute and Redeemer, bearing our sin in His own body on the tree, and to cast all the weight of our souls on Him. To enjoy that peace habitually, we must keep daily looking back to the same wondrous point at which we began, daily bringing all our iniquity to Him, and daily remembering that "the Lord hath laid on him the iniquity of us all" (Isa. 53:6). This, I am bold to say, is the Bible way of peace. This is the old fountain of which all the true sheep of Christ have drunk for eighteen hundred years and have never found its waters to fail. Holy men of all ages have agreed on one point, at least, in their respective creeds. And that point is this: that the only recipe for peace of conscience is to look by faith to Jesus suffering in our stead, the just for the unjust, paying our debt by that suffering and dying for us on the cross.

❖ From the sermon "Looking unto Jesus"

Conversion Is a Happy Thing

Whom having not seen, ye love; in whom, though now ye see him not, yet believing, ye rejoice with joy unspeakable and full of glory: receiving the end of your faith, even the salvation of your souls.
—1 PETER 1:8–9

A converted man is happy because he has peace with God. His sins are forgiven; his conscience is free from the sense of guilt; he can look forward to death, judgment, and eternity and not feel afraid. What an immense blessing to feel forgiven and free! He is happy because he finds order in his heart. His passions are controlled; his affections are rightly directed.

Everything in his inner man, however weak and feeble, is in its right place and not in confusion. What an immense blessing order is! He is happy because he feels independent of circumstances. Come what will, he is provided for; sickness and losses and death can never touch his treasure in heaven or rob him of Christ. What a blessing to feel independent! He is happy because he feels ready. Whatever happens, he is somewhat prepared. The great business is settled. The great concern of life is arranged. What a blessing to feel ready! These are indeed true springs of happiness. They are springs which are utterly shut up and sealed to an unconverted man.

Without forgiveness of sins, without hope for the world to come, dependent on this world for comfort, unprepared to meet God, one cannot be really happy. Conversion is an essential part of true happiness. Settle it in your mind today that the friend who labors for your conversion to God is the best friend that you have. He is a friend not merely for the life to come, but for the life that now is. He is a friend to your present comfort as well as to your future deliverance from hell. He is a friend for time as well as for eternity. Conversion is a happy thing!

✢ From the sermon "Conversion"

Self-Exertion

Strive to enter in at the strait gate: for many, I say unto you, will seek to enter in, and shall not be able. —LUKE 13:24

There was once a man who asked our Lord Jesus Christ a very deep question. He said to Him, "Lord, are there few that will be saved?" Who this man was we do not know. What his motive was for asking this question we are not told. Perhaps he wished to gratify an idle curiosity; perhaps he wanted an excuse for not seeking salvation himself. The Holy Spirit has kept back all this from us; the name and motive of the inquirer are both hidden.

But one thing is very clear, and that is the vast importance of the saying of our Lord to which the question gave rise. Jesus seized the opportunity to direct the minds of all around Him to their own plain duty. He knew the train of thought that the man's inquiry had set moving in their hearts; He saw what was going on within them. "Strive," He cries, "to enter in at the strait gate"! Whether there be few saved or many, your course is clear; strive to enter in.

Now is the accepted time. Now is the day of salvation. A day shall come when many will seek to enter in and shall not be able. "Strive to enter in" now.

I desire to call the serious attention of all who read this paper to the solemn lessons which this saying of the Lord Jesus is meant to teach. It is one which deserves special remembrance in the present day. It teaches unmistakably that mighty truth: our own personal responsibility for the salvation of our souls. It shows the immense danger of putting off the great business of religion as so many unhappily do. On both these points, the witness of our Lord Jesus Christ in the text is clear. He who is the eternal God and who spoke the words of perfect wisdom says to the sons of men, "Strive to enter in at the strait gate: for many, I say unto you, will seek to enter in, and shall not be able."

❖ From the sermon "Self-Exertion"

Doing Good Like Christ

God anointed Jesus of Nazareth with the Holy Ghost and with power: [he] went about doing good, and healing all that were oppressed of the devil; for God was with him.
—ACTS 10:38

Our Lord Jesus Christ was continually "doing good" while He was on earth (Acts 10:38). The apostles and all the disciples in Bible times were always striving to walk in His steps. A Christian who was content to go to heaven himself and cared not what became of others, whether they lived happy and died in peace or not, would have been regarded as a kind of monster in primitive times who did not have the Spirit of Christ. Why should we suppose for a moment that a lower standard will suffice in the present day? These are serious inquiries and demand serious answers.

There is a generation of professing Christians nowadays who seem to know nothing of caring for their neighbors and are completely swallowed up in the concerns of number one—that is, their own and their family's. They eat and drink and sleep and dress and work and earn money and spend money year after year. And whether others are happy or miserable, well or ill, converted or unconverted, traveling toward heaven or toward hell appear to be questions about which they are supremely indifferent. Can this be right? Can it be reconciled with the religion of Him who spoke the parable of the good Samaritan and bade us, "Go, and do thou likewise" (Luke 10:37)? I doubt it altogether.

There is much to be done everywhere. There is not a place in England where there is not a field for work and an open door for being useful, if anyone is willing to enter it. There is not a Christian in England who cannot find some good work to do for others, if he has only a heart to do it.

❖ From the sermon "Self-Inquiry"

Be Missionaries!

And he said unto them, Go ye into all the world, and preach the gospel to every creature. —MARK 16:15

I want all converted people to be missionaries. I do not want them all to go out to foreign lands and preach to the heathen, but I do want all to be of a missionary spirit and to strive to do good at home. I want them to testify to all around them that the narrow gate is the way to happiness and to persuade them to enter in by it.

When Andrew was converted, he found his brother Peter and said to him, "We have found the Messias.... And he brought him to Jesus" (John 1:41–42). When Philip was converted, he found Nathaniel and said to him, "We have found him, of whom Moses in the law, and the prophets, did write, Jesus of Nazareth!" And Nathaniel said unto him, "Can there any good thing come out of Nazareth? Philip said unto him, Come and see" (John 1:45–46)! When the Samaritan woman was converted, "the woman then left her waterpot, and went her way into the city, and saith to the men, Come, see a man, which told me all things that ever I did: is not this the Christ?" (John 4:28–29). When Saul the Pharisee was converted, "straightway he preached Christ in the synagogues, that he is the son of God" (Acts 9:20).

I long to see this kind of spirit among Christians in the present day. I long to see more zeal to commend the narrow gate to all who are yet outside and more desire to persuade them to enter in and be saved. Happy indeed is that church whose members not only desire to reach heaven themselves but desire also to take others with them! The great gate of salvation is yet ready to open, but the hour draws near when it will be closed forever. Let us work while it is called today, for "the night cometh, when no man can work" (John 9:4). Let us tell our relatives and friends that we have proved the way of life and found it pleasant, that we have tasted the Bread of Life and found it good!

❖ From the sermon "Self-Exertion"

The Lord Takes Pleasure in His Sheep

For the love of Christ constraineth us. —2 CORINTHIANS 5:14

The Lord takes pleasure in His believing people. Though filthy in their own eyes, they are lovely and honorable in His! They are altogether beautiful. He sees no spot in them. Their weaknesses and shortcomings do not break off the union between Him and them. He chose them, knowing all their hearts. He took them for His own with a perfect understanding of all their debts, liabilities, and infirmities, and He will never break His covenant and cast them off. When they fall, He will raise them again. When they wander, He will bring them back.

Their prayers are pleasant to Him. As a father loves the first stammering efforts of his child to speak, so the Lord loves the poor feeble petitions of His people. He endorses them with His own mighty intercession and gives them power on high. Their services are pleasant to Him. As a father delights in the first daisy that his child picks and brings him, even so the Lord is pleased with the weak attempts of His people to serve Him. Not a cup of cold water shall lose its reward. Not a word spoken in love shall ever be forgotten.

Their trials and temptations are all measured out by a wise physician. Not a grain of bitterness is ever mingled in their cup, which is not good for the health of their souls. Their temptations, like Job's, are all under God's control. Satan cannot touch a hair of their head without their Lord's permission nor even tempt them above that which they shall be able to bear. As a father has compassion on his children, so the Lord has compassion on those who fear Him. He never afflicts them willingly. He leads them by the right way. He withholds nothing that is really for their good. Come what will, there is always a need-be. When they are placed in the furnace, it is that they may be purified. When they are chastened, it is that they may become more holy. When they are pruned, it is to make them more fruitful. When they are transplanted from place to place, it is that they may bloom more brightly. All things are continually working together for their good!

✤ From the sermon "The Great Separation"

Consider the Pharisee and the Tax Collector Parable

And he spake this parable unto certain which trusted in themselves that they were righteous, and despised others: Two men went up into the temple to pray; the one a Pharisee, and the other a publican.

—LUKE 18:9–10

And now, beloved, let me urge upon all the lessons conveyed in this parable. It is a picture of a very large portion of professing Christians. Some, to be sure, are called by that name, but they never think at all about Christ or their own souls. It would make no difference to them if all the Bibles in the world were burned today, and of course they are going straight to destruction. But all others, rich or poor (there is no distinction) are either Pharisees or tax collectors. There is no halfway house; they either trust to themselves wholly or in part, which is much the same. Or else they are always self-condemned and have no confidence in anything they can do for justification.

You cannot search your heart too diligently, for this self-righteousness is the subtlest enemy of all. Beware of thinking, as the devil would have you, that the parable is a very good one for everybody else but does not exactly touch your case. Be sure, in this way you will lose your own souls. Let none forget the point of the parable: the Pharisee was not rejected because he was a moral man but because he was proud and self-righteous; the tax collector was not accepted because he was a sinner but because he was eminently penitent. True repentance is necessary for all, whatever be their lives and outward conduct. It is not your morality and your virtues, O you Pharisees, which hinder your salvation, but that proud feeling of something worthy in yourselves that prevents you from clinging simply and entirely to the cross and blood of Jesus Christ. Carry home, then, I entreat all of you, that as there is no way to salvation but Jesus Christ, so there is no character for entering that way but that of the tax collector and no prayer so acceptable in the sight of your Redeemer and your Judge as "God be merciful to me a sinner" (Luke 18:13).

✣ From the sermon "Self-Righteousness"

Family Gatherings at Christmas

For unto you is born this day in the city of David a Saviour, which is Christ the Lord.

—LUKE 2:11

Family gatherings at Christmas, we all know, are very common. Thousands of firesides are crowded then, if at no other time of the year. The young man in town snatches a few days from business and takes a run down to the old folks at home. The young woman gets a short holiday and comes to visit her father and mother. Brothers and sisters meet for a few hours. Parents and children look one another in the face. How much there is to talk about! How many questions to be asked! How many interesting things to be told! Happy indeed is that fireside which sees gathered round it at Christmas the whole family!

Family gatherings at Christmas are natural and right and good. I approve them with all my heart. It does me good to see them kept up. They are one of the very few pleasant things which have survived the fall of man. Next to the grace of God, I see no principle which unites people so much in this sinful world as family feeling. Community of blood is a most powerful tie. I have often observed that people will stand up for their relations merely because they are their relations and refuse to hear a word against them, even when they have no sympathy with their tastes and ways. Anything which helps to keep up family feeling ought to be commended. It is a wise thing, when it can be done, to gather together at Christmas the whole family.

Family gatherings, nevertheless, are often sorrowful things. It would be strange indeed, in such a world as this, if they were not. Few are the family circles which do not show gaps and vacant places as years pass away. Changes and deaths make sad havoc as time goes on. Our Christmas gatherings on earth must have an end one day. Our last earthly Christmas must come. Happy, indeed, is that Christmas which finds us prepared to meet God!

✣ From the sermon "The Family of God"

What Think Ye of Christ This Christmas?

Saying, What think ye of Christ? whose son is he? They say unto him, The son of David. —MATTHEW 22:42

Christmas is a season which almost all Christians observe in one way or another. Some keep it as a religious season. Some keep it as a holiday. But all over the world, wherever there are Christians, in one way or another Christmas is kept. Perhaps there is no country in which Christmas is so much observed as it is in England. Christmas holidays, Christmas parties, Christmas family gatherings, Christmas services in churches, Christmas hymns and carols, Christmas holly and mistletoe—who has not heard of these things? They are as familiar to English people as anything in their lives. They are among the first things we remember when we were children. Our grandfathers and grandmothers were used to them long before we were born. They have been going on in England for many hundred years. They seem likely to go on as long as the world stands.

Reader, I dare say the demands upon your time this Christmas are many. Your holidays are short. You have friends to see. You have much to talk about. But still, in the midst of all your hurry and excitement, give a little time to your soul. There will be a Christmas some year when your place will be empty. Before that time comes, suffer me as a friend to press home on your conscience the inquiry, What think ye of Christ? All men ought to think of Christ because of the office Christ fills between God and man. He is the eternal Son of God through whom alone the Father can be known, approached, and served. He is the appointed Mediator between God and man, through whom alone we can be reconciled with God, pardoned, justified, and saved. He is the divine person whom God the Father has sealed to be the giver of everything that man requires for his soul!

Reader, I tell you this Christmas that all men ought to think about Christ. There is no one in whom all the world has such a deep interest. There is no one to whom all the world owes so much. High and low, rich and poor, old and young, gentle and simple, all ought to think about Christ!

❖ From the sermon "What Think Ye of Christ?"

Do Not Neglect the Second Coming

And, behold, I come quickly; and my reward is with me, to give every man according as his work shall be. —REVELATION 22:12

I say that of all doctrines of the gospel, the one in which we are most unlike the first Christians in our sense of its true value is the doctrine of Christ's second coming. In our view of man's corruption, of justification by faith, of our need of the sanctifying Spirit—upon these matters I believe we would find that English Christians were much of one mind with believers at Corinth, Ephesus, Philippi, or Rome in olden times— but in our view of the second coming I believe we would find there was a mighty difference if we could but compare our experience.

We would find that we fell woefully short of them in our estimate of its importance and realization of its nature. We would discover, in one word, that we slumber and sleep about it.

The plain truth of Scripture, I believe, is as follows. When the number of the elect is accomplished, Christ shall come again to this world with power and great glory. As He came the first time in person, so He shall come the second time in person. As He went away visibly, so He shall return visibly. Then shall be fulfilled those words of Acts 1:11: "This same Jesus, which is taken up from you into heaven, shall so come in like manner as ye have seen him go into heaven"; and the words of Zechariah 14:5: "The LORD my God shall come, and all the saints with thee"; and the words of Enoch in Jude 14: "Behold, the Lord cometh with ten thousands of his saints." And the grand shortcoming of the church in these days has been and is this: that we ministers do not preach enough about this second coming, and private believers do not think enough about it. There are a few, but what are they? Many do not. We none of us live on it, feed on it, act on it, work from it, take comfort in it as God intended us to do. In short, the Bridegroom tarries, and we all slumber and sleep.

❖ From the sermon "The Ten Virgins"

God's Mind toward the World

For God so loved the world, that he gave his only begotten Son, that whosoever believeth in him should not perish, but have everlasting life. —JOHN 3:16

Let us consider God's mind toward the world: He "loved" it. The extent of the Father's love toward the world is a subject on which there is some difference of opinion. It is a subject on which I have long taken my side and will never hesitate to speak my mind. I believe that the Bible teaches us that God's love extends to all mankind. "The LORD is good to all: and his tender mercies are over all his works" (Ps. 145:9). He did not love the Jews only but the Gentiles also. He does not love His own elect only. He loves all the world.

But what kind of love is this with which the Father regards all mankind? It cannot be a love of delight, or else He would cease to be a perfect God. He is one who "canst not look on iniquity" (Hab. 1:13). Oh, no! The worldwide love of which Jesus speaks is a love of kindness, pity, and compassion. Fallen as man is and provoking as man's ways are, the heart of God is full of kindness toward him. While as a righteous judge He hates sin, He is yet able in a certain sense to love sinners! The length and breadth of His compassion are not to be measured by our feeble measures. We are not to suppose that He is such a one as ourselves. Righteous and holy and pure as God is, it is yet possible for God to love all mankind. "His compassions fail not" (Lam. 3:22).

Take comfort in the thought that God the Father is a God of infinite love and compassion. Do not hang back and hesitate under the idea that God is an angry being who is unwilling to receive sinners and slow to pardon. Remember this day that love is the Father's darling attribute. In Him there is perfect justice, perfect purity, perfect wisdom, perfect knowledge, infinite power. But, above all, never forget there is in the Father a perfect love and compassion. Draw near to Him with boldness because Jesus has made a way for you!

❖ From the sermon "Faith"

Distinction between Faith and Assurance

For the which cause I also suffer these things: nevertheless I am not ashamed: for I know whom I have believed, and am persuaded that he is able to keep that which I have committed unto him against that day.
—2 TIMOTHY 1:12

Reader, I believe it is of great importance to keep in view this distinction between faith and assurance. It explains things which an inquirer in religion sometimes finds hard to understand. Faith, let us remember, is the root and assurance is the flower. Doubtless you can never have the flower without the root, but it is no less certain you may have the root and not the flower. Faith is that poor, trembling woman who came behind Jesus in the press and touched the hem of His garment (Mark 5:27). Assurance is Stephen standing calmly in the midst of his murderers and saying, "I see the heavens opened, and the Son of man standing on the right hand of God" (Acts 7:56). Faith is the penitent thief crying, "Lord, remember me" (Luke 23:42). Assurance is Job sitting in the dust, covered with sores, and saying, "I know that my redeemer liveth" (Job 19:25). "Though he slay me, yet will I trust in him" (Job 13:15). Faith is the anxious, trembling voice: "Lord, I believe; help thou mine unbelief"! (Mark 9:24). Assurance is the confident challenge: "Who shall lay any thing to the charge of God's elect?… Who is he that condemneth?" (Rom. 8:33–34). Faith is Saul praying in the house of Judas at Damascus, sorrowful, blind, and alone (Acts 9:11). Assurance is Paul, the aged prisoner, looking calmly into the grave and saying, "For I know whom I have believed" (2 Tim. 1:12). "There is laid up for me a crown of righteousness" (2 Tim. 4:8).

Reader, whoever you may be, I exhort you never to be satisfied with anything short of a full assurance of your own salvation. Believe me, believe me, assurance is worth the seeking. You forsake your own mercies when you rest content without it. The things I speak are for your peace. It is good to be sure in earthly things—then how much better is it to be sure in heavenly things!

✤ From the sermon "Faith and Assurance"

God's Promise of Abiding

And the LORD, he it is that doth go before thee; he will be with thee, he will not fail thee, neither forsake thee: fear not, neither be dismayed. —DEUTERONOMY 31:8

Now, if I know anything of this world, it is a world of leaving, forsaking, parting, separation, failure, and disappointment. Think how immense the comfort of finding something which will never leave nor fail. Earthly good things leave us. Health, money, property, friendship all make themselves wings and flee away. They are here today and gone tomorrow. But God says, "I will never leave you!" We leave one another. We grow up in families full of affection and tender feelings, and then we are all thoroughly scattered. One follows his calling or profession one way, and another in another. We go north and south and east and west and perhaps meet no more. We meet our nearest friends and relations only at rare intervals, and then to part again. But God says, "I will never leave you."

We are left by those we love. They die and diminish and become fewer and fewer every year. The more lovely, like flowers, the more frail and delicate and short-lived they seem to be. But God says, "I will never leave you." Separation is the universal law everywhere, except between Christ and His people. Death and failure stamp every other thing, but there is no separation in the love of God to believers. The closest relation on earth, the marriage bond, has an end. Marriage is only "until death us do part." But the relation between Christ and the sinner who trusts in Him never ends. It lives when the body dies. It lives when flesh and heart fail.

Once begun, it never withers. It is only made brighter and stronger by the grave!

✤ From the sermon "Be Content"

The Frame of Mind in Which We Are to Run

Let us run with patience the race that is set before us.
—HEBREWS 12:1

The frame of mind in which we are to run: "Let us run with patience."
I take this patience to mean that meek, contented spirit which is the
child of real living faith, which flows from a confidence that all things
are working together for our good. Oh, it is a most necessary and useful grace! There are so many crosses to be borne when we have entered
the course, so many disappointments and trials and fatigues that, except
we are enabled to possess our souls in patience, we shall never persevere
unto the end. But we must not turn back to Egypt because some bring
up an evil report of the promised land; we must not faint because the
journey is long and the way lies through a wilderness. We must press
forward without flagging, not murmuring when we are chastened, but
saying with Eli, "It is the LORD: let him do what seemeth him good"
(1 Sam. 3:18).

O yes, beloved, we must run with patience, or we shall never obtain.
There may be many things we cannot understand, much that the flesh
could perhaps wish otherwise, but let us endure unto the end, and all
shall be made clear, and God's arrangements shall be proved best. Think
not to have your reward on earth; do not draw back because your good
things are all yet to come. Today is the cross, but tomorrow is the crown.
Today is the labor, but tomorrow is the wages. Today is the sowing, but
tomorrow is the harvest. Today is the battle, but tomorrow is the rest.
Today is the weeping, but tomorrow is the joy. And what is today compared to tomorrow? Today is but threescore years and ten, but tomorrow
is eternity. Be patient and hope unto the end.

❖ From the sermon "The Christian Race"

Come unto Me

Come unto me, all ye that labour and are heavy laden, and I will give you rest. —MATTHEW 11:28

Our years are passing quickly away. As each successive stage of the year comes round, we hear of gatherings and invitations. Easter and Christmas are times when friends invite friends to come and see them. But there is one invitation which demands attention every day in the year; that invitation is the one which I bring you this day. It may be unlike any that you have yet received, but it is of unspeakable importance—it concerns the eternal happiness of your soul.

Reader, do not shrink back when you read these words. I do not want to spoil your pleasures, provided always that your pleasures are not mixed with sin. I know that there is a time to laugh as well as a time to weep. But I do want you to be thoughtful as well as happy; to consider as well as to make mirth. There are some missing every Easter who a year before were alive and well; there are some every year gathering round Christmas firesides who a year afterward will be lying in their graves! Reader, how long have you yourself to live? Will another Easter or another Christmas find you alive? Once more I entreat you to listen to the invitations which I bring you this day. I have a message for you from my Master. He says, "Come unto me, all ye that labour and are heavy laden, and I will give you rest."

There is a good time coming for all who have come to Christ and committed their souls into His keeping. They shall remember all the ways by which they have been led and see the wisdom of every step in the way. They all wonder that they ever doubted the kindness and love of their Shepherd. Above all, they shall wonder that they could live so long without Him and that when they heard of Him, they could hesitate about coming to Him!

❖ From the tract *Come*

Topical Index

Scripture Index